Lovers,
Clowns, and
Fairies

Truly, the moon shines with a good grace.

Stuart M. Tave

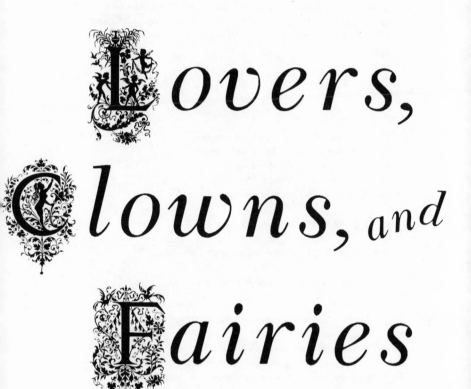

Lovers, Clowns, and Fairies

An Essay on Comedies

The University of Chicago Press

Chicago & London

STUART M. TAVE is the William Rainey Harper Professor in the College, and professor in the Department of English, at the University of Chicago. He is the author of *The Amiable Humorist: A Study in the Comic Theory and Criticism of the Eighteenth and Early Nineteenth Centuries* (Chicago, 1960); *New Essays by De Quincy* (Princeton, 1966); *Some Words of Jane Austen* (Chicago, 1973); and *Robert Bage's "Hermsprong"* (Pennsylvania State, 1982).

The University of Chicago Press, Chicago 60637
The University of Chicago Press, Ltd., London
© 1993 by The University of Chicago
All rights reserved. Published 1993
Printed in the United States of America

02 01 00 99 98 97 96 95 94 93   1 2 3 4 5

ISBN: 0-226-79019-3 *(cloth)*   0-226-79020-7 *(paper)*

Library of Congress Cataloging-in-Publication Data

Tave, Stuart M.
    Lovers, clowns, and fairies : an essay on comedies / Stuart M. Tave.
        p.   cm.
    Includes bibliographical references and index.
    1. English drama (Comedy)—History and criticism.   2. Humorous stories, English—History and criticism.   3. Characters and characteristics in literature.   4. Shakespeare, William, 1564–1616—Comedies.   5. Fairies in literature.   6. Clowns in literature.   7. Love in literature.   8. Comic, The.   I. Title.
    PR631.T38   1993
    823'.052309—dc20   92-42650
                                                              CIP

∞ The paper used in this publication meets the minimum requirements of the American National Standard for Information Sciences—Permanence of Paper for Printed Library Materials, ANSI Z39.48-1984.

Kai, Jacqueline, Rachel and Justin,
These are my lovers, above all uvvers,
These are my clowns when I'm in the downs,
These are the fairies I always can trust in.

A comedy and nothing but a comedy is a comedy.

Henry James

. . . where the word *Nose* occurs,—I declare by that word I mean a Nose, and nothing more, or less.

Tristram Shandy

God hath chosen the foolish things of the world to confound the wise.

Saint Paul

Contents

Preface

". . . definitions are hazardous," as the great lexicographer said, beginning with a maxim of civil law: things modified by human understanding, varieties of complication, changes of experience and accident, can scarcely be included in any "standard form of expression" because they are always altering their state. "Definition is, indeed, not the province of man," he tells us: beyond human faculties, the works of nature are too greatly extensive and diffused, the performances of art too inconstant and uncertain, to be "reduced to any determinate idea." "Definitions have been no less difficult or uncertain in criticism": imagination, licentious and vagrant, refusing restraint, always endeavors "to perplex the confines of distinction, and burst the inclosures of regularity," so that there is scarcely any species of writing "of which we can tell what is its essence, and what are its constituents." This is a deep and ominous preamble (and here much condensed) for a short periodical essay, before Johnson comes at last to his immediate problem: "Comedy has been particularly unpropitious to definers" (*Rambler* No. 125). It is a terrible and convincing warning, and reinforced by his own effort, that comedy is "such a dramatic representation of human life, as may excite mirth"—which does indeed avoid narrow limitations but does seem to be more indeterminate than particularly useful. (It is at least true that among Johnson's many definitions and critical dicta, so well and widely appealed to, this is not one often cited.) More recently Eco's William of Baskerville has thrilled us by following the trail of murdered men, not always understanding what he was doing, to the point where he had in his hand the lost second book of the *Poetics*—which would have had our answer, but it disappeared again, forever, and just as well, because those who ingested it were poisoned; like all of us Brother William must figure it for himself. We will never find the book or the definition with the essence. Each new finder is dissatisfied by what it is that his predecessors have not seen, because something is always missing, until he discovers and presents it for his equally dissatisfied successors. So if it does not seem like a promising move to begin with that revelation of the hidden truth, nor even offer a promised end, and if here it will be a while before we come to a pause to look back on where we have been, we must say something of what this attempt is about and what it is not about.

This is a book about literary works. It is not about jokes, or humor, or why people laugh, or the comic, or comedy. It is not about psychology, or philosophy, or anthropology, or theology. It is not even interdisciplinary, which is about as modest as one can get. It is not about comedy but some works of a kind that have been called comedies, and not all kinds; these are dramas and novels but mostly dramas because novels introduce other important problems. It tries to deal with a limited number of whole works and something of their relations, and for that reason brief references to other works have been cut, to make clear that the emphasis is not on excerpting local effects, that those effects are important only as they are part of a larger story.

It starts with a particular play. I suspect that a lot of writing about literature starts with a particular instance in mind, even when it is presented in the order of large pronouncements on generalities into which specific illustrations are tucked, which in turn, surprisingly, bear out the general idea (or are scolded for not doing so). My instance is *A Midsummer Night's Dream*. It is a beautiful play, in design and detail, and my interest is in these works as shapes of art. The mastery of that play's maker, in control in all points, gives us assurance throughout that however disordered the lives of the characters become he will be using his surprising skills to make all come right. His play has a symmetry in the development of the story it works out, a clarity of distinction among the characters it presents, a happy command of the languages they speak at every level of their varied abilities. Lovers, clowns and fairies, with their different natures and functions—of desire, foolishness, power—play their parts to perfection. The interchanging and interweaving of their fortunes are played out to their perfect fulfillment. The kinds of assumptions and values I am working are already evident, and more will follow. The story told by *A Midsummer Night's Dream* does seem to be a thing that appeals, because it is told again and again: things work out to a happy end, problems are solved, discord is resolved into concord, lovers marry, something of great constancy is achieved; but how that happens may be a mystery, not easily or wholly understood either by those to whom it happens or us who see it. Because it is a familiar kind of story it is difficult to tell, and any teller can make it trivial or trite, or dishonest. It has to be re-earned every time, made fresh, for as we know how it will go it must surprise us.

There are relatively few counters we are playing with here. John Stuart Mill in the crisis in his mental history was seriously tormented by the thought of the exhaustibility of musical combinations; the octave consists only of five tones and two semi-tones, he said, which can be put together in only a limited number of ways, of which but a small proportion are beautiful, and most of these must have been already discovered, so there cannot be much room for the new or richly beautiful. But his history moved one stage onward and he came to learn more of happiness and what could be done with what was available. There is much to be done with the limited number of terms we are using; it has seemed more useful not to increase units, to multiply categories and sub-categories and thus make discrete separations that satisfy the urge to neatness more than the shaded continuities of effects of the art, but rather to emphasize the myriad variations that have been worked with the parts and patterns of certain kinds of expectations. There is an endless number of ways authors can change the shapes of familiar stories and events, characters, voices, meanings, by the ways in which they remake them, shift emphases, rearrange, or offer and then withdraw, or omit, hoped for parts and patterns, by the ways they transvalue the process they unfold, and in this skilled originality play off the expectations of the audience. There may come a point when an audience schooled in certain modes thinks the proper contract is being violated and it becomes resistant in its response, will not accept what is being presented, and will begin to ask uncomfortable questions. Is this a comedy? Hasn't this deliberately deprived us of something that was promised, or gone beyond the bounds of what it claims to be? It is not a point at which useful arguments develop, as they become protective of territory and exclusive of strangers without legitimate credentials. A more useful way may be to worry less about boundaries, which cannot be held against the insistent incursions of authors, and try to make friendly comparisons and careful distinctions, so that the question becomes not whether the offending work is or is not a comedy but rather in what ways is it like or unlike other works with which comparisons seem helpful.

By beginning with a particular play we have a particular achievement as a reference. It is itself something to be tested. It is not a paradigm by which other works are judged as right or wrong as they more or less like it. All comedies do not aspire to the condition of *A Midsummer Night's Dream*. Some are very different, in that the several sorts of characters in them follow and depart from, in varying ways, the paths of the characters in that play, or the balances among the groups are not the same, or their stories do not come to the satisfactory ends found there. The comparisons remain useful to the extent that in those works where the initial anticipation proves to be mistaken, where there seem to be changed or even missing parts, where the fulfillment of the desires are not gratifying or not achieved, we are still dealing with a work where we are given indications that the audience or reader is one assumed to be knowing in the pattern of characters of a certain sort solving difficulties of a certain sort and finding a solution. We enjoy what the author does with our expectations as we pick up indications, earlier or later, small or large, that he is playing off these assumptions and that things are not going to be what we may have thought. Our perceptions, reactions, surprises, shocks, pleasures, are sharpened, multiplied, by the process. We are humbled, exhilarated, instructed.

I have found it useful to begin with *A Midsummer Night's Dream* because its tale of love, foolishness, and happiness has the familiarity of a long accepted line of recognizably similar works, before and after, and there is a value in beginning with a ready experience. We could start with *Volpone*, say, but there not only is the critical history more vexed but the author himself is aware, very self-conscious and pugnacious, that he will be thought to be violating what is acceptable practice. The kind of shape I start with, and

where I go from there, will be known to readers of C. L. Barber and
especially of Northrop Frye, from whom I have learned greatly
(and then departed in ways they could not approve). Others may
prefer another starting point and show other things, choose different kinds of comparisons; for that matter, A *Midsummer Night's
Dream* has had its variant (and dark) readings. Any mode will emphasize differently and omit what other readers will think important. As in this book individual interests and peculiarities will lead
into exploratory, or dead-ended, by-ways. And of course even
within the chosen limits the level of the analysis may be better or
worse. In one obvious underdevelopment, I talk of the languages of
the characters, but I do not do enough with them; I found that the
detail required for that was throwing off the proportions among various elements which I wanted to maintain. (And with *The Cherry
Orchard* I am dependent on translation, and have chosen one that is
most congenial to what I wanted to say.)

The order of the works discussed here is important and the chapters are designed to be read successively, because they do reflect
back and forth and what they say is not always apparent without that
reference. There is a vocabulary which runs throughout and, the
hope is, gains weight as it goes, so that the familiar observations
about the individual works have additional interest as they develop
less noted relations with other works. The vocabulary comes almost
entirely from the works themselves and from the qualities of their
casts of characters and the events those meet as they move through
their stories. The lovers in pursuit of their desires meet with difficulties in their course, problems they must overcome, some presented by other characters or forces, some within themselves.
There are restraints upon them, sometimes appearing as disabling
laws or illnesses. They do not see well, know how to understand
what it is they should do, which is a problem with their eyes, their
vision. Their course of love may take them on a journey, to another
place, to the freedom or the remedy, where they hope desires will
be fulfilled, but in their blindness they may lose themselves in what
is sometimes a darkness, a dream, a shadow; and the awakening may
require time, short or long as it is a measure of the difficulty of
change. That turn of time may be painful, for the end of the blindness can be a humiliating, a mortifying experience, a moment of

shock, that demands a giving up of an old life and self to permit the beginning of a new. But the ability to move, whether it be an impressive moral and intellectual change or a lucky chance that improves youthful fortunes, does tend to distinguish lovers from clowns. Clowns too have their hopes, sometimes pleasant, sometimes unpleasant, and our response to them will vary accordingly; but usually theirs are not such aspirations as we can sympathize with as we do with the young lovers, because, contrary to their own estimation, clowns are incompetent and unfitted for what they want. They are usually defeated, self-defeated, and even where they succeed it is in spite of themselves because they are incapable of change, of eye-opening. Those characters who are effective agents in promoting or hindering the movements of the lovers and clowns are here called fairies because, in their most powerful forms, they have a more than mortal power, in the first example Puck, an agent of a magical king. The fairies have the ability to control the lives of human creatures, may stand outside the human limiting conditions of time and space. These superior spirits, with their often undetected, sometimes literally invisible, opportunities of observation, command an effective insight, an ability to read minds, and are thereby able to predict and direct the actions of the mortals, reveal truths. They have the power to play with others' fortunes, have sport, sometimes stage a play with their unknowing cast; they can be excellent in mimicry to deceive, mislead, trick, make mischief, wild in their freedom, pushing the limits of life; they can be malicious, devilish. They have the magic which can change the vision, blind the eye with the potent charm; they know how to enchant, bewitch. From their height they can make fools, enjoy the spectacle, laugh at mortals who do not see the truth. But in other appearances they are helping figures, good fellows, who are capable of providing the solution to the problems of the mortals, having the power to remove difficulties, overcome laws, remedy illnesses, provide for happiness; and, in their most interesting way of doing this, they know how to return the blinded mortals, administer the counter-charm, the eye-opener, and lead lovers to the truth at the end of the journey.

The power by which this happens may not be fully explicable. It can manifest itself as a magic, a dream, perhaps a chance, a strangeness that tries and reshapes lives by taking them into another realm with other laws. It works by the transfiguring of minds (all together, where that is possible). Like the administering fairies these forces of change are variable forms which usually lead to the desired end; but then that is sometimes a mixed happiness, and like the fairies these forces go by paths of uncertainties, of shifting meanings, taking the mortals through mocking turns before allowing them to reach the end. In their course the characters may find that they have interchanged roles, that they have mistaken what they thought were their proper roles and are, it appears, proper subjects of laughter under the limits of the human condition on earth: lovers, clowns and fairies enter the dance and move in the circle. And, even if the mortals do not understand that story about themselves, we are instructed in the wisdom to know that it is about us.

In the succession of chapters some of these variations are followed, in an order that moves, generally, to the more and more problematic, or what appears so as seen from the point from which we have started. The advantages I gain in this scheme mean that I lose the uses of history. In another kind of study I have tried to do something with the many particulars of a history of comic theory and criticism in an extended period and in several of its contexts (*The Amiable Humorist*). I think too that there are historical applications for what is done in the present book. But there are values in the synchronic. There is, as we have been told, an important way in which literature has a simultaneous existence, and that way of reading is a moving part of the history of literature.

The editions of the texts used (given at the end of each chapter) are good modern reading editions, and so not always in the old spelling and punctuation form. The readers I have in mind are those who are literate and scholarly and have a familiarity with the plays and novels, but who are not specialists in each author and so will not be offended to see reminders of details in the plot and the dialogue. Similarly, the lists of books and articles at the end of each chapter are not extensive but are a sample of secondary sources with some relevance to the way the chapter has proceeded; they do not include important readings for the many other kinds of questions. Generally I have tried to include more recent things, from which those who are interested in further reading can trace back to earlier sources. Those who are knowledgeable in the literature on any of these plays or novels will know

those critics I have agreed or disagreed with, and where I have learned
much and where too little.

Barber, C. L., *Shakespeare's Festive Comedy: A Study of Dramatic Form
    and Its Relation to Social Custom* (Princeton, 1972 ed.)

Cowan, Louise, Introduction to her edition of *The Terrain of Comedy*
    (Dallas, 1984)

Frye, Northrop, "The Argument of Comedy," in D. A. Robertson, ed., *En-
    glish Institute Essays, 1948* (New York, 1949)

————, *Anatomy of Criticism* (Princeton, 1957)

Gardner, Helen, "Happy Endings: Literature, Misery, & Joy," *Encounter*,
    LVII, No. 2 (1981), 39–51

Goodman, Paul, *The Structure of Literature* (Chicago, 1954)

Grene, Nicholas, *Shakespeare, Jonson, Molière: The Comic Contract* (Lon-
    don, 1980)

Gurewitch, Morton, *Comedy: The Irrational Vision* (Ithaca, 1975)

Heilman, Robert Bechtold, *The Ways of the World: Comedy and Society*
    (Seattle, 1978)

Herbert, Christopher, "Comedy: The World of Pleasure," *Genre*, XVII
    (1984), 401–16

Hume, Robert D., "Some Problems in the Theory of Comedy," *Journal of
    Aesthetics and Art Criticism*, XXXI (1972), 87–100

Jagendorf, Zvi, *The Happy End of Comedy: Jonson, Molière, and Shake-
    speare* (Newark, Delaware, 1984)

Kaul, A. N., *The Action of English Comedy* (New Haven, 1970)

Knights, L. C., "Notes on Comedy," in *Determinations*, ed. F. R. Leavis
    (London, 1934)

Lauter, Paul, Introduction to his edition of *Theories of Comedy* (New York,
    1964)

Lehman, B. H., "Comedy and Laughter," in *Five Gayley Lectures, 1947–
    54*, University of California Publications: English Series 10 (1954)

Levin, Harry, *Playboys and Killjoys: An Essay on the Theory and Practice
    of Comedy* (New York, 1987)

Olson, Elder, *The Theory of Comedy* (Bloomington, 1968)

Polhemus, Robert H., *Comic Faith: The Great Tradition from Austen to
    Joyce* (Chicago, 1980)

Potts, L. J., *Comedy* (London, 1948)

Rodway, Allan, *English Comedy: Its Role and Nature from Chaucer to the
    Present Day* (Berkeley, 1975)

Sacks, Sheldon, *Fiction and the Shape of Belief* (Berkeley, 1966)

Chapter One

A league without the town

A Midsummer Night's Dream

A *Midsummer Night's Dream* is the perfect place to begin. Shaw the minor social scientist insisted that *A Doll's House*, in its utilitarian way, will have done more useful work in the world, but Shaw the major artist knew that "'A Doll's House' will be as flat as ditch water when 'A Midsummer Night's Dream' will still be fresh as paint . . ." ("The Problem Play," 1895). Only a major artist would use such flat phrases with the instinct that here they were bluntly and exactly right. *A Midsummer Night's Dream* is not only perfect in its detailed beauty and its practical workmanship but it works everything out perfectly.

To begin with, there is the arrangement of characters: they are disposed in three groups and there is never a question of who belongs to which. One is the Athenian court circle, Duke Theseus and his bride, Queen Hippolyta, Hermia and Lysander, Helena and Demetrius: all beautiful; all so classically and medievally and attractively named; all upper-class, the ruling center of the best society; all so well-spoken in blank verse and couplets and so witty when the occasion offers; and, most importantly, all in love. Then there is the lower class, "a crew of patches," fools, clowns, "rude mechanicals," uncultured artisans who labor with their hands, who "work for bread," whose absurd names identify them by the limited tools or qualities of their several occupations: Quince the carpenter, Flute the bellows mender, Snout the tinker, Snug the joiner, Starveling the tailor; and "the shallowest thick-skin of that barren sort," that dull-witted lot, Bottom the weaver, whose name combines so pleasantly both the mechanical trade and the level of mind (III, ii, 9–10, 13). Their uneducated prose gives them away as soon as they open their mouths. They are great misusers of words, especially when,

1

"Hard-handed men . . . Which never laboured in their minds till now" (V, i., 72–73), they try to play the "mimic" (III, ii, 19), to act out of their class, speak a finer speech, copy a higher art; and they get it all wrong, right down to the level of punctuation, masters of unintentional fallacies.

> We do not come as minding to content you,
> Our true intent is. (V, i, 113–14)

They are trying to imitate the manners of their betters to attract favorable attention to themselves and be rewarded accordingly. They can never elevate themselves, never change class, because they are such clowns. (In quarto and folio they are, by the convention of their roles, sometimes so identified—"Enter the Clownes"—and some of Bottom's speech prefixes are "Clowne" or variant spellings of that.) Finally there are, surprisingly enough, most remarkable creatures: with their names, both natural and romantically more than natural, Oberon and Titania, the Puck, Peaseblossom, Cobweb, Moth (Mote), Mustardseed; and with their powers, both overwhelming and delicate, of nature in the villagery and of romance. They are not subject to mortality, barely subject to time or space. Puck, swifter than arrow from the Tartar's bow, can put a girdle round about the earth in forty minutes (III, ii, 100–01; II, i, 175–76). He is "that merry wanderer of the night" (II, i, 43); wandering is usually a lost state for mortals, not being able to locate themselves, as it is with mortals of this play whom he misleads in the night; but not so for Puck, merry because free of the limiting condition. They are, these space-commanding creatures of the night, invisible. Their speech can be supernaturally lyrical, with no effort, when the occasion is there. They have magical powers and can lead the unknowing mortals in any direction, knowing as they do, invisibly present, what the mortals are thinking and, capable as they are, of altering those minds instantly. These are fairies. The three groups cannot be mixed; they are separate orders of beings and there is never a possibility of a member of one set moving permanently into another. If the Queen of Fairies falls in love with the Bottom of clowns that's marvellously absurd, and part of the secure fun in seeing that is the knowledge that this mismatch cannot possibly last for long.

So there we are with lovers, clowns and fairies, a complete cast, all we need, all perfect in their functions. What do they do? The lovers chase in a dance, running after one another, changing partners and then returning to first positions, working out the pattern of their pairing until they have achieved their desire. Hermia and Lysander are in love with one another and Helena loves Demetrius, who is the only piece out of place by his insistence on Hermia. If he would only fall in love with Helena all would be well, and since we are told that he was indeed once in love with her he may very well switch again. In fact that is what happens, so the problem has been solved in its simplest and most obvious solution—but only in the most complicated way, not by the one sensible move but by a complete scrambling of the original situation, so that we have lost such order as we had to start with. All is worked out to a happy end as we expected, by a means we could not have anticipated.

Hermia has a problem because of her father, Egeus; he wants her to marry Demetrius and he has an authority to enforce his demand. By the ancient privilege of Athens as she is her father's he may dispose of her either to Demetrius or to her death, according to the law immediately provided, and Theseus enforces the law. Theseus explains it to her carefully. To a daughter her father should be as a god, composer of her beauties to whom she is a form in wax "within his power" to make or mar. There is not much to choose between the two young gentlemen except that her father chooses Demetrius. "I would my father looked but with my eyes," she suggests; but no, "Rather your eyes must with his judgement look." She won't give in. This rather naughty little girl (of "stubborn harshness," her father says, and later events do let us see that he has something of a point), knowing already that the punishment for her disobedience is death, but still checking out her options, asks Theseus what is the *worst* that may befall her in this case if she refuses Demetrius. Not a foolish question it turns out, because there is a fate perhaps worse than death in this kind of play, life-long virginity. Theseus cautions her sensibly to think if she is the kind of young woman who can suffer that; "question your desires," he says, "Know of your youth, examine well your blood," whether she can endure the alternative of the livery of a nun in a shady cloister,

> To live a barren sister all your life,
> Chanting faint hymns to the cold fruitless moon.

They are thrice blessed that can master so their blood but she would seem to be a girl with the warm blood for this earth, likely to be "earthlier happy" by becoming the rose distilled than by withering on the virgin thorn or in that cool ambiguity of "single blessedness." She has said she does not know "by what power" she is made bold where so much power is being brought to bear upon her, but she evidently has something stronger than the godlike power arrogated by her father and ratified by ancient law which will now be executed by his Grace the Duke. She is ready to live and die in the single life rather than yield her virgin patent, her privilege, to a lordship her soul consents not to give sovereignty. Sensible Theseus tells her to take time to pause over these awful alternatives of disobedience, until the next new moon when he and Hippolyta his love will marry (I, i, 38–90). It's good advice from an experienced ruler, less convincing as coming from a man impatiently in love, and time will not make any difference. We know quite well by what power she is made bold and love will not be defeated.

That is clear enough for us to see and to say, but what is she to do? Hermia and Lysander discuss the problem, in a gracefully pathetic and not immediately relevant catalogue of lovers' crosses, a stichomythic series that lets us know the degree and kind of concern we must feel. They are not intellectuals but they do know, and it is rather a comfort, that their plight is not peculiar. All Lysander could ever read, could ever hear by tale or history, is the old story: "The course of true love never did run smooth," as he reports to Hermia, in his lovely gift not for original thought but imperishable words. It is certainly a wise saw applicable to any stage of civilization, before or after, as the more talented young Dickens, picking up the very latest technology in smooth transportation, was able to remind us once again in *Pickwick*, Chapter 8, "Strongly illustrative of the position that the course of true love is not a Railway." But such journeys do arrive safely at their desired end if lovers can devise the means, or some power devises for them. Hermia is restrained by a law that keeps lovers apart, the law of the state, of fathers, death, sterility. It is, she knows from the perspicuous Lysander's lecture—they do enjoy playing on the big stage—an "edict in destiny." In this immediate exemplar it is the law of Athens and he proposes that they run off to another place, where he will have another home with a more sympathetic widow aunt, "a dowager, / Of great revenue, and she hath no child. / . . . and respects me as her only son": just the sort of sentimental old lady who can handle this sort of difficulty and provide all good things. In that place "the sharp Athenian law / Cannot pursue us." The aunt's house is "remote seven leagues," so he proposes to meet Hermia "a league without the town" (I, i, 132–68). There they will begin their journey. They do meet and they do depart for that happy place where they will be free of frustrating law, where all problems will be solved and all loving desires fulfilled. But they don't have the boots for seven leagues. They do certainly find a place where other laws obtain, but it is not what they thought it would be and the laws are not what they could ever have anticipated or ever do understand; and their problems are both complicated and resolved by means more wonderful than anything they could have imagined. Young lovers have strong but limited imaginations. They will devise to steal through the gates of Athens, to meet in the wood,

> And thence from Athens turn away our eyes
> To seek new friends and stranger companies. (218–19)

New and stranger the companies will be ("strange companions," say quarto and folio). Young lovers find themselves, at the beginning of the journey of their lives, in a dark wood where the straight way is lost, under the moon, in a dream. Something has happened to those eyes we have been hearing about. We will hear much about eyes, both here and in subsequent works.

Meanwhile the other and lesser class of mortals of Athens, those clowns, have their own desires and their own difficulties which they too have to work out before the next new moon, in mounting that play they want to create and enact before the Duke and the Duchess on the wedding day at night. "Is all our company here?" The play is the "most lamentable comedy" about Pyramus and Thisbe, a very good piece of work, we are assured, and a merry (I, ii, 1–11). We are already convinced that this is a problem they will never solve, so utterly incapable as they are, but so thick that they are not even aware of their impotence and we can enjoy without any need to worry about them. Their problem, as they see it at first, is simply to find a good place to rehearse and so Quince, author and producer-director, distributes parts and tells all to meet him tomorrow night in the wood, "a mile without the town," by moonlight. There they will rehearse, for if we meet in the city, he says, "we shall be dogged with company, and our devices known." Bottom agrees that there they will meet and "rehearse most obscenely and courageously. Take pains be perfect" (80–86). In their kind, the best in their kind, they are always perfect. It is not certain if Quince's mile and Lysander's league are the same and it doesn't make much difference because they never run into one another or know that the other is there; but the wood is certainly the same place and the "company" they find there is certainly the same, new and stranger than either looked for, and their devices are known. Both young lovers and clowns come under the spell of the fairies.

What do fairies do? They are clever and mischievous, and the first thing we hear of Puck is that he is "that shrewd and knavish sprite / Called Robin Goodfellow." He enjoys laughing and jesting, as both another fairy and he tell us, scares maidens, misleads night wanderers; he's a great mimic, beguiles a fat and bean-fed horse by neighing in the likeness of a filly foal, and we will later see him doing just that sort of thing with a man or two infatuated with a girl or two (and indeed the man shall have his mare again—certain distinctions are not important to him); he has more than mortal powers of mimicry, animating objects both natural and artificial, lurking in the very likeness of a roasted crab apple in an old-woman's ale to bob against her lips and make her spill it on herself, or setting up this old favorite, always good for a "loffe":

> The wisest aunt, telling the saddest tale,
> Sometimes for threefoot stool mistaketh me;
> Then slip I from her bum, down topples she . . .

Then the whole choir hold their hips and loffe, and swear a merrier hour was never wasted there (II, i, 32–57). But this village humor of pulling chairs out from under old women, robust as it is, isn't half as much fun as the more intimate, inside, revealing tricks he can play. The fairies streak the eyes of the young men. The mortals think they are being most reasonable when they are most mistaken. "The will of man is by his reason swayed, / And reason says you are the worthier maid" (II, ii, 121–22): that is the bright Lysander, under the spell, wooing the wrong maid. Puck, agent of the Fairy King, has a juice, the juice of the little western flower, and maidens call it "love-in-idleness," which changes vision, makes lovers blind, makes them madly dote upon the next live creature that they see (II, i, 166–72). Lysander goes to sleep saying to Hermia, "end life when I end loyalty!" and jumps up saying, "And run through fire I will for thy sweet sake! / Transparent Helena" (II, ii, 69, 109–10). That is one blind young lover.

Under the fairy spell the lovers change partners in a pretty, choreographed movement. Lysander and Demetrius had both been in love with Hermia in their *pas de trois* and poor Helena had been without a partner, chasing Demetrius; but now Lysander with his altered eyes runs to Helena, who still chases Demetrius, who still chases Hermia, who is now chasing the now faithless Lysander, all in a circle; then Demetrius is given new eyes and both he and Lysander chase Helena in their *pas de trois* and poor Hermia is without a partner, chasing Lysander. One might think that Helena, who had been so unhappy when no one loved her, so unattractive as she thought herself, in her bad moments—"I am as ugly as a bear" (II, ii, 100)—would be delighted now when any man need only see her to love her; but she has never been so unhappy, certain that a cruel joke is being played on her by both the men and Hermia, her oldest and closest, only girl friend. Then the two young men grow hot in their claims to Helena and begin to chase one another in preparation for a fight. Hermia, totally confused by everyone's actions and never one to take things lying down (as we have seen, with an importunate father or an importunate lover), now grows hot with Helena, who she is certain has been the thief of love; and Hermia is eager to get her nails at that friend's eyes. All is in chaos with them, as mixed up couples and mixed up friends, and individually mixed to the point of loss of identity.

> O me, what news, my love
> Am not I Hermia? Are not you Lysander?
>
> (III, ii, 272–73)

And from that point, the lowest of their fortunes, all comes right, as Lysander returns to love and pair off with Hermia, and Demetrius is paired with Helena; and that in fact was the pattern of their configuration before the play began, so the change of partners in the dance has been worked out with a lovely symmetry. The choreography seems to have been designed by an artful nature long before these particular lovers were led through its moves; and other young partners will perform it on other stages.

It has all come right because Puck, at Oberon's direction, has changed Lysander's vision once again so that he now sees clearly which girl he ought to love. The fairies have a double power. If Puck at his entrance tells us how he pulls out chairs from under old aunts, in his last appearance he sweeps the dust behind the door, a tricky bit of housekeeping that makes all neat, as far as one can see. He has another name, Robin Goodfellow, an ambiguous propitiatory name for a trickster who can do both mischief and unexpected helpful deeds for people who should be helped. Having put these young lovers to quarreling with one another he uses his talents in mimicry both to stir them up and keep them far enough apart so they can do no hurt. Having set them at odds he makes these odds all even, and no more triangles.

> Yet but three? Come one more,
> Two of both kinds makes up four.

Having gathered them, unknown to one another, on the ground and sleeping, he works his medicinal magic once again.

> I'll apply
> To your eye,
> Gentle lover, remedy.

And that does the job, just as the proverb provides:

> Jack shall have Jill,
> Naught shall go ill:
> The man shall have his mare again, and all shall be well.
>
> (III, ii, 437–63)

Having charmed Lysander's eye with the juice of love-in-idleness to send him chasing the wrong girl he has Oberon's remedy, the chaste juice of Dian's bud, to clear the eye, make the boy see the right girl. That is the counter-charm.

These young lovers, for all their bright qualities, are not much for depth or complexity, only young lovers, and that *is* their character. They are easy to confuse with one another. "Thou shalt know the man / By the Athenian garments he hath on," Oberon had instructed Puck (II, i, 263–64), which we may think is not a wonderfully effective method of identification coming from the King of Fairies; but then to his eye there cannot be much essential distinction between one young mortal lover and another; and Puck by dropping the juice in the wrong man's eye makes what might be called a natural mistake, which pleases him. What difference does it make except to make mortal confusion more apparent? Helena has always been understandably insistent on the lack of distinction between her and Hermia. "Through Athens I am thought as fair as she" (I, i, 227), a fact Demetrius will see as soon as his vision is corrected. Helena knows they two have always been indistinguishable, working on one sampler, while sitting on one cushion, warbling one song, both in one key,

> As if our hands, our sides, voices, and minds
> Had been incorporate . . .
> Two lovely berries moulded on one stem . . .
>
> (III, ii, 203–14)

A reader needs a mnemonic device to keep them straight in his mind. On the stage, where they live, it is plan that one is tall, fair and timid, the other little, dark and fierce, but the point is that such details matter not at all; young men may fall in or out of love with the same details, finding them attractive or repellent from one moment to the next. To be young and in love is all that counts. With not much to choose between them we would not be greatly offended if they switched partners—as the young men do, shortly, several times—but since the pattern of pairing does seem to matter greatly to them we defer to their desires, even if we can see little reason why they can be satisfied only by so specific a solution.

With little difference or depth to begin with there is not much development to expect from them. It is pleasant to see, in the women, that under the pressures of the fairies in the night certain little suppressed qualities do pop out—like the revelation of the spitfire in Hermia, of which there had been a hint in the opening of the play. And then we hear the news that Helena (that less than dependable keeper of a friend's secret plan), for all her sweet-talk of two lovely berries molded on one stem, and for all her pathetic appeal to Hermia's feminine solidarity not to join with men in scorning a poor friend, has known of Hermia's keen and shrewish quality for some time and is now willing to tattle when it may do her own cause some service: "She was a vixen when she went to school" (III, ii, 215–19, 323–25). The young men do change as much as they are able and fulfill whatever potential was there. Each does see finally which young woman is the right young woman for him and that's rather more than they seemed capable of at the start. Their history may make us wonder a bit about future stability but we must accept, on high authority, that this is the end of the change. Back to Athens shall the lovers wend, Oberon assures us, "With a league whose date shall never end," a kingly decree then independently corroborated by the other ruler, who joins them, for in the temple with us, Theseus says, "These couples shall eternally be knit" (III, ii, 372–73; IV, i, 177–78). Of course these authorities, both fairy and human, have had their own problems in love, but that's all over now. Or at least this story is over and if other characters in every time and place will play this story again in their own lives, as they surely will, for these particular creatures we have come to a conclusion.

It seems that the young men have grown up, or so they insist, even if they do not understand how they managed to do that. "I wot not by what power," Demetrius says, in echo of Hermia's early declaration of an unknown strength, "But by some power it is." It is that same power of love: his mistaken love for Hermia, now melted as the snow,

> seems to me now
> As the remembrance of an idle gaud
> Which in my childhood I did dote upon,

and the object and pleasure of his eye is now only Helena (IV, i, 161–68). It is the same declaration of maturity which Lysander had made to Helena, when he abandoned Hermia:

> Things growing are not ripe until their season;
> So I, being young, till now not ripe to reason,

had been led to Helena's eyes (II, ii, 123–24). It is the sort of repetition which should leave us with an amused and healthy skepticism, but again our own vision should be wise enough to recognize and accept the distinction between the middle and the end of a story. Lysander was under the false charm and his words were the false words of the doting young man, Demetrius is under the true counter-charm and his words are the true words of the man in love. The sententious boy Lysander had been pompous in his certainty of reason, the no longer doting Demetrius is modest in his self-knowledge and limited understanding of what power it is, which makes him more credible. And of course we are not dependent only on his word. These are now young lovers who have become, to their capacities, small or large, ready to marry, and to marry under the auspices of those who have overseen their growing. They and their best bride-bed are blessed and they will have babies, not just any chance babies but, as we would expect in this play, perfect babies, promised by those who can make good the guarantee: the issue they create ever shall be fortunate.

> And the blots of nature's hand
> Shall not in their issue stand. (V, i, 387–88)

The accidents of love are so happily behind them and, so wonderfully, the accidents of natural gestation and time are suspended for them. That is worth a word more.

Time is peculiar in *A Midsummer Night's Dream*. For one thing, as Dr. Johnson said, "I know not why *Shakespear* calls this play a *Midsummer-Night's Dream*, when he so carefully informs us that it happened on the night preceding *May* day" (his annotation on IV, i, 110). It has been often explained by other annotators but it finally doesn't make much difference.

> Good morrow, friends, Saint Valentine is past;
> Begin these woodbirds but to couple now? (IV, i, 136–37)

We are told at the start that the play will end on new moon, and then the almanac says the moon will shine that night. But it really doesn't make much difference. And Shakespeare doesn't seem to have paid much attention to the time-scheme of the action. Theseus says in the first speech of the play that it will be four days and nights until the nuptial hour and Hippolyta repeats that, sensibly telling him not to be so impatient in desire, that the days will quickly turn to night and the nights will quickly dream away the time; she is right, the time goes quickly and is largely dreamed away. His prediction isn't true and neither he nor any of his subjects seems to notice that it cannot be much more than forty-eight hours (with one very long night). But then it really doesn't make much difference. No one can be confused by any of this except any foolish mortal who tries to stop the action to get the timing right. All this in a magnificently crafted, jewelled play. Time is dramatically quite unimportant in *A Midsummer Night's Dream*. We are given an expectation of a tight dramatic chronology which indicates tension—Hermia must make her decision and the lovers must work out their fates within four days, the clowns must get their play into production in that same short rehearsal schedule, the fairies must do their work before the night in the wood ends—but we in the audience can all hang loose. Time is unimportant because once we enter the wood, under the moon, in the dream, the complications and the resolution will all be moved instantly, magically. Puck drops the juice of the charm in the eye and the vision is distorted, he applies the antidote, the counter-charm, and the vision is clear. No time is needed in that more than mortal realm (and in fact these fairies don't have to run at the end of the black-browed night). Like everything in this play, changes are perfect, immediate.

We can believe in that magic because we can believe in these fairies. They speak a more than mortal language. But we believe too because it is not a meaningless stage-magician magic, mechanical tricks which seem to violate the order of nature and have no consequence, no revelation. "O strange! We are haunted!" (III, i, 86), but this is magic which makes palpable the reality which we then recognize as true when it is opened before *our* eyes. Bottom is translated for us—"Bless thee, Bottom, bless thee! Thou art translated!" (98) —into the ass's head he has always carried on those shoulders. We see his metaphor; it is a clever turn. As the translator explicates, ". . . those things do best please me / That befall prepost'rously"

(III, ii, 32, 120–21), back to front; and, in this instance, it shall be called Bottom's figure because the ass is foremost. But Bottom returns it upon us as well as upon his fellow clowns: "What do you see? You see an ass head of your own, do you?" (III, i, 97). Such simple magical sport with space—the best magicians need little paraphernalia to achieve great effects—changes the vision. What we see has always been there, and we know that, but we have never seen it with such eyes before. There is nothing much to *Gulliver's Travels,* as Dr. Johnson saw: "When once you have thought of big men and little men, it is very easy to do all the rest" (Boswell's *Life,* 24 Mar. 1775), and he is simply right. Quite simply, as we say, once you've read *Gulliver's Travels* and have seen that strange translation of space you will never see human beings on the same scale again. In their magical sport with time the fairies let us see, what we can now recognize in quick-time, or no-time, the common human processes we cannot see so brilliantly with our daily vision by a daily clock. Young lovers fall in and out of love with an unreasonable readiness and frequency, so we are not disbelieving but greet delightedly what is made more apparent here by the fairy spell. Lysander, in the wood, chases the wrong girl, but young men have been known to do that without supernatural intervention; Demetrius was doing it in the first act. One understands too, by way of further sharpening our daily vision, that the magic has entered this play before the fairies. "This man hath bewitched the bosom of my child," Egeus had been complaining as we started; the young man has given her rhymes, he has by moonlight been singing to her with feigning voice verses of feigning love, stolen the impression of her fantasy, her imagination (I, i, 27–32). Egeus hasn't got it all straight but in his stuffy way he is telling us about the sort of thing that goes on in the magical dream. It is also true that the kinds of transformations worked on the mortals in the dream are, at long last, what they have been always longing for. Helena wanted translation before it came upon Bottom. Sickness is catching, she said, and she'd give the world if she could catch Hermia's looks that way, her ear, her eye, her tongue, to make herself as attractive to Demetrius.

> Were the world mine, Demetrius being bated,
> The rest I'd give to be to you translated. (186–91)

And her wish is granted, they two being already so much alike that a
drop in Demetrius' eye makes all the difference.

The sport is taken one step more, because no one is exempt from
the magic. It is a funny foolish mortal show Puck is directing and
watching:

> Shall we their fond pageant see?
> Lord, what fools these mortals be! (III, ii, 114–15)

But his role, above the pageant of the laughter, is, even for him, impossible to sustain untouched. At least, as the fairies are themselves
dramatic creatures, participants in an action, they have, necessarily
by that condition it seems, their own problems, their lovers' quarrels, complications, resolutions, and they too play their roles in the
fond pageant. Oberon and Titania are not quite faithful, something
willful and petty, tricky and tricked, capable of mistakes in the
night. There is evidently some power which handles that show,
some "fate" which "o'errules," as Puck says (93), who sees to it that
Oberon and Puck slip from that glorious language to an imprecise
communication which leads Puck to drop the juice in the wrong eye:
some super-Puck who laughs and says, "Lord, what fools these
fairies be." All things circle in this play.

All desires are fulfilled and everything works out to a complete harmony and reconcilement of all opposites. Theseus and Hippolyta,
the mature lovers, have turned their war to love before the play
begins and have set a good example. The young lovers have been
sorted out and Theseus ratifies the obviously desirable arrangement
he finds. "I beg the law, the law upon his head!" Egeus demands
against Lysander, but Theseus is both a lover himself and a more
sensible judge and will not grant that. "Egeus, I will overbear your
will" (IV, i, 152, 176). Oberon and Titania have already settled their
difference in their way; that is important because the order of
nature, the order of human time, had been disturbed by their
quarrel—things won't grow up

> and the green corn
> Hath rotted ere his youth attained his beard;

this is a matter of not only unseasonable weather but of the medical
problems it brings, contagious fogs, murrain, rheumatic diseases,

distemperature (II, i, 88 ff). The kinds of immaturity and sickness
which have been giving Demetrius such troubles and which, now
"in health come to my natural taste," he recognizes (IV, i, 165–71),
have been cured by Puck's remedy; as the now loving amity of the
fairies helps make possible a healthful resolution of the human problems. The fairies dance, something they do so well. A dance of this
sort celebrates the attainment of desires, the ceremony when all
participate harmoniously, all are lovingly alive and active and all is
delightfully ordered: there is at once full freedom and full union, to
signal the happy solution and the restored or newly shaped kinetic
stability. In their double capacity the fairies lead the mortals "about
a round" and they dance in "a round" (III, i, 88; II, i, 140). The circle
is completed.

And the most discordant sounds harmonize, as even the dispersed company of clowns is reunited and is joyful. Bottom, that
perfect clown who has always thought that he can play any and every
role, who can create chords that would be impossibly self-
contradictory for anyone else, can roar you as gentle as any sucking
dove, has been at home among the fairies too because he has "a reasonable good ear in music. Let's have the tongs and the bones" (IV, i,
26–27). Shortly after this request is offered—we are getting a remarkable orchestration—there follows the very different fairy music and the dance that ends the dream. Which in turn is immediately
succeeded by the dawn and the hunting horns that will wake the
lovers. Theseus is there with his love and his hounds. "My love shall
hear the music of my hounds." He wants her to

> mark the musical confusion
> Of hounds and echo in conjunction.

As one who has been with Hercules and Cadmus once, when in a
wood of Crete they bayed the bear with hounds of Sparta, she has
heard such gallant chiding, when groves, skies, fountains and every
region seemed "all one mutual cry":

> I never heard
> So musical a discord, such sweet thunder.

In this friendly rivalry he will not be outdone because his magnificent hounds are bred out of that same kind and "matched in mouth

like bells, / Each under each. . . . Judge when you hear" (103–24).
It is at this point in the strange composition that he sees the sleeping
lovers and is surprised to find the clashing young men in such unity.

> I know you two are rival enemies:
> How comes this gentle concord in the world . . . ? (139–40)

They can reply only more amazedly, because no one can understand
the marvellous harmony of the dream and the wisest is he who hath
simply the best wit of any handicraft man in Athens, who knows it
hath no bottom.

But in fact not everything has been brought into a concordance,
because all this dance and all these wonders are accomplished by
the end of Act IV and there is still an act to follow. The clowns haven't
yet done their act. They've been looking forward to this performance to complete their happiness and gain their reward—Bottom
could not have scaped sixpence a day—and we've been looking forward, too; and some sort of general rejoicing, not for fairies only but
for the clowns and for the lovers young and not so young, would be
appropriate. The last act certainly is fun and worth the wait and it
couldn't very well have been offered before the resolution of the several problems. But that's a pretty long afterpiece, if that's what it is, a
bit much for a playwright who has been working with a delicate
shaping touch. In that shaping, of course, Pyramus and Thisbe does
seem right in the place where it is, because we have begun in Act I in
a world of reality, such as reality is in our base line in Duke Theseus'
Athens, then we have adjourned to a long middle passage in the
world of the fairies, wood within this wood, and now we return to
the home reality again; and that arrangement is, like everything in
this play, perfectly symmetrical. If anything, we are more real than
ever as we leave the fairy cobweb for the "palpable gross," for onion
and garlic eaters. But then to what reality are we returning? A very
strange reality, it seems, which is a play within the play and, as
scripted and presented, the most absurdly unreal thing we've seen,
a tragically disastrous parody of the course of true love. No problems
get solved here, either by Pyramus and his love or by their persona-
tors. This is, in its own effort, less credible than the dream. Which
should we believe?

It is a question worth debating and Theseus and Hippolyta talk it over, in two stages; which leads us to think that this marriage of two mature and experienced people, both like and unlike one another, whose acquaintance began in a less understanding dispute, will be a good marriage. The young lovers had been amazed as they came out of the dream, "Half sleep, half waking," "cannot truly say" at first how they came to be where they are. For a moment their eyes hesitate between a vision of the two worlds:

> Methinks I see these things with parted eye,
> When everything seems double . . .
>   Are you sure
> That we are awake? It seems to me
> That yet we sleep, we dream.

But in their youthful bounce it doesn't bother them much or stop them long in thought and, confident that they are now awake, off they go: "And by the way let us recount our dreams. [*Exeunt lovers*]" (IV, i, 143–44, 186–96). But Hippolyta is stopped by the recount: "'Tis strange, my Theseus, that these lovers speak of." Not so Theseus, who doesn't believe the dream at all: "More strange than true. I never may believe / These antic fables, nor these fairy toys." Lovers, madmen, have such seething brains, shaping fantasies, "that apprehend / More than cool reason ever comprehends," imagine more than any sane person can understand. His cool reason knows that "The lunatic, the lover, and the poet / Are of imagination all compact." Theseus is a very sensible man and a good ruler and has given his proofs, and by a life's experience he knows a thing or two about being in love. Hippolyta knows rather less but she has a more open mind on this subject, not certain in skepticism as he is, and not credulously insistent either:

> But all the story of the night told over,
> And all their minds transfigured so together,
> More witnesseth than fancy's images,
> And grows to something of great constancy . . .

If all the lovers had the same dream, a transfiguration of all minds that has a coherence, then there seems to be evidence of a story of life, a story with more meaning than the antic fable of seething brain, or of poet's eye rolling in a frenzy of art, those images of fancy so confidently dismissed by the single-visioned Theseus. She doesn't know what happened—how could she? who could?—but knows that even if she can't understand it something remarkable happened: "But howsoever, strange and admirable." She accepts the possibility of the inexplicable and wonderful, the shared dream of love. Theseus turns off the question: "Here come the lovers, full of joy and mirth," which, though it is not his intention, is as close to an explanation as we are likely to come (V, i, 1–28). To us who have been listening to this little inconclusive lovers' disputation it would appear that if the dream is more than cool reason ever comprehends and it more witnesseth than fancy's images—well, at that point, between reason and fancy, it is useless to argue in oppositions, for discords disappear in love and mirth. In this work we are suspended, perfectly, it seems, in a moment in a place of concordant reason-imagination, real-unreal, life-art. And now here come the clowns, full of life and art.

Theseus wants something more delightful than this dream he can't believe, to wear away the anguish of three hours before the wedding bed. Masques, dances, mirth, "What revels are in hand? Is there no play . . . ?" (V, i, 32–38). There is a choice of old stuff, pseudo-serious stuff, not sorting with a nuptial ceremony, but also on the menu he reads

> 'A tedious brief scene of young Pyramus
> And his love Thisbe; very tragical mirth'—
> Merry and tragical? Tedious and brief?
> That is hot ice and wondrous strange snow.

Theseus has found another question in harmony. "How shall we find the concord of this discord?" (56–60). That piques his interest, more than he asked for or could have thought possible, this kind of strangeness. He is told that it is a very poor play, really both brief and tedious, really tragical with a death which makes the eyes water, but "more merry tears / The passion of loud laughter never shed." That increases his curiosity. "What are they that do play it?" He is told that they are hard-handed men that work in Athens, men who never labored in their minds till now, and have now toiled to present this play for his wedding. "And we will hear it." He is told it is not for him, it is nothing, nothing in the world, unless he can find sport in their intents, so little ability so stretched with cruel pain to do him service. "I will hear that play." This is an impressive Duke. He knows that "never anything can come amiss / When simpleness and duty tender it . . . take your places, ladies" (61–84). His own lady is not pleased. The Queen of the Amazons is a gracious and feeling lady. We have seen her sensitive, thoughtful response to the dream, better than his confident assurance. She feels for these toiling men; she loves not to see wretchedness overcharged and duty in its service perishing. He honors her feeling but this is something in which he knows more than she. "Why, gentle sweet, you shall see no such thing." But the master of the revels has just said they can do nothing in this kind. "The kinder we"—witty man—"to give them thanks for nothing."

> Our sport shall be to take what they mistake;
> And what poor duty cannot do, noble respect
> Takes it in might, not merit.

It is not only these inarticulate simples who mistake, because experienced Theseus has seen great clerks in their premeditated speech, with practiced accent, shiver and look pale, not paying him welcome, "Make periods in the midst of sentences" (as Quince the Prologue will now do). "Trust me," he says, ". . . Love . . . and tongue-tied simplicity / In least speak most, to my capacity" (85–105). She should trust him, as a Duke of noble respect who knows how to value "might" and who knows how to watch a play. So it starts.

Those young lovers, Lysander and Demetrius, are witty fellows, very clever in their language, very witty spectators of the foolishness of that play and players they are watching. One might think they should be more thoughtful, more self-conscious at this replay of their own fond pageant. But no, that's all past—Oberon has in kindness erased the memory—for why should happy lovers be obliged to draw solemn lessons from their own conduct and not leave that to other, unseen, spectators? Hippolyta, not very happy with this whole idea of watching such incompetent actors on the stage, can't stand the thing. "This is the silliest stuff that ever I heard." She didn't say that about the dream. Theseus, enjoying himself thoroughly, instructs her in dramatic illusion: "The best in this kind are but shadows; and the worst are no worse, if imagination amend them." He knows how to transfer from his inward nature a human interest and a semblance of truth sufficient to procure for these "shadows of imagination" that willing suspension of disbelief for the moment, which constitutes poetic faith (*Biographia Literaria*, ch. xiv). She is the sensible one now and she won't have any of that: "It must be your imagination then, and not theirs." But he understands how to see shadows of this kind—"If we imagine no worse of them than they of themselves, they may pass for excellent men"— because he is ready to allow for imagination here. "Here come two noble beasts in, a man and a lion" (V, i, 204–10). Theseus disbelieves the fairy toy of the dream but willingly suspends disbelief to enjoy the play; to Hippolyta the play is silly but the dream is something of great constancy. Theseus has one kind of imagination, for a play of very tragical mirth, but he cannot extend that effort to the dream; Hippolyta, who cannot dismiss the dream, lacks the imagination to enjoy the play. For us spectators, needing both kinds of the faculty, because we know what we have witnessed and can deny neither scene, dream and play seem to bear a mutual effect, each gaining credibility for each, discords resolving in concord.

The art of the mechanicals cannot be dismissed. Fairies are poets, in their language and in their dramatic art, as inventors of amusing scenes in which they direct the actors who do not know how wonderfully they are being staged. That art needs an imagination of power; and even within Puck's play about lovers, in their own less knowing imaginations the distracted lovers themselves sometimes think that they are being made to play roles in scenes invented by one another. Clowns are lunatics trying to be poets, and do not have that imagination of power, that imagination which can take the forms of things unknown and turn them to shapes and give to airy nothing a local habitation and a name. Shapes and names give them endless problems. And Bottom fears they will be too real—"you think I come hither as a lion . . . No, I am no such thing; I am a man, as other men are"—or not be real enough—"Look in the almanac—find out moonshine, find out moonshine!" (III, i, 32–34, 40–41). In their chaos this company cannot find out that constancy of a story told by a shaping imagination. But then if we see how the best in this kind does it, the King of Shadows, we cannot think too badly of these less good shadows. We have been hearing and watching Oberon play a scene for well over a hundred lines when he informs us, at the moment when this remarkable confidence suddenly becomes necessary: "I am invisible" (II, i, 186). Yes, we say, we can see that now. It is a mutual endeavor. This shadow teaches us and, as Theseus instructs Hippolyta, our imagination must amend this shadow; we now see him with our eyes (perhaps he draws about him his invisibility robe) and we see with our imaginations, at once. So for all his clownish incompetence as an artist neither we nor anyone can simply look down on Bottom or his imagination. Theseus, the ruler by day, for all the excellence of his kind of imagination, does not have the imagination to see how much he has in common with this sweet Bottom who has been transported; Theseus, like the lovers and no more aware than they, has been watched over by the fairies: but Theseus, like Bottom and still less aware than he, has been loved, in one strange sense or another, by the Queen of the fairies. Bottom had given him and us, his two audiences, fair warning on our vision: "let the audience look to their eyes" (I, ii, 20). Bottom has wit; nay, he can gleek upon occasion. But he won't flaunt it, won't set his wit to so foolish a bird as a cuckoo, and more impressively, won't let the Queen of the fairies, in her unknowing irony, flatter his beauty or his wisdom. Not so, neither, but if he had wit enough to get out of this wood, as he says, he has enough to serve his own turn; and she may croon the fairy blandishment, "Out of this wood do not desire to go," and she may try to feed him with fairy fruit, "with apricots and dewberries, / With purple grapes, green figs and mulberries," but his great desire is to a peck of provender, to munch your good dry oats, or hay, for "Good hay, sweet hay hath no fellow" (III, i, 112–26, 144–45; IV, i, 29–31). He knows the limits of wit. If Bottom's senses and language have been more than ordinarily mixed in a dream, and the eye of man hath not heard and the ear of man hath not seen, and if his tongue is not able to conceive nor his heart to report what his dream was, if he has not the imaginative language to recount it, and if he thinks touchingly that only a ballad by that poet Peter Quince could do the job, he is not such an ass as to go about to expound this dream which, in either of its double senses, has no bottom. He has had an exposition of sleep come upon him. To the lovers all the deri-

sion shall seem "a dream and fruitless vision" (III, ii, 370–71), but he
has had what no other sees, except for us with whom he shares it. "I
have had a most rare vision. I have had a dream, past the wit of man
to say what dream it was" (IV, i, 200–09).

The wit of man in the night, in the dream, the shadow, under the
moon, has difficulties seeing all that is there and those varied, opposing and changing forces. The night is a time of fear and of love. The
moon brings the hours of beauty and of lunacy. Dreams are night-
mares, or, in their fulfillment of all desire, everything. Shadows are
the least substantial things, ghosts, at a remove, or two removes,
from reality, and they are the most substantial, the spirit, the essence, the revelation of the meaning. Shadows, like dreams, may be
airy nothing, like dreams may be strange and wonderful. They are
the stuff of art, that thing which is least real and most real, taking us
to the edge of another world. Puck in his last words invites the audience to meet him there, at the border:

> If we shadows have offended,
> Think but this, and all is mended:
> That you have but slumbered here
> While these visions did appear . . .

He invites us into the dream and the play and we have reason not to
trust him wholly; this may be his last and best trick. But he needs us
there, half-way, as we need him. The best in this kind are but shadows,
we know by now, and need imagination to help mend them.

> Gentles, do not reprehend;
> If you pardon, we will mend.

It is an extraordinarily modest request from one who seems to need
offer no apologies to us, who are all in his debt. But he insists on
having our friendship and we are ready to respond because he has so
much to offer in return.

> Give me your hands, if we be friends,
> And Robin shall restore amends. (V, i, 401–16)

It is all a special experience, in a created world carefully marked
off in time by the brief days and nights of confusion and celebration

preceding the nuptial hour, indeed by the immediate no-time magic of the fairies, carefully marked off in space by the roundel and fairy song that fence Titania's bower and hold out spotted snakes, thorny hedgehogs, spiders, beetles black and snails (II, ii, 1–30). It is essential that we know such things do live outside the charmed circle, look in upon us here because they are explicitly excluded, and that we know, as Puck tells us, there are ghosts wandering here and there home to churchyards, and damned spirits who go to and from their wormy beds (III, ii, 381–87). Ladies need not fear when lion rough in wildest rage doth roar because he assures all that he is Snug the joiner, and it is understood that he is a very gentle beast, and of a good conscience; but Puck reminds us before he sweeps the dust behind the door that there is another kind of beast and now that hungry lion roars (V, i, 211–19, 349). There are the disfiguring mole, harelip, scar, mark prodigious, those blots of nature's hand that frighten parents and at other times than now certainly may be upon their children (387–92). We have known from the beginning that in the history of the course of true love not everything has run smoothly at the end, that even if there were sympathy and no other tried to stop the course, war, death or sickness did lay siege to it,

> Making it momentany as a sound,
> Swift as a shadow, short as any dream,
> Brief as the lightning in the collied night,
> That in a spleen unfolds both heaven and earth,
> And, ere a man hath power to say 'Behold!',
> The jaws of darkness do devour it up.
> So quick bright things come to confusion. (I, i, 141–49)

The shadow, the dream, the night, may not be friends, the quickness of time may bring the brightness to confusion and not bring it back. Not all fairies are so helpful and even these we see have given proofs that they too can do harm enough. But if these have the charm to put their mischief upon the sight they are dependably there with the charm that takes off the blindness, opens the eye. They have the language—charm is a song, the carmen that casts the spell—and it is the magic of the language which creates that special circle of beauty, on the bank

> where the wild thyme blows,
> Where oxlips and the nodding violet grows,

and encloses it completely,

> Quite overcanopied with luscious woodbine,
> With sweet musk-roses and with eglantine.

There sleeps Titania (II, i, 249–53). It is, for that moment, verifiable
by the human senses (Bacon, writing of gardens, says the sweetest
smell in the air is yielded by the violet, next to that the muskrose,
then too sweet-briar, i.e., eglantine, then honeysuckles, i.e. wood-
bine; and among those few flowers that perfume the air most delightfully, being trodden upon, is the wild thyme). In that created
circle and in that way, with the shapes and colors and odors and
tastes and motions so specific and of such constancy, the reality of
that imagination cannot be denied; and in that way the play never
becomes sentimental but a most rare vision of completed aspiration.
We will learn more of sentimentality in the next and later chapters.

The text is the edition by R. A. Foakes, "New Cambridge Shakespeare"
(Cambridge, 1984). References are to act, scene and line numbers; where
successive quotations in the same paragraph are from the same scene the
act and scene numbers are not repeated.

Shaw is quoted from *Shaw on Shakespeare*, ed. Edwin Wilson (New
York, 1961), pp. xiii-xiv.

Barber, C. L., *Shakespeare's Festive Comedy* (Princeton, 1972 ed.)

Berry, Ralph, *Shakespeare's Comedies: Explorations in Form* (Princeton,
1972)

Bevington, David, "'But We Are Spirits of Another Sort': The Dark Side of
Love in *A Midsummer Night's Dream*," *Medieval and Renaissance
Studies*, VII (1975, published 1978), 80–92

Brown, John Russell, *Shakespeare and His Comedies* (London, 1957)

Calderwood, James L., *Shakespearean Metadrama* (Minneapolis, 1971)

Cope, Jackson I., *The Theater and the Dream: From Metaphor to Form in
Renaissance Drama* (Baltimore, 1973)

Dent, R. W., "Imagination in *A Midsummer Night's Dream*," *Shakespeare
Quarterly*, XV, No. 2, (1964), 115–29

Dunn, Allen, "The Indian Boy's Dream . . . Shakespeare's *A Midsummer
Night's Dream*," *Shakespeare Studies*, XX (1988), 15–32

Evans, Bertrand, *Shakespeare's Comedies* (Oxford, 1960)

Fender, Stephen, *Shakespeare: A Midsummer Night's Dream* (London, 1968)

Garber, Marjorie B., *Dream in Shakespeare* (New Haven, 1974)

Girard, René, "Bottom's One-Man Show," *The Current in Criticism,* edd. Clayton Koelb and Virgil Lokke (West Lafayette, 1987)

Huston, J. Dennis, *Shakespeare's Comedies of Play* (New York, 1981)

Kermode, Frank, "The Mature Comedies," in *Early Shakespeare,* "Stratford-Upon-Avon Studies" 3 (1961)

Kott, Jan, *The Bottom Translation* (Evanston, 1987)

Leggatt, Alexander, *Shakespeare's Comedy of Love* (London, 1974)

Nemerov, Howard, "The Marriage of Theseus and Hippolyta," *Kenyon Review,* XVIII (1956), 33–41

Nevo, Ruth, *Comic Transformations in Shakespeare* (London, 1980)

Summers, Joseph H., *Dreams of Love and Power: On Shakespeare's Plays* (Oxford, 1984)

Young, David P., *Something of Great Constancy: The Art of* A Midsummer Night's Dream (New Haven, 1966)

Zimbardo, R. A., "Regeneration and Reconciliation in *A Midsummer Night's Dream,*" *Shakespeare Studies,* VI (1970), 35–50

Chapter Two

These mountains make you dream of women

Man and Superman

Shaw too is interested in perfection, and in dreams. Like the strolling theatrical manager, who thrusts a few props from one pantomime into the service of another, "I have adapted this easy device to our occasion by thrusting into my perfectly modern three-act play a totally extraneous act in which my hero, enchanted by the air of the Sierra, has a dream . . ." (Epistle Dedicatory, pp. xvii-xviii). His perfectly modern three-act play is much superior in its dialogue and liveliness of ideas to others of its time, but in its structure and its kind it is a play of now or of any old time: the tale of young lovers who overcome the obstacles in their course and find their desired end, whether they understand their own desires or not, in marriage. As in *A Midsummer Night's Dream* we have two pairs of young lovers; and some of these, in this play one man in particular, are at first afflicted with problems of youthful blindness but then prove capable of enlightenment, of growing up. And certainly there are clowns, incapable characters, betraying themselves by their inability to speak the right language; there is a great variety of them (including, conveniently, even a rude mechanical), with a remarkable collection of stage dialects. No fairies, though, so we fall down on that point, and what are we to make of that?

The similarities are important indications of some things it might be worth looking at, but that is because they point also to important differences. The two pairs of lovers, unlike the pairs of *A Midsummer Night's Dream,* are certainly not minimally distinguishable from one another and easily interchangeable. The pattern of mating here cannot be as casual. In the first act when it is momentarily, and not really, suggested that Jack Tanner might be the unknown father of Violet Robinson's coming child, the notion that anyone could have entertained such a possibility is to her mind abominable; this is something deeper than a moral repugnance and her last words at the end of the last act are, with intense conviction, visceral as well as social, "You are a brute, Jack." The young men and the young women are quite different from one another, the men from the men, the women from the women, the couples from the couples, and they have therefore different problems. Violet is already secretly married, as we learn in the first act, and the problem she and Hector Malone have is that they must get the money from Hector's father to achieve their happiness. It is a while before they can do that; but that young lady always gets what she wants (she really doesn't want much—after all she married Hector) because she knows how to get it: having the son already pretty well under control the unshrinking Violet subdues the old man within a few minutes of meeting him and pockets the money, unstained by stooping or by gratitude. The problem of Jack Tanner and Ann Whitefield, the main couple because by far the more interesting, is more difficult. Nobody is trying to keep them apart; by the near-end of the play everybody, including Roebuck Ramsden, one of Ann's two guardians, who began with what certainly seemed to be a glorious, inexpugnable, dislike for Tanner, is like everyone else in encouraging the match. And Ann certainly loves Jack. The obstructing wall in the course of true love is Tanner and something important must happen in him before the end. In the first act we know that she is after him but he knows nothing. At the end of the second act he is told by his perceptive servant that she is after him, so he runs away. At the end of the third he knows that she has caught him and he can't escape. It is not until the end of the fourth and final act that he knows he loves her. Unlike the swift moves of *A Midsummer Night's Dream* the action here goes in stages, by incremental knowledge, takes time.

Tanner is a remarkably intelligent, knowing, witty man. He certainly has a flow of words. He has written a book. Shaw, as he lets you know, unlike other authors who only tell you that their hero is an author, actually shows you, publishes, the book. It is a convincing proof. Who can believe that David Copperfield could ever write a book, much less anything as good as a novel by Dickens? But *The Revolutionist's Handbook and Pocket Companion* by John Tanner, M.I.R.C. (Member of the Idle Rich Class), really sounds as bright as if it had been written by Shaw. Tanner has ideas, forward-looking ideas, able to change the society of England at the start of the twentieth century. He is very up-to-date in all the ways of 1903. He owns one of the new automobiles; it can go eighty-four miles an hour; it is on the stage and it moves, though not 84 mph, to be sure, because he doesn't understand it and really can't drive it or fix it himself and it scares him. He knows a lot about a lot—politics, economics, social questions, family problems, morality, poetry, insect life, sex. Tanner's ideas are genuinely interesting, certainly well expressed, to be taken as seriously as Shaw's. Like the very best in his art—Shakespeare, Congreve, Jane Austen, for example—Shaw can make a great fool of a fool; but like them he gets his finest effects not from setting up such easy marks, where we can all join in looking down, but from inventing superior characters with sparkling minds, not less than you or I but a great deal smarter and more marvellously articulate than we can ever hope to be, and then showing us, now privileged and humbled us, how foolish they can be.

Tanner is effective in many ways. The play begins with dialogue between Ramsden and Octavius Robinson: a long, affectionate handshake which tells the story of a recent sorrow common to both, the death of Mr. Whitefield, we gather after a bit, old Ramsden's friend and young Octavius's sort of second father:

> RAMSDEN: . . . Well, well, Octavius, it's the common lot. We must all face it someday. Sit down. . . .
>
> OCTAVIUS: Yes: we must face it, Mr Ramsden. But I owed him a great deal. He did everything for me that my father could have done if he had lived.
>
> RAMSDEN: He had no son of his own, you see.

And this goes on with "now he is dead—dropped without a moment's warning. He will never know what I felt" (handkerchief and cries unaffectedly); and with "How do we know that, Octavius? He may know it: we cannot tell"; and with mutually comforting extravagant compliments from Mr. Whitefield which each survivor reports to the other. It is the expected exposition to start a perfectly modern play and it is intolerable. It must be expected because Ramsden is an impressively "respectable" man and because Octavius is "really an uncommonly nice looking young fellow. He must, one thinks, be the jeune premier; for it is not in reason to suppose that a second such attractive male figure should appear in one story" (I, 4–5). Transparently, we have been set up by these dull commonplaces, as we realize with relief, when their conversation turns to a friend of Octavius, a man who Ramsden declares has written a book which is the most infamous, scandalous, mischievous, blackguardly book that ever escaped burning at the hands of the common hangman. "I have not read it: I would not soil my mind with such filth . . ." (7). We certainly want to meet that mischievous friend of nice Octavius; Octavius doesn't take him seriously (and we never do find out why Tanner wants Octavius as friend), but we know now that we deserve and are going to get something more novel and more interesting than a jeune premier. Tanner is announced by the maid, and is refused entrance to the house by Ramsden, who is then told by the maid that Tanner is not at the door but already upstairs. Tanner blows in and the level of speech and life rises instantly. The play begins.

He understands readily how Ramsden's mind works, its historical and social origins, and he can predict its reactions and language.

> RAMSDEN: I have no—
> TANNER: You have no desire for that sort of notoriety. Bless you, I knew that answer would come as well as I know that a box of matches will come out of an automatic machine when I put a penny in the slot: you would be ashamed to say anything else. (I, 15–16)

Ramsden has such conventional notions about Ann, his Annie who is such a wonderfully dutiful girl, to whom her dead father's wish would still be sacred, who has never once given her own wish as a reason for doing anything or not doing it, only her father's or mother's: "It's really almost a fault in her. I have often told her she must learn to think for herself" (6). He intends that Annie's wishes shall be consulted in every reasonable way. "But she is only a woman, and a young and inexperienced woman at that." Clever Tanner, who has no illusions about the innocence of that young woman, or her ability to think for herself, or how she gains her ends by that device of duty, can offer only an amused condescension: "Ramsden: I begin to pity you" (14). Tanner is right about that, too,

having got to a level of Ramsden's mind that Ramsden himself has
just glimpsed without profit, in a moment when even his patience
with Ann has given out: "That girl's mad about her duty to her parents" (8). Tanner is even generous enough to make common cause
with Ramsden, in self-understanding and acknowledgment of defeat, when Ann has forced them, with the stroke of her paw, into
accepting the joint-guardianship appointed for them by her father's
will. "I feel that I am too young, too inexperienced, to decide," she
says, "My father's wishes are sacred to me." "Ramsden," Tanner offers, "we're beaten—smashed—nonentitized, like her mother,"
but Ramsden doesn't understand (20, 22). Tanner also understands,
whimsically, how Octavius's mind works, his desire to be a poet,
write a great play. "With Ann as the heroine?" "Yes: I confess it."
And of course Tanner has strong advice, that the play is all right but
if the poet is not careful, by Heaven, Ann will marry him, eat him
up, as women do these things in their fury of creation. The excellence of the advice, which in its depth is always more than personal,
like most of Tanner's analyses is rather upsetting to the shallow
minds he has to deal with. "You come out with perfectly revolting
things sometimes," is Octavius's response, and it is only by making it
a fixed rule never to mind anything Jack says that his friends manage
to accept him (22–25). But he has a liveliness of mind and a readiness
to move others into action which is refreshing and fascinating.
When the dreadful secret of Violet's pregnancy is revealed and para-
lyzes almost everyone else and the shock brings out the worst in
them, Tanner takes charge in an efficient way and tells everyone
what else to do; he outrages Ramsden, we are happy to see, but he
does even better than that, bringing the distraught man to realize
that Violet is really being treated very badly by them.

　　If we are looking for a fairy, in the sense of a Puck-like character
who has a higher level of knowledge and power because he is capable of reading minds, of understanding others better than they
understand themselves and who can therefore direct them, sport
with them, or arrange for the solution of their problems, here he is.
A little earlier in the act when he was playing with Ramsden he had
shown, as Ramsden said uncomfortably, "a malicious humor" (I, 28),
that mischief-making ability. Now, in the crisis of Violet's case, he is
doing the good-fellow bit. But within a few minutes, before the end

of the first act, he has fallen flat on his face. He knows so much about biology and the fulfillment of woman's highest purpose and greatest function, the crowning of completed womanhood in the bearing of a child, defiant though she may be of every social convention and its condemnation; but he knows nothing about women. He defends and congratulates Violet for having known that she was right to follow her instinct, that vitality and bravery are the greatest qualities a woman can have, and that not being legally married matters not one scrap, and so forth, when he is not only in ignorance of the facts of her situation but he is utterly mistaken in crediting "vitality" to her character; and he is utterly offensive to her. Judging himself to be so unlike the rest of her judges, he has in fact been thinking "like the rest," as she says, thinking that she has been "a wicked woman." Worse than that: "You think that I have not only been vile, but that I share your abominable opinions" (45).

His own problem lies deeper than that unseeing tumble into Violet's contempt, because at this point in the first act we've seen already that for all his superior understanding of Ann as "woman" he really doesn't understand Ann. Even the knowledge that he too has been beaten, smashed, nonentitized by her is not an insight into Ann or Jack. He knows how women go after men, warns foolish Octavius, who thinks that he is the pursuer and Ann the pursued: "Fool: it is you who are the pursued, the marked down quarry, the destined prey. . . . You are doomed" (II, 54–55). But his talk of his own free exemption has never bothered Ann, who is always pleased to tell him how well he talks, which always brings him to the point where *"he collapses like a pricked bladder,"* is *"heavily let down"* and must collect *"his scattered wits"* (I, 39; II, 60). He is not ashamed of "my real self" (I, 15), but she knows one thing more of that than he does.

We are dealing not with a Puck who knows so much more than the others that he can control their lives. Tanner may think he is playing that more than mortal role and he may have moderate success in it but what we have, more adequately described, is a blind young lover. He is "prodigiously fluent of speech," as we are told upon his first entrance, but then, as we see, that is part of the problem with a man who is "excitable—(mark the snorting nostril and the restless blue eye, just the thirty-secondth of an inch too wide open), possibly a little mad" (I, 9). It will take a good actor to make that thirty-secondth of an inch visible to the second balcony, but if he is good he will find ready ways. The man is blind because he sees a little too much. His far-sighted eye sweeps the horizon and all abstract knowledge but cannot take in what is at the end of his nose. With his eye flashing and working himself up into a sociological rage he demands to know why Ann will not call her soul her own, why she will tell a lie because her conventional mother has made her do that. "Oh, I protest against this vile abjection of youth to age!" (Actually, he learns shortly after, it was not the mother's lie, it was Ann's). Break your chains, get your mind clean and vigorous, he cries, offering the liberating journey to that distant, wonderful place—come with me for a fast ride in a motor car, to Marseilles, across to Algiers, right down to the Cape if you like: "That will be a Declaration of Independence with a vengeance. . . . That will finish your mother and make a woman of you." She accepts, thoughtfully. There wouldn't be any harm in that: "You are my guardian: you stand in my father's place, by his own wish"; nobody could say a word against their traveling together, it will be a delightful excursion and she'll come. He is aghast—"Youll come!!!"—utterly appalled. If there is no harm in it there is no point, he insists, but she knows that's absurd and since he wishes it she will come on this lovely holiday he offers. "You really are good—much better than you think. When do we start?" (II, 59–61). Yes, he is her guardian, standing in her father's place, in the traditional role of the foolish old man who stands, ineffectively, as an obstacle to the satisfactory completion of the course of true love. He doesn't yet know how he came to fall into that role, but he certainly is the man who is obstructing his own desire. He has yet to learn what that desire is; and Ann has always known that foible: "I dont for a moment think that Jack knows his own mind" (IV, 156). If he has given Violet too much credit he gives Ann too little.

If there are no fairies in *Man and Superman*, and Jack Tanner is a failed self-appointed candidate for that role, their mischievous work is still being done, and done too as they do it a league without Athens, invisibly. Lovers, clowns and fairies obviously have many variants of characters within these categories of large convenience. But, more interestingly, it is also true that one man in his time may play many roles. And, one point more: lover, clown and fairy are not characters only but dramatic functions with a life of their own; and if they find no other place to dance, the fairies will dance in the mind, with most delight in the circle they love best, the mind of him who in his own conceit is the shrewd and knavish sprite.

The career of Jack Tanner is worth following. He can be foolish, like any blind young lover, but he is not a clown. He really is bright, a hope for the future, someone who ought to be better than he is and capable of being better. We want to see him succeed; it would be a loss if he didn't come to know more than he does, perceive more accurately, fulfill his potential, even if he doesn't yet understand what that means. What he shares with the clowns in his world is a faulty vision of the world, each one thinking he is a severe critic of a deficient society, an advanced man, one who knows what the world-to-come should be. Where he differs from them is where his grand and faulty vision of life is bound with, bound by, his own life as a lover; and though their notions too are all shaped by the limitations of their lives he, unlike them, is a young lover capable of coming to see that truth about himself and acting on the knowledge.

In each act of the play Shaw throws in another character, or two, or more, sort of like the Dickens he knew so well. In Act I we have met Roebuck Ramsden, with his appropriate given name marking a Victorian who starts radical and ends reactionary. (Roebuck is also the name of one of Farquhar's rakes and later, at the end of Act III, we learn that the buck and the ram are another and less public part of Ramsden's life.) He is more than a highly respectable man, the president of highly respectable men. His age is important, Shaw tells us, because everything depends on whether his adolescence belonged to the sixties or the eighties (how pleasant to transfer that astute dictum to a later century). He was born in 1839 and was a Unitarian and Free Trader from his boyhood, and an evolutionist from 1859, so that he thinks of himself as an advanced man and fearlessly outspoken reformer. His mind and his study are framed for us by the busts and portraits of Bright, Spencer, Cobden, Martineau, Huxley, George Eliot, autotypes of allegories by G. F. Watts. He will not allow Tanner to treat him as a mere member of the British public, prejudiced and narrow. It touches him on his most sensitive point: "You pose as an advanced man," he retorts; "Let me tell you that I was an advanced man before you were born." That is too easy for

Tanner: "I knew it was a long time ago" (I, 15). Ramsden is the outdated nineteenth-century liberal still thinking he is ahead. He is,
and he speaks in the language of, a gentleman. "You know that I am
not a bigoted or prejudiced man. . . . But I draw the line at Anar-
chism and Free Love and that sort of thing" (8).

In the second act we meet two other advanced men. First there is
Enry Straker, Tanner's chauffeur, the New Man, as Tanner nomi-
nates him, who knows machinery, and on whom Tanner is therefore
dependent. Like all good servants he has also an experienced common sense and insight lacking in his employer (though a traditional
virtue, in this play, has a weak side too). Enry has been educated not
as a contemptible gentleman at a university but as a working engi-
neer at the Polytechnic, and is not a poetic Socialist but a scientific
one. This original lower class New Man does not try to imitate the
language of the upper class and cultivates his dialect. But as the perceptive Tanner also notes, "This man takes more trouble to drop his
aitches than ever his father did to pick them up. It's a mark of caste
to him. I have never met anybody more swollen with the pride of
class than Enry is" (II, 50). Still worse, we see in the next act, he
has a conventionally stuffy family pride which is really very old-
fashioned, an intellect which reaches forward into the twentieth
century and social prejudices which reach back into the dark ages.
In a crisis he behaves "just like a miserable gentleman" (III, 83, 139).
So the New Man is an interesting variation but a rather simple inversion, at best, and certainly nothing of much promise for the future of
humanity. The second self-appointed representative of a new world,
entering in the second act, is Hector Malone, the young American
with his elevated moral sentiments. "English life seems to him to
suffer from a lack of edifying rhetoric (which he calls moral tone);
English behavior to shew a want of respect for womanhood; English
pronunciation to fail very vulgarly in tackling such words as world,
girl, bird, etc." (II, 62). His American r's in "morl," or as we hear
later in "Worker," impart an overwhelming intensity to simple and
unpopular words; but in fact, Violet knows well, he is about as fit to
become a worker as is Octavius, and he is, as the missing husband of
Violet, another moral impostor (IV, 152–53). The truth is, Hector's
culture is nothing but a state of saturation with English exports of
thirty years ago, reimported and hurled at the heads of the English.

"When he finds people chattering harmlessly about Anatole France
and Nietzsche, he devastates them with Matthew Arnold, the Auto-
crat of the Breakfast Table, and even Macaulay . . . there is intel-
lectually nothing new to be got out of him . . ." (II, 62–63).

Act III, with Mendoza and his friends and fellow brigands, offers a
small crowd of dogmatic prophets of the future, Anarchist, Social-
Democrat in both sulky and rowdy varieties, the dregs and scum of
society (the dregs assuming they are the scum at top); they speak in
several kinds of debased Cockney and French tongues, Christian
and Sheeny. Their dominant leader is urbane and witty, diplomatic
and dignified, capable of violence if need be, the very well-spoken
Mendoza; his language is romantic, capable of powerfully soporific
poetic sentimentality. In the dream that follows we meet his semblance in the Devil, the smooth and dangerous deadly master of the
saccharine dialect, the leader of the best society in hell.

Act IV brings Hector Malone Sr., the billionaire American, that
paternal-power new world type, who might buy up the Alhambra,
and who knows he could do better with it than the Spanish government. His immediate ambitions are limited to using his money to
buy English abbeys and to work vengeful change on the English society which starved his mother: this to be achieved in marrying his
son into that society by way of social profit. He is Irish in birth and
the original material of his speech was perhaps the surly Kerry
brogue, now degraded by his life in the big cities. His practical bent
is displayed in his purchase of shares in Mendoza, Limited, estab-
lishing a partnership with the brigand. They will make good partners because he too is such a sentimental ninny, as Violet discovers
quickly and exploits with no mercy. None of these clowns we have
been meeting act by act, contrary to their self-assurance, is in touch
with reality.

Tanner is different from all of these because he does come upon
reality, though it is not the reality he thought he had in front of him.
Learning from Straker at the end of Act II that he is the man Ann is
after—"[wildly appealing to the heavens] Then I—*I* am the bee, the
spider, the marked down victim, the destined prey" (II, 70)—he
jumps into his automobile, in this crisis actually starts it up, and rolls
offstage: he will escape, go off on his journey to the continent to find
a new place where he will be free. He cuts cleverly to Spain, clev-

erly because the expedition of the proposed mental Declaration of
Independence, on which he had foolishly invited Ann, was to have
gone to Monte Carlo. He arrives in the Sierra Nevada, in the evening and there he is stopped by Mendoza, a friendly and intelligent
type with whom he gets on well. Politically and socially they have
much in common and they are easily frank with one another, which
does them both credit. "I am a brigand: I live by robbing the rich."
"I am a gentleman: I live by robbing the poor. Shake hands" (III, 77).
As with his other friends and acquaintance Tanner is full of good
advice; and when it develops that Mendoza's present life is the consequence of a problem with a woman, a terribly sad, hopeless, infatuation with a woman who had the most magnificent head of hair he
ever saw, who had humor, intellect, could cook to perfection, and
who would not have him, Tanner tries to talk him into good sense,
into forgetting her. Interestingly enough, this variable and capri-
cious cruel fair, "in a word, enchanting," is in fact a cook and, it turns
out, is Louisa Straker, sister of Tanner's rude mechanical. "A dramatic coincidence!" as Mendoza exclaims with delight, it fits so well
with the romantic tale of his love. "You are Enry, her favorite
brother!" "Oo are you callin Enry? . . . For two pins I'd punch
your fat edd, so I would." Enry, who had been amused initially at
what he recognized as a romantic "six shillin novel sort o woman, all
but the cookin. Er name was Lady Gladys Plantagenet, wasnt it?" is
offended by this liberty with his sister's name and the implication
that she was keepin company with Mendoza. But Mendoza, a man
of letters, is not put off.

> I loved Louisa: 40,000 brothers
> Could not with all their quantity of love
> Make up my sum.

"And so on. I forget the rest." His affliction has reduced Mendoza to
the composition of affecting poetry, as in

> O wert thou, Louisa,
> The wife of Mendoza,
> Mendoza's Louisa, Louisa Mendoza,

(and so on; we can forget the rest). "That is real poetry," he explains
in equally moving prose, "—from the heart—from the heart of

hearts. Don't you think it will move her?" There is no answer because his language has put Tanner to sleep (III, 81–86).

He had warned Tanner about sleeping here, when Tanner had
told him to put his poetry in the fire and not to sacrifice his career
to a monomania. How can Mendoza look round at these august
hills, divine sky, taste this finely tempered air, Tanner asked, and
then talk like a literary hack on a second floor in Bloomsbury? But
Mendoza understands this sort of thing better than Tanner, knows
that the Sierra is no better than Bloomsbury when once the novelty
has worn off. "Besides these mountains make you dream of women
—of women with magnificent hair." Tanner has taken no Louisa, no
woman, no entangling locks, to these mountains; he has escaped
that. "They will not make me dream of women, my friend: I am
heartwhole." It is a boast, we anticipate with pleasure, that will certainly precede a fall. Any may, any woman, who says "I am heartwhole" is going to take one of Cupid's best darts; no one elects
himself to an estate above the human condition. Mendoza warns
him, "Do not boast until morning, sir. This is a strange country for
dreams" (III, 84–85).

And so Jack Tanner, not the first blind lover to find himself, something of himself, in a strange country to which he has escaped, is not
the first to find himself in a dream, outside the daily laws of his life.
Instead of his universe "there is nothing: omnipresent nothing . . .
no time nor space, utter void." In this world beyond human life, no
time, no space, is revealed a man in the void: "an incorporeal but
visible man, seated absurdly enough, on nothing" (III, 86), as Shaw's
king of shadows skips over his problem in dramatic imagination, as
easily and shamelessly as Shakespeare's had done with his "I am invisible." More than that, this incorporeal man may be expected to
have a most rare vision, a dream that hath no bottom. With nothing
of his own to sit on, he has what would be, in Montaigne's experience, a unique opportunity of his privileged condition—to take a
seat "au plus élevé trône du monde" and not have to say, like us mortals who lust to sit high, "si ne sommes assis que sur notre cul." That
freedom does later turn out to be his case, but at the moment he is in
the depths of hell. A strange hell it is, too, and he cannot understand
why he is there. He is not John Tanner but Don Juan Tenorio. There
are four characters in the dream, Don Juan, Doña Ana, the Devil

and the Statue, each with a close resemblance to one of the characters we have met in the waking state, Tanner, Ann, Mendoza,
Ramsden; but they are not the same characters. There is echo upon
echo of lines of dialogue between perfectly modern three-act play
and totally extraneous dream, so we have no doubt of close connections in thoughts and tendencies; but they are not the same because
the place and the time, and therefore the action, are not the same.
On earth characters tend to have more in common, be more like one
another in their shared humanity, but in hell, where they are incorporeal, and less human, their essential qualities of spirit have freer
play and their differences become more visible. In Don Juan there
is a curious suggestion of Tanner but a "more critical, fastidious,
handsome face, paler and colder, without Tanner's impetuous cre-
dulity, and without a touch of his modern plutocratic vulgarity" (87),
so that the resemblance and even an identity are essentially qualified into this higher level. The Devil, on the other hand, though
"not at all unlike Mendoza" is "not so interesting" as that attractive
chief, the "one man on my journey," as Tanner later says, "capable
of rational conversation" (96, 139). The Devil looks older than
Mendoza, as one would expect, but age would seem to have brought
only premature baldness; and in spite of an effusion of good-nature
and friendliness, he is peevish and sensitive, "does not inspire much
confidence in his powers of hard work or endurance, and is, on the
whole, a disagreeably self-indulgent looking person," though of
course clever and plausible (96).

There is an important dramatic action in the dream in hell. If Don
Juan is puzzled to be where he is, we should not be surprised to see
him there, because we have seen already that characters who get
lost in the middle of the journey of their lives often find themselves
in a dark wood where the straight way is lost, where their vision
changes and they must, if they can, find the path to set out for
heaven. It is the common language of those on earth, and especially
lovers, to talk of themselves as being in heaven or hell, as the immediate circumstances of their course to or from the fulfillment of their
desires seem to demand. We have heard that language when Hermia
is pressed to look with her father's eyes and finds that it is "O hell! to
choose love by another's eyes"; or when, in the Athens that had
seemed a paradise, her love for Lysander has ironically "turned

a heaven unto a hell"; or when Helena wants to follow Demetrius "and make a heaven of hell" by dying on the hand she loves so well (I, i, 140, 207; II, i, 243). And so in the dream in hell in this play there is an important dramatic action as a quartet of characters sing in argument to save or change their lives: and at its end two of them, having made their decisions, make climactic moves, enter on journeys, one from heaven to hell, one from hell to heaven; and one other cries out in longing for a change; and one other, who has suffered a political defeat, will never be able to change and will always be happy.

Like other hells this one is initially a surprising place to its tenants, because like other hells it is well designed to provide just what most of them have always wanted, whether they knew it or not; and in this one they feel no pain. The truly damned are happy in hell. The newly arrived old lady will be perfectly happy and at home here, Don Juan assures her, because she has reached a place (very like a paradise or end of a comedy, a perfect place) where all desires are fulfilled. Hell is in fact very little different from earth, as he tells her. "As saith the poet, 'Hell is a city much like Seville'" (or London, as Shelley did say). There is only one difference between hell and earth and that will be developed because it is that which makes hell so much more desirable to almost everyone; the lady does not yet understand, so Juan must explain it all. He initiates her with a preliminary gesture by telling her that she will find that her old age, seventy-seven, is not tolerated in hell because "It is too real" and in hell we worship Love and Beauty. She can choose any other age and he suggests twenty-seven as a new fashion. So she becomes twenty-seven, *"Whisk!"* (III, 90–92). She still does not understand and now, recognizably the Doña Ana he knew and who recognizes him, she begins to talk of love, which revolts him, bores him. In hell they do not know what they are talking about. "They think they have achieved the perfection of love because they have no bodies. Sheer imaginative debauchery! Faugh!" (94). Ana at this point is not yet at home, for the wrong reasons.

The two characters who are at home in hell are those who now make their entry, the Statue and then, of course, the Devil, who is the leader of the best society here. The Statue has a problem because he has been sent to heaven by some "irony of fate" (as the

Devil calls it in the wonderfully comforting language of hell), but the
Statue is a cheerful fellow and doesn't complain. "I was a hypocrite;
and it served me right to be sent to heaven." But he has now decided
rightly to join the Devil, for he knows where he belongs, where his
happiness lies—with the Devil in hell who calls upon the world to
sympathize with joy, with love, with happiness, with beauty, the
language that nauseates Don Juan, that cold selfish egoist, as the
Devil calls him, who is a social failure in hell. Juan too can go to
heaven if he wants; Ana is surprised to hear that she too can go (if her
taste lies that way, the Devil tells her contemptuously), and she does
not understand why everyone doesn't go to heaven. Her father the
Statue can tell her that: it is because heaven is the most angelically
dull place in all creation; that's why. The Devil adds that he himself
was not turned out but left and organized this place because the
strain of living in heaven is intolerable. He could go back any time
he desired, often goes back there. "Have you never read the book of
Job?" There is no barrier between "our circle" and "the other one."
Ana still cannot understand, because surely there must be a great
gulf fixed. But the gulf is not literal, the Devil explains, but only, in
his terms, which are a debased reduction as we shall soon learn, the
difference between the angelic and the diabolic temperament: as,
for example, in England, where he has the largest following. Englishmen, who are free to do whatever the government and public
opinion allow them to, may choose the race course or the concert
room: the concert room is admitted to be the higher and so forth,
more ennobling place, but lovers of racing do not flock to the concert
room to suffer the weariness the Statue has suffered in heaven. Ana
wants to go to heaven at once but it is explained further to her that
just as at concerts there are rows of weary Englishmen who are there
not because they like the music but because they think they ought to
like it, so there are those who sit in heaven not because they are
happy there but because they think they owe it to their position,
thinking they are moral when they are only uncomfortable; if she
goes to heaven without being naturally qualified for it she will not
enjoy being there. She cannot accept that exclusion from the best
people and must be told that the blest, once called the heavenly
host, the saints, the fathers, the elect of long ago, are now the

cranks, faddists, outsiders of today (III, 97–101). All this continuing obtuseness on her part, as both a new and virtuous arrival, makes it convenient to explain to her the basic facts of the distinction between hell and heaven and, though it is irrelevant to the present discussants, we hear that distinction which marks off what is most important for us: earth.

Don Juan is going to heaven, he says, because it is without lies, pretenses: "heaven is the home of the masters of reality" and that is why he is going there. Ana is going there for happiness, she says, having had quite enough of reality on earth. That gives Juan his opportunity for his first long exposition and we must listen because it lays out the essential points. The levels of hell and heaven and earth are levels of reality. Hell is the home of the unreal and thus of the seekers of happiness; heaven is the home of the masters of reality; earth is the home of the slaves of reality. Earth is a nursery (and, we may interject here, it provides the immature stage, the stage from which the brighter young lovers in comic works rise to become fully grown), a nursery where men and women play at being great figures, heroes, heroines, saints, sinners. But on earth they cannot live in this fool's paradise because they have bodies: all the physical needs and corruptions, death above all, make them slaves of reality; thrice a day meals must be eaten and digested, thrice a century a new generation must be engendered, all driven to the demands and prayers of the animal. Hell is the successful fool's paradise because it is the successful escape from the tyranny of the flesh, in which one becomes a ghost, appearance, illusion, convention, deathless, ageless: in a word, bodiless. This state, no body, no time, eliminates the problems of earth, the social, political, religious, best of all perhaps, the sanitary. By escaping all these problems of reality you can then call appearance beauty, emotions love, sentiments heroism, aspirations virtue, as you did on earth, and here you face no contradictory facts. The characteristic literature of hell then is romance, perpetual romance, universal melodrama: it is sentimental. The literature of earth, where there is always the ironic contrast of needs and pretensions, is human comedy. Ana, still foolish, thinks that if hell is so beautiful then heaven must be glorious, but she has missed the point: if heaven is the home of the masters of reality, it is a place where you live and work instead of playing and pretending, face things as they are. "But heaven," as Juan adds with a pretty much universal truth, "cannot be described by metaphor" (III, 102–03).

We never see heaven in this play; it is not amenable to metaphor because it cannot be seen. There is no body in heaven, but unlike hell it is not a projection of pleasures of the body. It is the place to enjoy the contemplation of Life: "the force that ever strives to attain greater power of contemplating itself," the transcending of the blindness where imagination piles up illusions to hide the realities (III, 103–04). For the Devil this boasted force of Life, the brain that strives for vision, for a higher life, is rather, as the observation of life on earth demonstrates, the power of Death, the human ingenuity that invents a more efficient engine of destruction. But the weak side of the Devil, as Juan knows, is that he has always been a "gull," taking man at his own evaluation, man flattered to be bold and bad when in fact he is a coward (105–07). The Devil is a deceptive fairy as the effective Tempter of the Statue and most of mankind, but to those on their way to heaven he has always been a fool at last, the biggest in the world. As always, the Devil is an Ass, the Bottom of the universe, and Don Juan, the genuinely superior spirit, above the human condition, sees clear through him. To Juan's knowledge the coward is transformed when he fights for a universal purpose, an idea: a man will die for a Catholic or catholic idea, for liberty, or more than liberty: "men will die for human perfection" (108–09).

Don Juan is a creature who not only strives for but has within his reach, literally, those things for which the characters of comedies can only wish, or only attain metaphorically—perfection, the complete fulfillment of desire, all potentialities realized. Life's continual effort is to achieve higher social organization and completer self-consciousness, to become "the ideal individual being omnipotent, omniscient, infallible, and withal completely, unilludedly self-conscious: in short, a god," with "not only self-consciousness but self-understanding" (III, 111–13). It is the attainment of the myth. What Juan wants is work for a philosopher, the man who seeks in contemplation to discover the inner will of the world (114); the literature of heaven is philosophy. On earth the literature is human comedy because that is where men and women live and must work within the conditions of the nature of that place.

Don Juan has come to philosophy because all other sorts of men were tedious failures, the men who had prowled round him when he was on earth, the doctors, divines, politicians, the romantic artist. The artist with his songs and paintings and poems indeed did bring Juan great delight and some profit, taught him to hear better, see better, feel more deeply. But unhappily the artist led him into the worship of Woman, making him believe that the music, the beauty and the emotions were in her; and she, with her instinctive cunning kept silent and allowed him to glorify her, to mistake his own visions, thoughts and feelings for hers (III, 114–15). In effect, as we can see, though he did not, it was Woman, on earth, who made him a character in a human comedy. Ana, not very bright in philosophic dialogue, understands this point, in a concrete way, better than the others. You all, she says to her male audience, want to marry lovely incarnations of music and painting and poetry; but they don't exist, and if flesh and blood is not good enough for you, you must go without. Women have to put up with flesh-and-blood husbands—and little enough of that too, sometimes—and you must put up with flesh-and-blood wives. The squeamish, hellish, Devil and the Statue don't like that, but it's true, she says, for all that; "so if you dont like it you can lump it" (116). It is an uncharacteristic vulgar outburst for a high-born lady, but exactly suited to her audience. Juan, unlike the other two, quite agrees, for she has put his whole case against romance into a few sentences. The romantic man with his artistic nature (that man's own term for his own infatuation) had taught Juan to use his eyes and ears, but the beauty worshipping, happiness hunting, woman idealizing, wasn't worth a dump as a philosophy of life. So, as Ana perceives—she is more on her own turf now—Woman taught him something too, with all her defects. She did more, he says: she interpreted all the other teaching for him. Now we hear of Don Juan as a young lover on earth. When he had reached his desire he found there was an "astounding illumination!" He had been prepared for infatuation, intoxication, "for all the illusions of love's young dream." This was an unusual young lover, no Lysander or Demetrius he, eyes streaked with the magic juice, reason anesthetized, because never was his perception clearer, his criticism more ruthless. "I was not duped: I took her without chloroform." And Ana, always with an eye on the reality in matters of this sort: "But you did take her"; and Juan, who knows all this already, replies with his most important speech. "That was the revelation. Up to that moment I had never lost the sense of being my own master." But as we know from what he has already said, on earth no one is the master of reality. Until that moment of revelation he had never consciously taken a single step without the examination and approval of his reason.

> I had come to believe that I was a purely rational creature: a thinker! I said with the foolish philosopher [on earth, of course, there are such], "I think; therefore I am." It was Woman who taught me to say "I am; therefore I think." And also "I would think more; therefore I must be more." (116–17)

That, I think, is the point where the perfectly modern three-act play, as the story of Jack Tanner, ends at the end of the last act. When Don Juan stood face to face with Woman every fiber in his young brain said No on every issue, but "Life seized me and threw me into her arms as a sailor throws a scrap of fish into the mouth of a seabird." That moment did not make him happier, which the foolish romantic Devil thinks was the result, but it did make him wiser. "That moment introduced me for the first time to myself, and, through myself, to the world." That, we note, is the moment of knowledge which a comic hero finally arrives at. He sees. In this particular play, "I saw then how useless it is to attempt to impose conditions on the irresistible force of Life" (III, 117–18). But that is one important variant of the general principle of understanding and accepting, with open eye, one's truth and proper fulfillment. Jack Tanner wants to think more; therefore he must be more: as a character in his comedy he must see that he is in love and he must marry and he must be a father.

It is not the end of Don Juan's story, because he, at the end of this dream in hell, walks off, leaves the woman, makes his journey to heaven, where she cannot follow (except as she too may be translated). The law of his life, Juan says, is the working within him of Life's incessant aspiration to higher organization, wider, deeper, intenser self-consciousness, and clearer self-understanding (III, 127). It is the absence of that instinct in you, he says to The Tempter, that makes you "that strange monster called a Devil," diverting men from their real purpose to that palace of eternal deadly pleasures which makes them the false, wretched creatures they are. It is a bad moment of truth for the Devil; he is *"mortified"* at this uncivility, as Juan in this palace of lies recites the litany of synonym-distinctions to uncover the realities beneath the appearances of the Devil's friends: not beautiful, only decorated, not clean, only shaved and starched, he says, and continues in a brilliant series of several dozen lessons in the language of a clear moral vision. The unchangeable Devil of course cannot learn anything from the mortification of being shown the truth, incapable of opening his eye. Under the pressure of losing a client he descends to the devilish version of revelation, the ingratiating salesman's intimacy of "Don Juan: shall I be frank with you?" He has been so before, of course, as far as he went, yes, but Juan's impatience now in pushing beyond the limits and so going to heaven brings the Devil to "confess": men get tired of everything, of heaven no less than of hell, and all history is nothing but the record of this oscillation between extremes, each epoch a swing of the pendulum, each generation imagining that a swing from heaven to hell is an emancipation, from hell to heaven an evolution. When Juan has been wearied a thousand times by this, like the cynical Devil, where he now sees a fulfillment of upward tendency he will then see "nothing but an infinite comedy of illusion." This puts Juan out of all patience because it means there is nothing to learn, no significant movement, no real journey to be made, only an endless circle of illusion, never a fulfilling ending to a comedy. But Juan strives to understand himself, possessed with a purpose beyond his own: "This is because the philosopher is in the grip of the Life Force." So the Devil wishes him every happiness, a readiness to receive him again if he repents and feels a need for warmth of heart, sincere unforced affection and all that. Juan turns back that greasy language, which really makes Señor Satan angry because that is the language on which he builds his fool's paradise. But for Juan "though there is much to be learnt from a cynical devil, I really cannot stand a sentimental one" (128–33).

Jack Tanner too says "I am in the grip of the Life Force" (IV, 167), but he is not a philosopher and he cannot depart for heaven because he has a body, in time and space, on earth, in the comedy where he must find his fulfillment. If Ana ends the dream with the pretentious blasphemy of "I believe in the Life to Come" and crying to the universe "A father! a father for the Superman," the next sound we hear as she vanishes into the void and reality returns is "a live human voice crying somewhere"; and as the cry becomes distinct "it says *Automobile, Automobile*" (III, 136). At the beginning of the twentieth century, and if you don't like it you can lump it, a vehicle of the real life to come on this earth.

Tanner's ending in a marriage can be seen as a defeat and he himself talks about it in those absurd overblown terms, apostasy, profanation of the sanctuary of his soul, sale of his birthright, shameful surrender, ignominious capitulation (IV, 166), but it is no such thing. It is the best thing that could have happened to him, not happiness, as he rightly insists to the end, not the romantic illusion, but better than that. When he finds out from Straker, at the end of Act II, that he himself, and not Octavius, is the bee, the spider, the marked down victim, the destined prey, Straker confirms his analysis: "thats what you are and no mistake; and a jolly good job for you, too, I should say" (II, 70). Straker is quite right because to be married to Ann Whitefield is a jolly good job for Jack Tanner. Straker doesn't understand any better than the Tanner of Act II why it is that, but Tanner will find out and, more significantly, Tanner will make it a good job for him and for her.

Ann Whitefield is a woman very much worth loving, and like such a woman she has different effects on different men. To old Ramsden she is the wonderfully dutiful girl, helpless, always ready to be guided by his experienced wisdom. To young Octavius she is enchantingly beautiful, transfigures the world for him, makes the puny limits of individual consciousness infinite by a mystic memory of the race, back to the paradise from which it fell. She is to him "the reality of romance," "the unveiling of his eyes," "the abolition of time, place, and circumstance" and all that (I, 16). In the language of the dream, Octavius is the man who would be happy in hell, forever in illusion, and who, when he thinks Ann has broken his heart, will be happy enough here on earth, "a sentimental old bachelor" for her sake, as she tells him (IV, 157). Ann is uninterested in this nonsensical worship. She is indeed a well-formed creature, perfectly ladylike, graceful, comely, with ensnaring eyes and hair, knows how to devise her costume. But none of this is sufficient to explain Ann's "charm" and even without all these advantages "Ann would still make men dream" (I, 16). She is a vital genius, which is easy enough to tell us in a stage direction but rather more difficult to show; Shaw shows us. For one thing, he gives us the other young lady, to play off her. Violet is hard as nails, as Ann says of her, with some admiration for Violet's businesslike effectiveness in getting her own way always without having to make people sentimental about her (IV, 159); but there is no vitality in her, only the tiny resolute mouth and chin, and the ruthless elegance of equipment, including the very smart hat with a dead bird in it. Her withering disposal of old Miss Ramsden, spoken with the full authority of a just married idle young woman in contempt of an old maid "without any serious duties and respon-sibilities," is excruciating. Not much vital life there, but the wed-ding ring before which all must cower. There is no fun in her, no mercy either, but there is some fun in Ann (I, 43–46). The charm and the dream are there in Ann, not only the illusion but the truth it hides.

Ann seems to be in so many ways a false creature, and she is, per-fect in her way. She is "a perfectly respectable, perfectly self-controlled woman, and looks it; though her pose is fashionably frank and impulsive." What is worse is that she is quite aware of what she is doing and sees it as quite sensible and quite right, certainly quite effective. "She inspires confidence as a person who will do nothing she does not mean to do; also some fear, perhaps, as a woman who will probably do everything she means to do without taking more account of other people than may be necessary and what she calls right." What the weaker of her sex sometimes call a cat. On her first entrance nothing can be more decorous (I, 16–17). The studious in-decorum of Tanner's response is absurd, bravado, tell-tale weak-ness. And while he is lecturing Octavius on the vitality of woman, the blind fury of creation, and the struggle of the mother woman and the artist man—and instructing him that the artist's work is "to shew us ourselves as we really are. Our minds are nothing but this knowl-edge of ourselves" (24)—she is showing us what knowledge of him-self he has. While he champions Violet's cause with fervor and ignorance, Ann acts with a quiet and sensible detachment, she of course secretly knowing the undreadful truth and using the occasion to dispose of the others and keep Tanner for a private conversation.

She hopes he doesn't mind being her guardian. He doesn't yet know, nor do we, how that has been arranged. He thinks it has been his own fault because of a large speech he once made to her father (about youth and age) and he has now discovered that her father made a particular application; that's not a bad guess, though wide of the mark, and characteristic of Tanner's fate. What he won't know until the end is that Ann has arranged his fate, for her own purposes, even more directly. At this point he thinks he is simply the latest addition to her collection of scapegoats, but once again it's a clever mistake because he doesn't really understand the role he plays in this human comedy. His stupid old joke, as it is to her, doesn't stop Ann ("Do please drop it"). He had been staring gloomily at Ramsden's bust of Herbert Spencer, now he studies her in the same way, with as much understanding of his evolution, that is, his usual partial knowledge. He realizes how unreal his moral judgments are. She seems to him to have absolutely no conscience—only hypocrisy, and she can't see the difference—"yet there is a sort of fascination about you. I always attend to you, somehow. I should miss you if I lost you" (31). He won't lose her; she'll see to that.

But she knows he's not easy. She tries to establish a claim by their long relation, since they were boy and girl, but he refuses to be held to that measure, evidently because he remembers it all as a time when she, a Lady Mephistopheles, tempted and controlled him, insatiably curious as to what a boy might be capable of, diabolically clever at getting through a boy's guard and surprising his inmost secrets. He does have a partial understanding that in her power over him she has something of the Puck-like, devilish, mind-reading force. It does him no good, of course, because his eyes are, in his mode, too wide open. She never exercised that power with Octavius; he is suddenly struck by the remembrance that for some reason, obvious enough to us, she never tempted that boy. The Tanner boy told her all his secrets and she never told him anything. He didn't want to talk about her, she says, he wanted to talk about himself. "But what a devil of a child you must have been" to know that weakness and play on it (I, 32–33), and that's true because she does have that genuine secret of play. What Ann did not and does not understand, however, is that the boy broke off their confidences and became "quite strange" to her, not because of other girls, which she could understand, but because of that strange thing she could not understand; what is beyond her is that he found something of his own, a soul, the birth of a moral passion, became, in his own grand estimation, a reformer, an iconoclast, shattering creeds, demolishing idols. She, too feminine she says, is bored by senseless destruction. But for him this sort of destruction clears the ground, gives space and liberty, prepares for creation, the creation he adores in flora and fauna and even in her; it was creative instinct that led her to attach him and with bonds that have left their mark to this day. With the sort of irony that always dogs reluctant lovers, he says "Yes," the old childish compact between them was an unconscious love compact, and that of course suddenly chases the boredom from her face. But his half-knowledge of passion is still a moral passion only and he can still defend himself, unknowingly, in confusing her by being silly: "one never knows how to take you," she says (34–37). She knows how to take him, but it will take her a little time to figure that out.

He had developed a jealous sense of his own individuality, his emancipation from her, from woman and her instinct to keep him from getting loose. "No woman shall ever enslave me . . ." (I, 38). It is not a fully convincing line of a free man, since he finds it necessary to repeat it, to Octavius in the next act—"I am neither the slave of love nor its dupe" (II, 54)—and both times it is in protection against the same woman; he is by his own admission "the slave of that car" of his, which is also the subject of his troubled dreams at night, and he is "Enry's slave" (49, 56). Trivial or important these are all preliminary manifestations of that larger general revelation of the dream, that he is, like all human beings, a slave of reality. His declarations of freedom don't bother her, because "I dont mind your queer opinions one little bit." He is intelligent enough to know she doesn't mind because she knows they don't matter any more than the boa minds opinions. She puts her boa round his neck, throwing away even her hypocrisy, but she is never hypocritical with him, she says, and puts her arms round his neck. He, the overwise man, pities Octavius, thinking she is "only playing" with "me," because he is not, as she sees, really a clever man. If he seems to understand the things she doesn't he is a perfect baby in the things she does understand; and men make more mistakes by being too clever than by be-

ing too good, she adds, with contempt for both him and Octavius
and the whole male sex. He never feels safe with her—"there is a
devilish charm"—then breaks off from that truth, in a futile attempt
for safety, "or no: not a charm, a subtle interest [*she laughs*]." She
understands him, as she usually does in important matters: he is a
flirt, always abusing and offending people but never really meaning
to let go his hold of them (I, 39–41), which is a lot better than his own
understanding of himself.

They are a well-matched couple. She must put forth the best in
herself before she can succeed, and he will be the better for it. Before she catches him he will know much more of the truth about himself. And she will know more of the truth about herself because he
will force it from her. Ann knows that Octavius is not a man for her,
with all his illusions about her, not all of them to her liking either
since they depend on an assumption of feminine incapacity. She has
no real interest in his romantic notions, though she is willing to play
on them, and knows that even if she were willing to accept him she
would soon disillusion him. But she does not dread disillusioning
Jack and her face lights up with mischievous ecstasy at the absurd
thought: "I cant: he has no illusions about me. I shall surprise Jack
the other way." She can't disillusionize him because she won't have
to live up to an ideal, but "Oh, I shall enrapture Jack sometimes!"
(IV, 157–58). Octavius knows too little, Jack too much, as Mrs.
Whitefield says (161), but Jack is teachable. He has not the slightest
intention of marrying Ann, he tells Mrs. Whitefield, emphatically.
But Mrs. Whitefield, nonentity that she is, does understand slyly
that "She'd meet her match in you, Jack. I'd like to see her meet her
match." He thinks not, sees no match for her except a man with a
poker and hob-nailed boots and not even then. Mrs. Whitefield
knows more: "No: she's afraid of you. At all events, you would tell
her the truth about herself." And that indeed is one thing he can do,
as feeble Mrs. Whitefield has always longed to do. That is, he can
tell her the truth about herself in terms of her own professed moral
code. To begin with, he explains to her less articulate mother, Ann
says things that are not strictly true, is in short a liar. Having
plunged Octavius into love without any intention of marrying him
she is a coquette. Her treatment of her mother makes plain that she
is a bully as well. She can't bully men as she bullies women so "she

habitually and unscrupulously uses her personal fascination to make men give her whatever she wants. That makes her almost something for which I know no polite word." "Well," says Mrs. Whitefield in her kind of mild expostulation, "you cant expect perfection, Jack" (162–63). No, he can't. Most marriages, Ana had said to Juan, are "perfectly comfortable." "'Perfectly' is a strong expression, Ana," said he. "What you mean is that sensible people make the best of one another" (III, 120), and that wasn't good enough for him. Unlike the free Don Juan and his desire for perfection, Jack Tanner will have to take a flesh-and-blood wife. In this trumped-up indictment he has brought against Ann she is no different from anyone else, as he admits, but she will admit nothing, insisting on the conventional code; he can stand anything except her confounded hypocrisy. "That's what beats me." Mrs. Whitefield is carried away by hearing her own opinion so eloquently expressed; she has been given the word she could never find her herself. "Oh, she is a hypocrite. She is: she is. Isnt she?" And this she can improve into "Ann ought to marry you . . . it would serve her right." (IV, 163–64). It certainly would. The hypocrisy doesn't beat him because that's the truth he at last forces from her, that consummate actress.

It is evident, and it becomes more apparent to him, that some force other than his will is pushing him into marriage. There are social assumptions, the conventions he despises and talks against. There have been, from the start, the conventions of comedies, too: as when he says, "I cant control her . . . I might as well be her husband" (I, 11), a serious improvement on the trivial complaint of Wilde's Lord Augustus, "Well, really, I might be her husband already" (*Lady Windermere's Fan*, end of Act II). The two sets of conventions have old and related origins, which he doesn't realize. Mrs. Whitefield is confused by the scientific advances of the modern world, which of course he knows all about, and he is kind in his condescension. "Yes: life is more complicated than we used to think." But she startles him by knowing the one important fact, that of course he'll marry Ann whether Mrs. Whitefield likes it or not—. "It seems to me," he interrupts, "that I shall presently be married to Ann whether I like it myself or not" (IV, 161–62). "The sooner you get married too, the better," Violet tells him, with her usual contempt. "You will be much less misunderstood." And she is right. "I

quite expect to get married in the course of the afternoon," he answers restively. "You all seem to have set your minds on it" (165).

But the deeper pressures, which make social and comic conventions, are what he has yet to see. "Ann: I will not marry you," he
explodes. "Do you hear? I wont, wont, wont, wont, WONT marry
you." She is confident the end must be near and she is placid. He
knows it's in the air; others leave them alone together, Ramsden
beams, Octavius refers him to her mother and offers a blessing,
Straker openly treats her as his future employer. Jack knows the fu-
tility of escape, having run away only to be stopped by a lovesick
brigand and run down like a truant schoolboy. If he doesn't want to
be married, he needn't be, Ann says, turning away, sitting down,
much at her ease. He follows her, not at ease. Men don't want to be
hanged but they let themselves be without a struggle for life (he
does have that backwards, the understanding of his life and fate).
"We do the world's will, not our own. I have a frightful feeling that I
shall let myself be married because it is the world's will that you
should have a husband." No, not quite, we see; not that she should
have a husband, but that she should have him. "But why me? me of
all men!" To him marriage is apostasy, violation of his manhood, acceptance of defeat, all those protective words he has deployed to
keep himself from sharing the human fate. "Why are you trying to
fascinate me, Jack, if you don't want to marry me?" He is coming to
see that there is more at work than the conventional pressures, or
rather that they are the immediate form of the basic force. "The Life
Force. I am in the grip of the Life Force" (IV, 166–67), in an uncertain memory of the dream.

"I dont understand in the least," she says, "it sounds like the Life
Guards." And she is right to mock him not only because she is interested in the present concrete man and not his distant abstractions,
but because, though she can't know this, he is not the bodiless philosopher of his dream. He, as her match, is the flesh-and-blood
man, though he does not understand that. Why doesn't she marry
Octavius, he asks? She lets him in on the "secret" he has never seen,
that Octavius will never marry. Hasn't he noticed that that sort of
man never marries? Tanner is astonished. No, she points out, men
like that always live as comfortable bachelors with broken hearts,

adored by their landladies, and never get married: "Men like you
always get married." And now finally it begins to end, as he smites
his brow to let in the light. "How frightfully, horribly true! It has
been staring me in the face all my life; and I never saw it before" (IV,
167). It is the classic line of the moment of eye-opening. It's the
same with women, Ann explains with a fair equality; the poetic temperament's very nice, but it's an old maid's temperament. "Barren,"
he says; "The Life Force passes it by." Now he's talking her language. "If thats what you mean by the Life Force, yes." He tries the
names he has used for accusation, as defensive talismans. "Infamous, abandoned woman! Devil!" She reminds him of "Boa-
constrictor!" Then he does better—"Hypocrite!"—because that
one is true, the eloquent expression of the truth which so carried
away Mrs. Whitefield, and that one she has never been willing to
admit. The truth is being forced. She answers now, softly, "I must
be, for my future husband's sake." "For mine! *[Correcting himself
savagely]* I mean for his." She of course ignores the correction, because the truth is closer for both of them. Yes, for his own sake, and
he'd better marry a hypocrite; women who go about in rational dress
(and I take it the phrase is not limited to gendered clothing) are in-
sulted, get into all sorts of hot water, and their husbands are dragged
in too and live in further dread: wouldn't he prefer a wife he could
depend on? No, for him hot water is the revolutionist's element and
you clean men as you clean milk pails, by scalding them. It is his
familiar talk, which she has never minded one little bit and which
she has never needed to answer, but now she is ready to dispose of
it easily. "Cold water has its uses too. It's healthy." He needs that
douche and it tells him more of her and her equal powers than he
knew, and it brings him to despair: "Oh, you are witty: at the supreme moment the Life Force endows you with every quality." But
if she can change roles and be witty then he can do the same and be a
hypocrite; her father appointed him her guardian, not her suitor,
and he will be faithful to his trust. But he has never known, in any
way, the full story of his life and now this last bit is revealed to him,
quite properly, in a bit of immemorial stage-convention business
about a hidden will, here elevated slightly to a painful pun. It was
she whom her father consulted before making his will and, says she,

"I chose you!" "The will is yours then! The trap was laid from the beginning." And how long ago that beginning was Ann really knows: *"[concentrating all her magic]* From the beginning—from our childhood—for both of us—by the Life Force" (167–68). The magic is there in the mountains of Spain as it is in the wood a league without the town, and as it was there, before it was recognized, in Athens or in London.

In dramatic terms the Life Force has an important function. It is the love-juice, the potent and universal force that is more than an individual desire, though that individual desire is the form in which it manifests itself in any one life or paired lives. It is the enchantment, the charm and then the counter-charm. It is what produces the blindness of the lover and then, in its true significance, produces the turn. It is the magic of the eye-opener that reveals the true love by the moment of self-knowledge. Shaw is a poet, with his eye in a fine frenzy rolling, and he gives to airy nothing a local habitation and a name that pleases him as having a more early twentieth-century juiciness than love-in-idleness or Dian's bud, the juices of those little flowers of the late sixteenth century; but in the drama the Life Force plays its part as self-knowledge.

Tanner has no defenses now but stubborn and useless words. "I will not marry you, I will not marry you." "Oh you will, you will." And for his mindless "no, no, no," she has only her "yes, yes, yes" (that treble affirmative position, evidently urgent in women of several sorts around 1903, or 1904). It leaves her coaxing, imploring, almost exhausted: "Yes. Before it is too late for repentance. Yes." That is an unwitting mistake because he is struck by the echo from the past. "When did all this happen to me before? Are we two dreaming?" The memory is there because he knows it not only from personal experience and he is thrown back into the timeless dream where he learned that. But to her he is slipping away again, into the generalities where he has always tried to dwell, and this time is her last grasp and she can't hold on. She loses her courage and with an anguish she does not conceal can now say only, "No. We are awake; and you have said no: that is all." He has won and he replies *"brutally,"* the triumphant man, "Well?" "Well, I made a mistake: you do not love me." So she hasn't caught him and he hasn't been defeated and he hasn't been duped or enslaved. But the Life Force has done its magic, it has opened his eyes, and he understands himself. "*[seizing her in his arms]* It is false: I love you. The Life Force enchants me: I have the whole world in my arms when I clasp you" (IV, 169). (O my, how these poets do bring back to life such dead lines and their metaphors, giving them new meaning! "For you in my respect are all the world," as lovers said in the wood a league without Athens, II, i, 224) But he is still regretting his freedom, honor, self, one and indivisible, and such stuff as he has never understood properly. She tells him his happiness will be worth them all, but this is part of a nonsense he has never desired. Both have a favored nonsense they speak, but the truth must come. He will not sell all that for happiness, he insists, forcing her to give up her last pretense and speak her truth. "It will not be all happiness for me," she says; "Perhaps death." That clutch holds and hurts, sets him groaning (the sound of childbirth). "What have you grasped in me? Is there a father's heart as well as a mother's?" (169). Yes, it seems there is. He has been talking, talking so well, about vitality in women as a blind fury of creation and how a man is nothing to them but an instrument of that purpose (I, 23); Don Juan has pursued that line too, and bodiless Juan can get away with that, but Jack shall have Jill and all that follows on earth, where thrice a century a new generation must be engendered because there is a father's heart too. He has been introduced for the first time to himself, and, through himself, to the world. If he is a slave of reality, as he must be, he has not been enslaved as the dupe of a woman. He is in the grip of the Life Force and, like all young lovers, it is "I wot not by what power / But by some power it is" (*Midsummer Night*, IV, i, 161–62). He understands that now better than anyone and he understands her better than anyone, which makes him a superior man—which is what she wanted, which is true even if she didn't understand what that would mean. He has not sold freedom and honor and self; he has become free, free from his ignorance of himself, free from his ignorance of his own desire, to grow up and fulfill that self, by marrying this woman here and now. It is only in this way that he can move from this point to an unknown possibility. And those who may still think, in that old canard, that Shaw is sexless, may try this climax:

TANNER: If we too stood now on the edge of a precipice, I
   would hold you tight and jump.
ANN: [*panting, failing more and more under the strain*] Jack;
   let me go. I have dared so frightfully—it is lasting longer
   than I thought. Let me go: I can't bear it.
TANNER: Nor I. Let it kill us.
ANN: Yes: I dont care. I am at the end of my forces. I don't care.
   I think I am going to faint. (IV, 169)

It is a tour de force, a comedy and a philosophy, perfectly modern
three-act play and totally extraneous middle act of the enchanted
hero in his dream, detachable parts, separately actable and usually
separated. As in *A Midsummer Night* the half-remembered strange
dream is validated as something of great constancy:

MENDOZA: Did you dream?
TANNER: Damnably. Did you?
MENDOZA: Yes. I forget what. You were in it.
TANNER: So were you. Amazing! (III, 136).

Here, however, the prosy play can work with or without the poetic
dream; the middle and its myth of perfection isn't necessary for the
solution, because here you can't expect perfection at the end; but
the young lover, to the extent that he remembers the dream, understands at that lofty level what is happening to him, and more importantly, we understand who he is and what he is doing at the end of
his comedy.

ANN: [*looking at him with fond pride and caressing his arm*]
   Never mind . . . Go on talking.
TANNER: Talking!
   Universal laughter.

   The text is in Shaw's *Collected Works*, "Ayot St. Lawrence Edition," Vol.
X (New York, 1930). References are to act and page number; where successive quotations in the same paragraph are from the same act the act number
is not repeated. In quotations from Shaw's more extensive stage directions,
the short-essay type, italics and roman have been reversed.
Bentley, Eric, *Bernard Shaw 1856–1950*, Amended Edition (New York,
   1957)
Berst, Charles A., *Bernard Shaw and the Art of the Drama* (Urbana, 1973)

Bertolini, John A., *The Playwriting Self of Bernard Shaw* (Carbondale, 1991)

Brustein, Robert, *The Theatre of Revolt: An Approach to Modern Drama* (Boston, 1964)

Crompton, Louis, *Shaw and the Dramatist* (Lincoln, 1969)

Dukore, Bernard F., *Bernard Shaw, Playwright: Aspects of Shavian Drama* (Columbia, Mo., 1973)

————, "Shaw's 'Big Three'," *Shaw: The Annual of Bernard Shaw Studies*, IV (1984), 33–67

Gibbs, A. M., *The Art and the Mind of Shaw: Essays in Criticism* (New York, 1983)

Gordon, David J., *Bernard Shaw and the Comic Sublime* (New York, 1990)

Grene, Nicholas, *Bernard Shaw: A Critical View* (New York, 1984)

Morgan, Margery M., *The Shavian Playground: An Exploration of the Art of George Bernard Shaw* (London, 1972)

McDowell, Frederick P. W., "Heaven, Hell, and Turn-of-the-Century London: Reflections upon Shaw's *Man and Superman*," *Drama Survey*, II (1963), 245–68

Nethercot, Arthur H., *Men and Supermen: The Shavian Portrait Gallery* (Cambridge, Mass., 1954)

Sterner, Mark H., "*Man and Superman:* Drama as Clash between Social and Spiritual Exigencies," *Text and Presentation*, IX (1989), 141–48

Valency, Maurice, *The Cart and the Trumpet: The Plays of George Bernard Shaw* (New York, 1973)

Vogt, Sally Peters, "Ann and Superman: Type and Archtetype," *Fabian Feminist*, ed. Rodelle Weintraub (University Park, Pa., 1977)

Wisenthal, J. L., *The Marriage of Contraries: Bernard Shaw's Middle Plays* (Cambridge, Mass., 1974)

Chapter Three

What are men to rocks and mountains?

Pride and Prejudice

A young lover in *A Midsummer Night's Dream* or in *Man and Superman* who finds the course of true love becoming too difficult to negotiate has the option of escaping to a country where he, or she, imagines this matter can be better ordered. But time and place are not so magically disposable in *Pride and Prejudice*. The story here is familiar: we are presented with two sets of young lovers who have problems which must be worked out, and here too are those who try to direct their lives for them, and varied clowns doing their own foolish acts, before the lovers can attain the deserved happiness we expect for them; but here their solutions cannot be sought in another world among the powers of more than mortal spirits.

As in *Man and Superman* the lovers are not interchangeable pairs, as Elizabeth points out to her kind and less perceptive sister. When Jane and Bingley have finally come together in their felicity Jane wants everybody to be as happy as she:" "If I could but see *you* as happy!" she says to Elizabeth. "If there *were* but such another man for you!" It does not seem possible to her that there could be a second Bingley in the universe, but for Elizabeth that limitation is just as well. "If you were to give me forty such men, I could never be so happy as you. Till I have your disposition . . . I never can have your happiness." She'll have to shift for herself and perhaps with very good luck she may meet with another Mr. Collins in time (III, xiii, 350). Elizabeth's time has not been and will not be so empty and desperate as that, but certainly as she has not her sister's disposition a duplicate of her sister's fortune cannot fulfill her desires. Her sister's difficulties in the course of true love have been rather simple as she and Bingley fell in love very quickly, to say the least, and were kept apart only by the interference of others; or if there is a defect in

Bingley which made him vulnerable to such interference in the happiness of himself and the woman he loves it is because, as Elizabeth says gently now, "He made a little mistake to be sure; but it is to the credit of his modesty" (350). She has had, for herself, a different opinion of Bingley's weakness and he would never be the man for her. There is certainly no sign that he has learned anything or will ever be any different. Like him Jane is not one to profit much by experience: she does not ever comprehend why the false Miss Bingley wished to be intimate with her, "but if the same circumstances were to happen again, I am sure I should be deceived again" (II, iii, 148). She and Bingley are well matched, they being two of a kind, so easy, Mr. Bennet says, every servant will cheat them (III, xiii, 348). Two of a kind is not Elizabeth's style. And if there are external problems in the matching of Elizabeth they are not what delays her happiness. Unlike the story of Jane the story of Elizabeth takes time because it takes time for Elizabeth to learn and to change, and the story is complicated further because it takes time for Darcy to learn and to change and because those processes are continually affected by one another.

We have here too, as in our previous tales, interfering elders who are busy breakers and makers of matches; and, as before, these are ineffective clownish figures with none of the power of their pretensions to arrange the fates of others. Mrs. Bennet is one of the best ever in this role, a legend for all time—that mother whose main business in life is match-making, with five daughters and slender means, but so eager and silly that she is marvellously incompetent at her business, simply by being herself. She is a grand hazard in the course of the true loves of Jane and Elizabeth; she also pushes Elizabeth as hard as she can to take that clown Mr. Collins (commending him for speaking so sensibly to Mr. Darcy and for being a remarkably clever young man, I, xviii, 101); she pushes her favorite Lydia into a danger where Lydia, the likest to her mother, succumbs, thereby immediately prostrating her mother and then quickly throwing her into ecstasy. But then in a year Mrs. Bennet has surprisingly married off three of five, a commendable, statistically remarkable, record. "Three daughters married! . . . Oh, Lord! What will become of me. I shall go distracted" (III, xvii, 378): one of those great fools who succeed so well in spite of herself. Then there is that other clown, Lady Catherine—Mr. Darcy has already been forced to see that he too has relatives to blush for, "ashamed of his aunt's ill breeding" (II, viii, 173)—that other match-making mother. This one has arranged the marriage for her own daughter and nephew when they were children, and she has not been in the habit of brooking disappointment: "depend upon it I will carry my point" (III, xiv, 358). Her superb effort to break the engagement of Darcy and Elizabeth, which in fact doesn't yet exist, helps bring that match to its happy conclusion. "Lady Catherine has been of infinite use," Elizabeth says, "which ought to make her happy, for she loves to be of use" (III, xviii, 381).

But then Elizabeth and Darcy, the young lovers very like Jack Tanner in this respect, also think of themselves as superior spirits with strong confidence in their own abilities to oversee the lives of others. They know how to read minds and characters and thereby to predict conduct and to determine proper matches for their friends. What they know least is the proper marriage for themselves, knowing least their own minds and characters. Like Shaw, Jane Austen has a special delight in such interesting people, handsome and clever, and sometimes rich, the most attractive people we have ever met: those who are so bright they think they are Puck, and who must discover that they are really mortals in love, much in need of the time and place of the eye-opening experience.

Emma might have been a better example for this chapter. She has charm, the charming Miss Woodhouse, and though that is a commonplace compliment, and though there is a false charm, as it is offered in Augusta Hawkins, there is a reality in Emma's which is validated by that contrast. It is made convincing not only by what we can see for ourselves but by the denial of Mr. Knightley, early in the novel: "But I . . . who have had no such charm thrown over my senses, must still see, hear, and remember" (I, v, 37). He, unlike Miss Taylor (as was) and most of those within Emma's circle, has kept his senses clear, which is not always gratifying to Emma. But it is borne in on us at the start how effective she thinks she is. If Mr. Knightley, hearing her abuse the reason she has, in breaking the match between Harriet Smith and Robert Martin, thinks it would be better to be without reason than misapply it as she does, Emma has a higher certainty of her knowledge of love and of the minds of men: men fall in love with girls like Harriet (or what Emma thinks Harriet is) and Emma confers on her the power of choosing from among many. And, playful with Mr. Knightley, as we have seen her from the start (I, i, 10), she informs him of how bewitchment works on men. "'To be sure!' she cried playfully. 'I know *that* is the feeling of you all.'" She knows that such a girl as Harriet is exactly what every man delights in, what at once "bewitches his senses" and satisfies his judgment. We know Mr. Knightley's senses are neither charmed nor bewitched, but Emma is certain that "Were you, yourself, ever to marry, she is the very woman for you" (I, viii, 63–64), a delightful promise. And so it is not surprising that a few pages later Emma then begins to create a play and assures Harriet that Mr. Elton's sweet verses of courtship are certainly for her: "It is a sort of prologue to the play . . . and will soon be followed by matter-of-fact prose," as indeed it will be. Harriet, with a better sense of uncertainty, but now overridden, is more like the open Hippolyta—"The strangest things to take place!" To Emma it is nothing strange or out of the common course but so evidently, so palpably, desirable; what courts her pre-arrangement immediately shapes itself into the proper form. Her Hartfield, under her rule, seems to have a magic quality, seems to have "a something in the air," she says, "which gives love exactly the right direction, and sends it into the very channel where it ought to flow." She has the right text—

The course of true love never did run smooth—

and she is the right editor. "A Hartfield edition of Shakespeare would have a long note on that passage." She has her map of misreading, because under her direction, she expects, all will run smooth, and she will be distressed later to find that the text of her own play will run closer to Shakespeare's. There may be some without common sense who will not find agreeable Harriet's match with Mr. Elton, she says, but "we are not to be addressing our conduct to fools" (I, ix, 74–75). She is, like Puck, above that mortal condition. The charade of courtship found on the table was, she tells her father, "dropt, we suppose, by a fairy"; but it is so pretty, her father says, that he can easily guess "what fairy brought it." Nobody could have written so prettily but Emma, a pretty confusion that helps to define her status among the fairies. Emma only nodded and smiled (78).

She can indeed laugh: Harriet may so wonder that Miss Woodhouse should not marry, "so charming as you are!" but "Emma laughed and replied, 'My being charming, Harriet, is not quite enough to induce me to marry; I must find other people charming—one other person at least.'" And, free from the charms of others, in maiden meditation fancy free, as we may offer our own quotation for the Hartfield edition, she has very little intention of ever marrying at all. "I must see somebody very superior to any one I have seen yet, to be tempted," and she would rather not be tempted. The fact is "I cannot really change for the better." If she were to fall in love that would be a different thing, but "I have never been in love; it is not my way, or my nature; and I do not think I ever shall." So she would be a fool to change such a situation as hers (I, x, 84).

We may be certain that such exemption from the human condition is not a role a young lady or man can play for long on this earth. By the end of Volume I Emma has learned that she has been in error, that she did not see into Mr. Elton's mind, though the misread signs were fairly obvious even to her unimaginative brother-in-law, that she has been foolish, wrong in taking so active a part in bringing any two people together, adventuring too far, assuming too much, making light of what ought to be serious, and, not being tricky Puck, "making a trick of what ought to be simple." She is ashamed and resolved to do such things no more (I, xvi, 137). But of course she is not done; she is still "acting a part" on a succeeding matter (I, xviii, 145); or she is rebuking Mrs. Weston for trying Emma's specialty—"My dear Mrs. Weston, do not take to match-making. You do it very ill," without seeing why Mrs. Weston's suggestion of Mr. Knightley and Jane Fairfax is so irritating to her—and then running off into ridicule of the possibility by expertly imitating Miss Bates as Mr. Knightley's prospective relative. "For shame, Emma! Do not mimic her. You divert me against my conscience" (II, viii, 225). She has some real talents in this Puckish line of acting and of mimicry and of seeing into others and directing them, but that is part of her problem since she enjoys the power and cultivates it until her limits close in on her painfully. By the late stages of her third volume the faith of Miss Smith, her most malleable creation, who is still certain that Miss Woodhouse "can see into everybody's heart" is no longer gratifying (III, xi, 404).

Emma has been a disinterested fairy, exerting her talents to be helpful, enjoying the fun of match-making. "It is the greatest amusement in the world!" But Mr. Knightley knows she is not good at it and is more likely to do harm to herself than good to others (I, i, 11–13). He is better in foretelling things than she, as she is forced to see at several times and, most painfully, when it appears that she has unwittingly brought together Harriet and Mr. Knightley. The discovery of her blindness is mortifying. She had believed herself "in the secret of everybody's feelings," had "proposed to arrange everybody's destiny," and proved to be universally mistaken: and, incompetent fairy that she was, "she had not quite done nothing—for she had done mischief" (III, xi, 411–13). Happily she is still mistaken in foretelling the results of these evils, for Harriet, that clown, will always bounce, and Mr. Knightley, that superior spirit administering the counter-charm, with no charm thrown over his senses, had doted on her, faults and all (III, xvii, 462).

But for our purposes we will stay with *Pride and Prejudice*. It's a story that enables us to follow more readily the pattern we've been working with, both in the symmetrical contrasting of the two main sets of young lovers, and in the way in which the primary couple play off one another to bring about their eye-opening changes. Elizabeth, of course, is the central and most active character, and it is the mind and fortunes of her spirit we follow in its wit and its wanderings. We pick up the bright and attractive quality of Elizabeth from the beginning, her first encounter with Darcy when, catching her eye, he makes the mistake of underestimating her powers of temptation and leaves her with no very cordial feelings towards him: she tells the story "with great spirit" among her friends; "for she had a lively, playful disposition, which delighted in any thing ridiculous" (I, iii, 12). With all the right equipment, the liveliness, playfulness, the delight in all that is ridiculous, the imagination, this young lady is a spirit who will change his vision and tell his story in another way. The result is confirmed in the final chapter when Georgiana Darcy listens with astonishment bordering on alarm at Elizabeth's "lively, sportive, manner" of talking to him, now the object of open pleasantry; by Elizabeth's instruction Georgiana's mind receives knowledge which has never before fallen in her way, how a woman may take liberties with her husband (III, xix, 388). We, not as naive as the

young sister and with more opportunities for observation, have seen
this spirit in its liberty, the "easy playfulness" of manner by which
Darcy is caught (I, vi, 23), the continual "liveliness," "lively imagination," "lively talents" and the "spirits soon rising to playfulness" and
"liveliness of your mind" Darcy learns to admire (III, xviii, 380).
Others do not notice the effect of the first meeting of Darcy and
Wickham, but characteristically Elizabeth sees and is astonished.
"What could be the meaning of it?—It was impossible to imagine; it
was impossible not to long to know" (I, xv, 73). When she arrives at
Hunsford to visit Charlotte and Mr. Collins she anticipates quickly
how her visit will pass, for "A lively imagination soon settled it all"
(II, v, 158). If she cannot find out a secret in an honorable manner
she is quite capable of "tricks and stratagems" to find it out (III, ix,
320). To the uncomprehending, like Mrs. Hurst and Mrs. Bennet,
her look and manner may seem even "wild" (I, viii, 35; ix, 42), a
shocking free spirit.

She has more than the manner, or the art to please by her easy
playing and singing, or the lightness to run across the fields when
she has an important mission, for she has the superior power of
the mind reader. We see that early, just after the great spirit of her
response to Darcy, as Jane, who has had better dancing, expresses
her admiration for Bingley. "He is just what a young man ought to
be," with sense and good humor, Jane says, "and I never saw such
happy manners!—so much ease, with such perfect good breeding!"
Elizabeth sees quickly what Jane is really thinking of, besides these
proper social qualities. "He is also handsome," she replies, "which a
young man ought likewise to be, if he possibly can. His character is
thereby complete." And she gives her approval: "Well, he certainly
is very agreeable, and I give you leave to like him. You have liked
many a stupider person." Jane is easy to read, though no one appreciates her goodness and its weaknesses better than Elizabeth: "Oh!
you are a great deal too apt you know, to like people in general. You
never see a fault in any body." (Jane is the sort of girl who, in another
time, might become a school-teacher because, as the happy saying
goes, she likes people.) "With *your* good sense, to be so honestly
blind to the follies and nonsense of others!" (I, iv, 14). When she sees
Jane's smile of sweet complacency and glow of happy expression in
Bingley's company, "Elizabeth instantly read her feelings." Loving

sister that Elizabeth is, her own concerns of the moment give way to Jane's happiness (I, xviii, 95). But that lively mind stays sharp in its understanding of the minds of even those she loves. Jane's honest blindness to the faults of others leads her to faulty assumptions— that Bingley's sisters can only wish his happiness and if he is attached to her she cannot believe they would influence him against her, the only woman who can secure his happiness. Elizabeth knows a defective syllogism when she sees one: "Your first position is false. They may wish many things besides his happiness . . ." (II, i, 136).

Elizabeth ranges more widely than her family out into the neighborhood, has rather a vocation for seeing into thoughts and characters, is therefore capable of predicting action. If Bingley says that whatever he does he does in a hurry, that he may depart Netherfield in five minutes, "That is exactly what I should have supposed of you," Elizabeth replies. "You begin to comprehend me, do you?" "Oh! yes—I understand you perfectly." He would like to take that for a compliment, "but to be so easily seen through," he is afraid, is pitiful. She can make better distinctions than that: it does not necessarily follow that "a deep, intricate character" is more or less estimable, she tells him, "than such a one as yours." She doesn't give a name to such a one as his, though shallow and simple do seem to be implied. Bingley continues immediately, "I did not know before . . . that you were a studier of character. It must be an amusing study." She is a connoisseur: "Yes; but intricate characters are the *most* amusing. They have at least that advantage." Even in a country neighborhood, where there are few subjects, a confined society, people themselves alter so much there is something new to be observed forever (I ix, 42–43): she has a delighted sense of the effects of time on character.

It is amusing and she dearly loves a laugh. There is a sisterly resemblance to Lydia, but Lydia is louder and more violent ("Lord! how I laughed! . . . I thought I should have died. . . . any body might have heard us ten miles off!"), whether her enjoyment is a silly joke or a good journey to an unthinking immoral end (II, xvi, 221–22; III, v, 291). Elizabeth has a discriminating appreciation of levels and occasions. Her enjoyment is often private, as she sees into how others are making fools of themselves: she turns away "to hide a smile," from Darcy's assurance of his "real superiority of

mind" (I, xi, 57); "nor could she think, without a smile," what Lady
Catherine's indignation would have been if Elizabeth had been presented to her ladyship as the future niece (II, xiv, 210); "and she
could hardly suppress a smile" when Darcy later seeks the acquaintance of some of her relatives, perhaps thinking them people of fashion (III, i, 254). Mr. Collins's proposal brings her closer to an open
expression, when the idea of Mr. Collins, "with all his solemn composure, being run away with by his feelings," makes her "so near
laughing" that for the moment she can't stop him (I, xix, 105). Some
of these opportunities, as with Collins, or Sir William Lucas, are
rather too easy, as she knows. "Elizabeth loved absurdities, but she
had known Sir William's too long" (II, iv, 152). It is more impressive
to hear that the sensible Mrs. Gardiner, who knows her nieces well,
can say to her of Jane's disappointment in love that "It had better
have happened to *you,* Lizzy; you would have laughed yourself out
of it sooner" (II, ii, 141). Elizabeth is admirable, for she has that
awareness of herself too as object. If observant Mrs. Gardiner then
points out that it would be better if Elizabeth did not *remind* her
mother to invite Wickham, she understands immediately: "'As I did
the other day,' said Elizabeth, with a conscious smile" (II, iii, 145).
If Darcy says, with some truth, that she finds great enjoyment in
occasionally professing opinions which are not in fact her own,
"Elizabeth laughed heartily at this picture of herself" (II, viii, 174).

But she is herself best able to draw for him the picture of
Elizabeth as the witty laugher. Miss Bingley is incapable of punishing what is, in her trivial language, a shocking speech of Darcy's, but
for Elizabeth "Nothing so easy, if you have but the inclination." She
knows we can all punish one another: "Teaze him—laugh at him.—
Intimate as you are, you must know how it is to be done." Witless
Miss Bingley does not know that, even her intimacy has not yet
taught her; his temper may defy teasing, "And as to laughter, we will
not expose ourselves, if you please, by attempting to laugh without a
subject. Mr. Darcy may hug himself." That absurdity will not pass
with Elizabeth, who knows that all mortals are subjects. "'Mr.
Darcy is not to be laughed at!' cried Elizabeth. 'That is an uncommon advantage, and uncommon I hope it will continue, for it would
be a great loss to *me* to have many such acquaintance. I dearly love a
laugh.'" Darcy is not prepared to hug himself, for he knows the gen-

eral principle that "The wisest and the best of men, nay, the wisest and the best of their actions, may be rendered ridiculous by a person whose first object in life is a joke." But Elizabeth is as well read in eighteenth-century comic theory as he. Certainly, she replies, there are such people, "but I hope I am not one of *them*. I hope I never ridicule what is wise or good. Follies and nonsense, whims and inconsistencies *do* divert me, I own, and I laugh at them whenever I can.—But these, I suppose, are precisely what you are without." And from there she draws him out until she must turn away to hide the smile (I, xi, 57). Her diversions are impeccable in principle and skillful in execution. As with the family resemblance and distinction in the laughter of Lydia, her sport in exposing follies and nonsense has her father's talent but is essentially different. For one thing, he lacks depth and his range is limited to hitting easy marks. He does well with Mr. Collins, who is deserving of the ironic contempt which we enjoy, but Mr. Collins is such an obvious fool that he walks with happy cooperation into the wit-traps Mr. Bennet sets for him. Mrs. Bennet, who, in her way, appreciates her husband's ability to give what she calls "one of your set downs" (I, iii, 13), is herself the continual victim of his traps, but she, and her younger daughters too, are hardly worth the effort. Worse yet, there is a cynical disappointment in this treatment of his wife, whom he chose for foolish reasons and without accepting responsibility thereafter for the consequences of his choice. The effect is not amusing and creates a family with unhappy defects, "hopeless of remedy." He is "contented with laughing at them," and never exerts himself (II, xiv, 213). He sees into others, this man who is "a mixture of quick parts, sarcastic humour, reserve, and caprice" (I, 1, 5), but not into himself (except for one moment in his life which he knows will pass soon enough, III, vi, 299).

Elizabeth sees with a better eye. The eyes are the first thing that catch Darcy, make her an object of some interest in his eyes who had at first scarcely allowed her to be pretty and looked at her only to criticize: he no sooner made it clear to himself and his friends that she had hardly a good feature in her face "than he began to find that it was rendered uncommonly intelligent by the beautiful expression of her dark eyes." What he is beginning to see of course is a superior mind and his own "critical eye" is forced to a better discrimination

(I, vi, 23). It is the first indication the obtuse Miss Bingley receives of his admiration. She thinks, watching him exchange a few words with Elizabeth, that she can read his mind, that "I can guess the subject of your reverie." Darcy knows her better: "I should imagine not." Miss Bingley assumes they think alike, that she is quite of his opinion in contempt of present company, but her conjecture, as he tells her, is totally wrong: "I have been meditating on the very great pleasure which a pair of fine eyes in the face of a pretty woman can bestow." She immediately fixes her eyes on his face and desires to know who is the lady inspiring such reflections and when he replies, with great intrepidity, that it is Miss Elizabeth Bennet she is astonished. "How long has she been such a favourite?—and pray when am I to wish you joy?" Darcy is the one who can read the mind: "That is exactly the question which I expected you to ask." This is a bit unfair to Miss Bingley, because after all it is he who had misled her and has now changed his own mind, but we don't mind anything unfair to Miss Bingley. What is of more interest to us is, first, that she is an easy read, and he is making his read by an easy generalization about what he calls "A lady's imagination," so he doesn't get much credit for that; and, second, that he is still quite ignorant of who Elizabeth is and what will be the effect, how much greater and different the pleasure and how unsuspected the pain, which she will have on him. But for us it is a pleasure to see this sign of a better vision in him (I, vi, 27). Miss Bingley continues to act blindly when Elizabeth turns up at Netherfield after the active cross-country walk—hair untidy, blowsy, petticoat six inches deep in mud as the ladies see her—and Miss Bingley whispers to Darcy that this adventure must have rather affected his admiration of her fine eyes. "Not at all," he replies; "they were brightened by the exercise" (I, viii, 36). Poor Miss Bingley cannot let it alone and is at it again in the next chapter, forcing even more precise detailed observations from Darcy. "As for your Elizabeth's picture, you must not attempt to have it taken, for what painter could do justice to those beautiful eyes?" No, Darcy agrees, "It would not be easy, indeed, to catch their expression, but their colour and shape, and the eye-lashes, so remarkably fine, might be copied." It is lovely to see Elizabeth, who of course hasn't heard this, conclude the chapter by laughing at them all and refusing to spoil their picturesque grouping. "Good bye," and she runs gaily off (I, x, 53).

But the fact is those fine eyes, bright and beautifully expressive of an uncommon intelligence, and they are all of that, with their quick sight into the minds of others, are not always properly observant or accurate. They do not see Darcy and his thoughts very well, even, or especially, when she is his object. "Occupied in observing Mr. Bingley's attentions to her sister, Elizabeth was far from suspecting that she was herself becoming an object of some interest in the eyes of his friend." She notices that Darcy is attending to her conversation with others. What does he mean by listening? she asks Charlotte. Charlotte, who is an accurate observer, pretends to no more than she sees: "That is a question which Mr. Darcy only can answer." Elizabeth is more sharp: ". . . if he does it any more I shall certainly let him know that I see what he is about. He has a very satirical eye," and if she doesn't begin to become impertinent herself she will soon grow afraid of him (I, vi, 23–24). But she does not see what he is about and his eye is not now satirical, and she does grow mistakenly impertinent in self-defense. Darcy deserves it all, and at the moment he doesn't himself know what he is about, but our concern is for her and her overconfidence in her sight and for the insufficient self-defense to which it leads.

Darcy is not the only young lover who gives her difficulties in understanding, because even Mr. Collins, so much simpler to see through and to escape, in some ways rather an enjoyable object, even he in his strange way does puzzle her. Mr. Collins is a wonderful clown, a gentleman and a stranger who announces himself before he arrives, in the language of his letter, with its formal pretensions to the higher literacy, its ideas of healing the breach and offering the olive branch, its ponderous sentences. He has no noun without its adjective, "valuable rectory . . . earnest endeavour . . . grateful respect," no word where two will do, "bounty and beneficence . . . rites and ceremonies . . . promote and establish," and he has the loftier diction, "subsisting," and "demean myself," with the happy ambiguity of that last. As he says, "I flatter myself . . .". "He must be an oddity, I think," Elizabeth says. "I cannot make him out.— There is something very pompous in his stile . . . Can he be a sen-

sible man, sir?" "No, my dear; I think not," says Mr. Bennet, "I have
great hopes of finding him quite the reverse. There is a mixture of
servility and self-importance in his letter, which promises well. I am
impatient to see him." This polite young man's appearance fulfills
the promise of his language, heavy looking, air grave and stately,
manners very formal (I, xiii, 62–64). Mr. Bennet cultivates him and
brings him out. When he solemnly discloses his feelings for Elizabeth
she is near laughing, to be sure, but when the critical moment
comes—"And now nothing remains for me but to assure you in the
most animated language of the violence of my affection"—she has a
problem, because he is so fixed in his form that she cannot make him
understand her language. He is so confident of his understanding of
the minds and motions of ladies that, "with a formal wave of the
hand," he dismisses her own words of declination: "it is usual with
young ladies to reject the address of the man whom they secretly
mean to accept, when he first applies for their favour . . ." "Upon
my word, Sir," she says, she is perfectly serious in her refusal. She
considers the matter finally settled and, rising as she speaks, she
wants to quit the room; but no, her word cannot mean, he will speak
to her again, not accuse her of cruelty at present, "because I know it
to be the established custom of your sex to reject a man on the first
application . . ." "Really, Mr. Collins . . . you puzzle me exceedingly . . . I know not how to express my refusal in such a way as may
convince you of its being one." But, once more, in words we have
heard before in his letter (and once more earlier in the present dialogue), "You must give me leave to flatter myself, my dear cousin,
that your refusal of my addresses is merely words of course." He
must conclude that she wishes to increase his love by suspense, "according to the usual practice of elegant females." What can she say?
"Can I speak plainer?" she asks, ". . . as a rational creature speaking
the truth from her heart." "You are uniformly charming!" cries he.
And to such perseverance in willful self-deception she can only immediately and in silence withdraw (I, xix; 106–09). Mr. Collins is the
fool who sees himself as the master of language and reading of minds
and as the irresistible lover. And he does play the lover with success.
If he is told that his first possible choice, Jane, is already spoken for,
he can turn to Elizabeth, and when he finds that she really is unwilling, he could turn readily to the third sister, who might have been

prevailed on to accept him. Mary had appreciated, judiciously, the composition of his letter (I, xiii, 64), the solidity of his reflections often struck her, and though he was by no means so clever as herself she thought he could improve himself by such an example as hers (I, xxii, 124). But clever Mr. Collins surprises them all by his proposal to Charlotte when even Charlotte had little dared to hope that so much love and eloquence awaited her so quickly. "In as short a time as Mr. Collins's long speeches would allow" she accepted him, to the satisfaction of both (121–22). He runs his course in three days, not quite as fast as Puck in one night switches lovers around, but a creditable performance for a mortal playing both roles. (And really in not much more time than the whole of *A Midsummer Night's Dream*).

For Mr. Collins, that unchangeable clown, time can have no meaning—and he has done remarkably well for himself. He appears very fortunate in his choice of a wife, Darcy says. Yes indeed, Elizabeth can confirm; "his friends may well rejoice in his having met with one of the very few sensible women who would have accepted him, or have made him happy if they had" (II, ix, 178). Fortunate Mr. Collins has found a sensible woman for whom time has no meaning; to the bright-eyed Elizabeth's astonishment it is her intimate friend, a character she discovers she has never understood. Charlotte had never deceived her. Charlotte had been quite clear in advice about Jane's slowness with Bingley: "if she were married to him to-morrow, I should think she had as good a chance of happiness, as if she were to be studying his character for a twelve-month." Charlotte needs no time, no affection, no movement in feeling or knowledge; knowing does not advance felicity in the least and "it is better to know as little as possible of the defects of the person with whom you are to pass your life." Elizabeth, we know already, delights in anything ridiculous: "You make me laugh, Charlotte; but it is not sound. You know it is not sound, and that you would never act in this way yourself" (I, vi, 23). Charlotte knows quite well how she would act and does not lose the opportunity of "fixing" her man (21). "You are uniformly charming," Mr. Collins had declared to Elizabeth, and we can assume that he used the same uniformity with Charlotte, but Charlotte's own eye cannot be and has no need to be charmed. If Mr. Collins entreats her to name the day that is to

make him the happiest of men, the lady feels no need to trifle with
his happiness. "The stupidity with which he was favoured by nature,
must guard his courtship from any charm that could make a woman
wish for its continuance; and Miss Lucas, who accepted him solely
from the pure and disinterested desire of an establishment, cared
not how soon that establishment were gained" (I, xxii, 122). It is a
long time before Elizabeth becomes at all reconciled to the idea of
so unsuitable a match; she had always felt Charlotte's opinion of
matrimony was not exactly like her own, "but she could not have
supposed it possible that when called into action, she would have
sacrificed every better feeling to worldly advantage." It is a most humiliating picture. And to this is added the distressing conviction
that it is impossible for her friend to be tolerably happy in that lot
she had chosen (125).

When she visits Mr. and Mrs. Collins at Hunsford she "looked
with wonder" at her friend who can have so cheerful an air with such
a companion. Charlotte knows how to manage that air, by wisely not
hearing or seeing her husband. It costs only a faint blush, because it
is certainly "not unseldom" when such wisdom is not possible, and
Elizabeth, seeing her composure in bearing with her husband, has
"to acknowledge that it was all done very well" (II, v, 156–57). By the
time the visit ends Elizabeth sees Charlotte more clearly, in that
friend's acceptance of a permanent diminishment of life. "Poor
Charlotte!—it was melancholy to leave her to such society!—But
she had chosen it with her eyes open." Charlotte does not seem to
ask for compassion. She keeps busy: her home and housekeeping,
parish and poultry and all their dependent concerns "had not yet
lost their charms" (II, xv, 216). Charlotte is no blind lover, makes her
choice with her eyes open, takes the consequences and does as well
as can be done with them. The charm that needs no time was not in
love but in the home, the parish and the poultry; and yet they too, it
seems, like all charms, may be not fixed but subject to time.

Elizabeth is never liable to the charm that needs no time as it appears in the grave and stately air of clownish Mr. Collins, but there is
another stranger who has an air and to whom she is blind. It takes
little or no time, she later realizes, "a first interview . . . and even
before two words have been exchanged" (III, iv, 279). Wickham
charms her. Her first sight of him comes when she is walking in

Meryton with her sisters, so that her vision is merged for that moment with Kitty's and Lydia's. "All were struck with the stranger's air, all wondered who he could be . . ." Kitty and Lydia, determined to find out, lead the way across the street and it is found that Mr. Wickham has accepted a commission in the corps: "This was exactly as it should be; for the young man wanted only regimentals to make him completely charming." The thought and the words sound not like Elizabeth's but her silly sisters', but this time she is with them. His gentlemanlike appearance, the fine countenance, good figure and very pleasing address, is followed by a happy readiness of conversation—a readiness at the same time perfectly correct— "and the whole party" are still talking together very agreeably when Darcy comes by (I, xv, 72). At that point the more perceptive Elizabeth does notice a difference, but it will be a while before she can understand what that means. At their next meeting when Wickham talks "she is very willing to hear him," and her curiosity is unexpectedly relieved by the conversation of this man who is more than ready to tell her about Darcy. She has a quick ear for the pompous style of Mr. Collins, but what does she hear in the words of Wickham?

> His father, Miss Bennet, the late Mr. Darcy, was one of the best men that ever breathed, and the truest friend I ever had; and I can never be in company with this Mr. Darcy without being grieved to the soul by a thousand tender recollections.

When a girl like Elizabeth Bennet hears that sort of language she should be trying to hide a smile, be near laughing. But this agreeable handsome man is saying what she wants to hear. She honors his feelings, "thought him handsomer than ever as he expressed them." "She could have added," this observant studier of character, "'A young man too, like *you,* whose very countenance may vouch for your being amiable.'" He speaks well, does all gracefully (I, xvi, 78, 80–81). The man was completely charming upon his entry into her life and the next time she thinks of that is at the moment when she reads the letter with the mortifying truth about him and remembers: "She could see him instantly before her, in every charm of air and address," but could remember no substantial good; she is now struck with the impropriety of what he communicated to a stranger "and wondered it had escaped her before" (II, xiii, 206–07). The last time she hears of his charm is in Lydia's language—"and what do you think of my husband? Is not he a charming man? I am sure my sisters must all envy me" (III, ix, 317), which completes the circle of the first meeting with him. As for Wickham and his several roles, he begins by playing the charming deceiver, proves to be unsuccessful as lover, and ends by marrying a fool in, to that degree, an appropriate match.

That discerning eye which gives Elizabeth such amusing power to see through character has difficulties with strangers. She may laugh at her dear Jane who is at first so uncertain in deciding the truth about Wickham and Darcy; but Jane, for her own weak reasons, does say rightly that they can't conjecture the causes or circumstances, and she will not give in: "Laugh as much as you chuse, but you will not laugh me out of my opinion." Bright Elizabeth has no difficulty seeing the truth, can't believe that Wickham should invent such a history—names, facts, everything mentioned without ceremony— her hard evidence. "Besides, there was truth in his looks." To simple Jane it is not so simple. "It is difficult indeed—it is distressing— One does not know what to think." "I beg your pardon;—one knows exactly what to think" (I xvii, 85–86). More difficult and distressing, however, is Charlotte, her intimate friend who turns out to be strange. "The strangeness of Mr. Collins's making two offers of marriage within three days, was nothing in comparison of his being now accepted" (I, xxii, 125). "It is unaccountable! in every view it is unaccountable!" If Jane, in her ineffective way, tries to defend Charlotte, Elizabeth will have none of it. "You shall not defend her, though it is Charlotte Lucas. You shall not, for the sake of one individual, change the meaning of principle and integrity, nor endeavour to persuade yourself or me, that selfishness is prudence, and insensibility of danger, security for happiness" (II, i, 135–36). That is clear enough, but when Wickham's attentions are over and he becomes the admirer of someone else—the sudden acquisition of ten thousand pounds is "the most remarkable charm" of this young lady—Elizabeth, "less clear-sighted perhaps in his case than in Charlotte's," does not quarrel with him for his wish of independence. "Nothing, on the contrary, could be more natural . . ." (II, iii, 149–50).

That stranger who gives most trouble is Darcy, another confidently superior spirit whose eye has its own problems in seeing what lies beyond his assured vision. His first remark, when he looks at her, catches her eye, withdraws his own, and speaks coldly of her, is reason enough for her to remain with no very cordial feelings towards him (I, iii, 11–12). At the point when she can't help observing how frequently his eyes are fixed on her she hardly knows how to suppose she can be an object of admiration to so great a man, but that he should look at her because he dislikes her is "still more strange." What she cannot see is that her eye has now caught his "and Darcy had never been so bewitched by any woman as he was by her." If she does not understand him it is in part because he does not understand his own mind; he really believes that but for the inferiority of her family connections he should be in some danger (I, x, 51–52). Her dislike makes her the ready dupe of Wickham's invented history: "'How strange!' cried Elizabeth. 'How abominable!'" (I, xvi, 81). Wickham's tale of injustice makes her wonder that the very pride of Darcy has not made him just, if from no better motive than that he would be too proud to be dishonest—a sharp insight of Elizabeth at her best, now lost in strangeness. Neither she nor Darcy performs very well in this area. "I should like to know how he behaves among strangers," Colonel Fitzwilliam says to her, and Elizabeth can tell him how dreadful Darcy is in his unwillingness to dance with, or even seek an introduction to, young ladies outside his own party. Darcy is by now prepared to admit he might be more forthcoming, "but I am ill qualified to recommend myself to strangers." Shall we ask him, she says to Colonel Fitzwilliam, why an intelligent and experienced man is ill qualified to recommend himself to strangers? Because he will not give himself the trouble, Fitzwilliam answers for him. Darcy's answer is that he has not the talent some possess, of conversing easily with those he has never seen before. Elizabeth, at the pianoforte, says she cannot perform as well as many women she has seen, but she has always supposed it to be her own fault, because she would not take the trouble of practicing. Darcy turns that to a compliment: "We neither of us perform to strangers" (II, viii, 174–76). They do have that in common; and what they both must find, and each will show the other, is that it takes trouble and practice to learn the art.

What is strange, as we have seen before and will see in later chapters, is in simplest terms what is outside the limits of one's ability to understand, for lack of experience or of vision. But in different tales those limits and the response to them have different meanings, and in this story they present a moral test: to stop with that deficiency of comprehension, not move to extend one's ability, is the mark of a mind either uncommonly weak or uncommonly clever. Mrs. Bennet, who sees nothing that is not beyond her, is the best example of the one and Elizabeth, who sees everything clearly, of the other. The family resemblance here is that, in their unlike ways, they both sit down with their grievances, very discontented with the ways in which other people have insisted on acting beyond their powers of comprehension, acting badly of course. Elizabeth has got to move from this and with the right moves, as the response to the perception of the strange will be a reduction or an increase of life.

She does not like Darcy's unwillingness to move in the dance, and rightly so, but she does not do very well at that liveliness herself. If he refuses her as partner she then refuses him, as she had said she would, and both of them deserve that moment. But when, at the Netherfield ball, he takes her so much by surprise in his next application for her hand, "without knowing what she did, she accepted him." She is left to fret over her own want of presence of mind with this man she says she is determined to hate. When she takes her place in the set, "They stood for some time without speaking a word." Her first dances of the evening had brought distress, with awkward and solemn Mr. Collins who is "often moving wrong without being aware of it"; but now neither she nor Mr. Darcy is capable of making the right move. The dance, as we have seen in *A Midsummer Night's Dream,* is not simply the celebration at the end when the lovers in the action fall into the right places, but it is part of the process by which they change positions in coming to find the right partners for themselves. In the present tale, where young lovers cannot easily find a way of running off to the wood, the dance is properly the best opportunity they have for private conversation, for coming to understand one another. These two must learn the language in which to talk to one another and, as the most articulate speakers and speakers of the best language in their society, at this point neither is good at this dance. Neither will break the silence, till Elizabeth, in an unpromising counter-move, fancies that it would be the greater punishment to her partner to oblige him to talk. She puts him through a mock-rehearsal of the trite commonplaces of dance-conversation, which again he deserves. "Do you talk by rule then, while you are dancing?" he asks. "Sometimes. One must speak a little, you know," though for *some*, conversation ought to be arranged that they may have the trouble of saying as little as possible. The pace is picking up, moving from talk by rule to talk of persons present. Is she talking of her own feelings, he asks, or what she imagines to be his? Both, says she, making things more interesting by bringing them together: she has always seen a great similarity in the turn of their minds, that they are each unsocial, taciturn, unwilling to speak unless they expect to say something that will amaze the whole room. It is a deft cut, under cover of a proffered identity. He understands that it is not meant for herself (part of the irony is that she's rather closer to the whole truth than she intends); and he won't accept it for himself either, though "*You* think it a faithful portrait undoubtedly." "I must not decide on my own performance."

No, she should not, because this small success is going to tempt her to more dangerous performance. After another silence Darcy refers to their recent meeting in Meryton and, "unable to resist the temptation," she takes that as her opening to make him talk about Wickham. She sees that the hit goes home, "but he said not a word, and Elizabeth, though blaming herself for her own weakness, could not go on" (she is not seeing her right weakness). She has stopped the conversation and when at length he speaks of Wickham it is in constraint. She pushes the emphasis, to how Wickham is likely to suffer all his life from Darcy's treatment. "Darcy made no answer . . ." They are given a short interlude, and a proper punishment, by an interruption from the foolishly well-spoken Sir William Lucas—who compliments Darcy on his very superior dancing, not often seen, except in the first circles, and adds, in a courteous afterthought, that his fair partner does not disgrace him. Sir William, with equal adroitness, offers them congratulations on what he assumes is their common pleasure in the forthcoming marriage of Jane and Bingley; and that does strike Darcy forcibly. But he will not interrupt, Sir William says, for he will not be thanked for detaining Darcy from "the bewitching converse" of that young lady, whose

"bright eyes" are also upbraiding him. Such talk of bewitching converse and bright eyes could not be less to the moment. The interruption has made him forget what they were talking of, Darcy
says, less than candidly. "I do not think we were speaking at all,"
Elizabeth replies; "Sir William could not have interrupted any two
people in the room who had less to say for themselves . . . and what
we are to talk of next I cannot imagine." Books? he tries again. No,
she's sure they have nothing in common there. Besides, she can't
talk of books in a ballroom; "my head is always full of something
else." It certainly is, and she is now talking "without knowing what
she said, for her thoughts had wandered from the subject," as then
appears by her "suddenly exclaiming." Her head is stuffed full with
Wickham, which does not improve her ability to see, and her exclamation is directed at Darcy's blindness. You "never allow yourself to
be blinded by prejudice?" "I hope not." She continues the cross-
examination, to make out his character, but she does not get on at
all, she says, is puzzled exceedingly—which should give her pause
if she means it, and give them both more time, but it was only a few
pages ago that she had already known exactly what to think. He asks
her not to sketch his character at present, as he has reason to fear
that "the performance would reflect no credit on either," and it
would not, because neither is performing creditably at present
(I, xviii, 9–94). They will have to converse more of performance.

They will have to make better use of their time, the time needed
to move with more credit in this dance. There is no magic here
which will produce instantaneous effects, no other realm in which
time and space will be suspended, for here they are marked with a
careful precision. The chronology of this tale was worked out by its
author and can be followed with an almanac (Chapman's Appendix,
400–07), because time is a measure of change, month by month and
day by day, and Elizabeth Bennet, not yet one-and-twenty, must be
changing in this daily world if she is to become a woman, capable of
love and worthy of being loved, which here means capable of understanding that world and herself. She is not a clown and there is no
chance that she will not change, no choice of standing still. She has
the lively mind and the eyes that see and only someone so bright
could go so far astray, could use that power so mistakenly; this wit
must move either for the better or the worse, and if she does not

move in the right direction she will corrupt, will be amusing and destructive, her father's daughter. She has come to a stopping point, when all those other people whom she has understood so well have unexpectedly refused to act as they should and disappointed her so: when Charlotte has accepted Mr. Collins; when Bingley has gone from Jane; when "The more I see of the world, the more am I dissatisfied with it" (II, i, 135). And now Wickham too has defected, to a young lady whose "most remarkable charm" was the sudden acquisition of ten thousand pounds. Of course she does know that she wasn't distractedly in love with Wickham because she doesn't feel the accepted symptoms of the deserted romantic heroine, and Kitty and Lydia take his loss more to heart than she does: "They are young in the ways of the world, and not yet open to the mortifying conviction that handsome young men must have something to live on, as well as the plain" (II, iii, 149–50). That is the witty Elizabeth we like to hear, turning the wit on herself as she has before, but there's now also something of the self-protective role of the worldly-wise disillusioned lady, which doesn't become her. She hasn't known yet what it is to love, as she sees, but then she doesn't know yet the ways of the world either, or what it is to be mortified.

She seems to be standing still, as the almanac moves on and for the first time we hear almost nothing of the days because Elizabeth is going nowhere. The next sentence and chapter begins: "With no greater events than these in the Longbourn family, and otherwise diversified by little beyond the walks to Meryton, sometimes dirty and sometimes cold, did January and February pass away." Elizabeth is looking forward to March, when she will visit Charlotte and Mr. Collins, for though she had not at first thought seriously of going there it now seems to be a greater pleasure; there will be a novelty in it, and with Jane away in London, and home as it is, "a little change was not unwelcome for its own sake" (II, iv, 151). The first stage to Hunsford is a journey of only twenty-four miles, to see Jane and the Gardiners in London, and there, as we see under the questioning of the sensible Mrs. Gardiner, the previous little note of a disillusion is sounding more like a cynicism. Mrs. Gardiner wants to hear about Wickham and his new affair, where Wickham seems to have been indelicate and the lady deficient in sense or feeling. Elizabeth keeps turning away from Mrs. Gardiner's careful distinctions, trying to

blur the moral lines between money and affection—which had been
so certain when she looked at Charlotte's pursuit of Mr. Collins's
establishment, but are of little meaning now that she looks at
Wickham's pursuit of the willing girl with ten thousand pounds.
Well, have it as you choose, she says in unfair exasperation with her
persistent aunt, "*He* shall be mercenary, and *she* shall be foolish."
Elizabeth has had enough of men. "I am sick of them all. Thank
Heaven! I am going to-morrow where I shall find a man who has not
one agreeable quality, who has neither manner nor sense to recommend him. Stupid men are the only ones worth knowing, after all."
Mrs. Gardiner loves her niece and will not let go. "Take care, Lizzy;
that speech savours strongly of disappointment" (153–54). It does
and the word is a strong one, as Elizabeth understands, the balked
desire which can become spleen, a sour moroseness. Lizzy is not
standing still but slipping back. She will need more than a short
journey and it will have to be a journey to a better end.

She has the unexpected happiness of an invitation to join her aunt
and uncle on a tour of pleasure in the summer: "We have not quite
determined how far it shall carry us," says Mrs. Gardiner, "but perhaps to the Lakes." We will be interested in finding how far north
this will carry Elizabeth and her need to be carried is loud in her
response. "My dear, dear aunt," she rapturously cries, "what delight! what felicity! You give me fresh life and vigour. Adieu to disappointment and spleen. What are men to rocks and mountains?"
So Elizabeth, unable to solve her problems at home, sees happiness
in the opportunity to run off to another place, where she can leave
behind all those frustrating people and find felicity, be given new
life, not with men, not even Mr. Collins, but with rocks and mountains. "Oh! what hours of transport we shall spend!" We do hope not
and hope that she will make better use of her hours on the journey;
and we can have faith in Elizabeth from what we have seen of her
and from her present insistence on what she wants it to be when she
returns from the journey. "And when we *do* return, it shall not be
like other travellers, without being able to give one accurate idea of
any thing. We *will* know where we have gone—we *will* recollect
what we have seen." It shall not be jumbled together in their imaginations and they will agree when they describe what they have seen
(II, iv, 154). For Elizabeth this will not be a dream and she wants to

get it all clear and get it all together, unlike other travelers. But like other runaways who want to escape into that better place she will find her journey more strange than anything she could have imagined.

At this moment of excitement she is only at the first stop in her first journey, and she is still expecting to see at the next stage a stupid man, the only kind worth knowing. Off she goes and "Every object in the next day's journey was new and interesting to Elizabeth," her spirits in a state for enjoyment and "the prospect of her northern tour . . . a constant source of delight" (II, v, 155). Her time at Hunsford is both instructive and amusing as she sees and understands better the life of Charlotte at the Parsonage and is introduced to Lady Catherine and the honors of Rosings. But she also sees, and it was not an expected part of her journey, much more of Mr. Darcy. In going from Hertfordshire to Kent she is more on his ground, at the home of his aunt, with his cousin Colonel Fitzwilliam, with more and better opportunities to talk and to learn about him. Charlotte, who has a better eye for this sort of thing, watches Darcy as he looks at Elizabeth a great deal, and once or twice she suggests to Elizabeth the possibility of his being partial to her; "but Elizabeth always laughed at the idea" (II, ix, 181). She dearly loves a laugh, as she had told him, but now with his love he will astonish her beyond expression (II, xi), and from this point in her story Elizabeth's moments of laughter will be not amusing but painful; there will be more tears, and those begin by the end of this chapter. Her response to his declaration is resentment and anger, which he well deserves because he too still has a long way to go. His response to her rejection is his own anger and astonishment.

Elizabeth has been quick to read the blindness in others, in the Jane she loves for Jane's too generous feelings, in the Darcy she thinks so ill of for his ungenerous feelings (pp. 64, 78, above), and when she receives Darcy's letter she will have her moment to define her own blindness. "Her feelings as she read were scarcely to be defined." She read in a way "which hardly left her power of comprehension" to a point "when she read with somewhat clearer attention," and her feelings become "yet more acutely painful and more difficult of definition" and the oppression of emotion makes her put the thing away hastily, protesting that "she would never look in it

again." She walks on, but it will not do and "in half a minute" the
letter is unfolded again "and collecting herself as well as she could,
she again began the mortifying perusal . . . and commanded herself so far as to examine the meaning of every sentence." It takes
time and she is now down to the critical half-minutes. She does not
want to see and (like Mr. Collins) "for a few moments, she flattered
herself" that her wishes did not err; but she reads and re-reads line
by line and every line proves more clearly what she has not been
able to see before (II, xiii, 204–05).

> She grew absolutely ashamed of herself.—Of neither Darcy
> nor Wickham could she think, without feeling that she had
> been blind, partial, prejudiced, absurd. . . . "I, who have
> prided myself on my discernment! . . . How humiliating is
> this discovery!—Yet, how just a humiliation!—Had I been in
> love, I could not have been more wretchedly blind. . . . Till
> this moment, I never knew myself." (208)

It is the familiar moment when the young lover moves from blindness to self-knowledge (and for her the time is still not fulfilled). As
we have seen it before it requires the administration of an eye-
opening agency, Dian's bud in the hand of Puck or the Life Force in
Nature. Jane Austen's word for that is "mortification," the just humiliation Elizabeth feels and repeats in this speech, and, as she
reads on, "the terms of such mortifying yet merited reproach" which
bring their sense of severe shame. But in her day-to-day world there
is no designated superior power to drop the juice into the eye;
Elizabeth must do it for herself, a difficult and a painful task. Happily, she has one other to help her, the man who writes the letter she
must learn to read, as indeed she has been teaching him, both of
them unknowingly. Both of them have been proud powers of superior discernment into the minds of, and the proper matches for, the
mortals they see, but there will be none to help open their eyes except as they may be able to do it for each other. It is a process of
mutual mortification.

We have seen mortification before and we will see it again, in both
its trivial and its painful forms. The Devil of *Man and Superman* is
mortified when Don Juan speaks a truth (p. 45 above) but in the life
of the Devil it is only a brief embarrassment, without effect because

the Devil is a clown incapable of profiting from the truth about himself. To Hermia the law of Athens brings a literal threat of mortification if she does not depart from her love and change to another; but it is a foolish law, with the worse alternative that she may wither on the virgin thorn, and we are happy to see her simply escape from death and emerge with a better life and love. The more interesting mortification which must be faced by the lovers of *Pride and Prejudice* can be understood profitably only by characters who are capable of feeling the justice of a wound to their pride and self-esteem. It is not easy and it is part of a movement that takes time. It is here a necessary condition for the satisfactory coming together of the lovers, forcing a self-recognition that requires giving up a part of the character for which each has felt self-esteem and taking on a changed character, the end of the old and blinded self and the beginning of the renewed and more liberal life. The inception, the turning-point, and the resolution of the changing relations of Elizabeth and Darcy are marked by mortifications: the first rousing effect each has on the other; the proposal and letter; and the elopement of Lydia, the event that brings the conclusive proofs of affection. The series begins at their first encounter as Darcy sees her and withdraws his eye because she is not handsome enough to tempt him to the dance; Elizabeth could easily have forgiven *his* pride, she says, "if he had not mortified *mine*" (I, v, 20). A few pages on she becomes an object of some interest in his eyes when he finds the intelligence and beauty in hers: "To this discovery succeeded some others equally mortifying," as he is now forced to acknowledge that his critical eye has been mistaken and is now caught by her form and her manner (I, vi, 23). But neither has yet been able to benefit from this; the effect has not been strong enough, in good part because neither is in a moral position to make the other feel the effect. The occasions multiply upon Elizabeth, especially in that ball at Netherfield, in "the dances of mortification" she has, with badly timed liveliness, prepared for herself with Mr. Collins (I, xviii, 90), in the several ways in which the members of her family make her blush with shame and vexation, as though they had made an agreement to expose themselves as much as they could; and, more importantly, in the confident ways in which she has made her own unknowing contributions to this carnival of fools by her style of dancing with Mr.

Darcy. All this does not come home to her until, at the eye-opening
moment she reads Darcy's letter and the memory it brings of the
"mortifying" family conduct at the Netherfield ball (II, xiii, 209).
The proposal and letter bring, as at the start of their course, a moment of reciprocal wounded pride, but now to better effect. She has
been quite right to reject him; he would not be a good husband. He
has not, even in proposing, she tells him, behaved in a "gentleman-
like manner" and he is startled to be told that truth, and more than
startled. "You could not have made me the offer of your hand in any
possible way that would have tempted me to accept it": this he must
hear from the woman whose pride he mortified by saying she was
not handsome enough to tempt *him*. He is astonished and he looks
at her with "mingled incredulity and mortification" (I, xi, 192–93).
Her accusations of his treatment of Wickham are ill founded, but, as
he later says, his behavior to her merited the severest reproach. It
takes time to work, as the incredulity goes but not the mortification.
The recollection of what he said, his conduct, his manner, his expression, is for many months inexpressibly painful to him. Her re-
proof, that he had not behaved in a gentleman-like manner—the
words remain with him—had been a torture, and it was some time
before he was reasonable enough to allow their justice. Realizing the
pride and selfishness of a lifetime is a hard lesson and he owes much
to her who taught him. "By you, I was properly humbled" (III, xvi,
367–69).

His letter produces more immediately a change in her life. That
fresh life and vigor she had desired so ardently from her journey will
follow his effect. One of the first things she hears on her return home
is Lydia's happy news that the wretched Wickham is not going to
marry the young lady with the ten thousand pounds; evidently the
lady has been sent safely away by worried relatives, but Lydia is certain he never cared three straws about her: "Who *could* about such a
nasty little freckled thing?" "Elizabeth was shocked to think that,
however incapable of such coarseness of *expression* herself, the
coarseness of the *sentiment* was little other than her own breast had
formerly harboured and fancied liberal!" (II, xvi, 220). It is a new
moment for her, that recognition of sisterly similarity under the apparent superiority of language. That wit which dearly loved a laugh,
amused at Mr. Darcy's uncommon advantage of immunity, looks dif-

ferent to her now. She had meant to be uncommonly clever in taking such a decided dislike to him, without any reason, she tells Jane, for it is such a spur to one's genius, "such an opening for wit . . ." One may abuse a man without saying anything just, "but one cannot always be laughing at a man without now and then stumbling upon something witty" (II, xvii, 225–26). We will be seeing the effects of mortification, of different kinds, in some of the succeeding works; and we will see it again in the course of Elizabeth's life, because she has not yet come to the end of her journey. She has yet to reach Pemberley, where, in one reward of improvement she can eventually leave the mortifying society of her family (III, xviii, 384).

On her second journey, with its promised rapture of the hours of transport in the rocks and mountains of a north without men, she does not get quite as far as she had hoped, that longed-for place. It is a stranger journey than she had expected and another vision. When she sees Darcy's home ground it is she who is now the stranger. "Every disposition of the ground was good" and the home itself she sees, with admiration of his taste, as she compares it with the Rosings where she saw him in her first journey, has less of splendor, and more real elegance. "'And of this place,' thought she, 'I might have been mistress! With these rooms I might now have been familiarly acquainted! Instead of viewing them as a stranger . . .'" She sees family portraits, "but they could have little to fix the attention of a stranger" and she walks on in quest of the only face whose features are known to her until at last it arrested her: "she beheld a striking resemblance of Mr. Darcy, with such a smile over the face, as she remembered to have sometimes seen, when he looked at her. She stood several minutes before the picture in earnest contemplation . . ." Now, with a gentler sensation towards the original than she had ever felt, she walks out, and—this is an earned sight— "suddenly" she sees the original. ". . . so abrupt was his appearance that it was impossible to avoid his sight. Their eyes instantly met . . ." It is for him too a startling moment and each has cause for the deepest blush. But she is overpowered again by shame and vexation, because it may seem as if she has purposely thrown herself in his way again. "How strange must it appear to him! In what a disgraceful light might it not strike so vain a man!" (III, i, 246, 250–52). He is stranger than she yet knows.

She is astonished at such a change as she sees in him, that he not merely once loved her but that he loves her still well enough to forgive all her manner and the unjust accusations in her rejection (III, ii, 265–66). But this is not enough and the promising indications that the course of true love is about to reach its desired end are suddenly stopped, by Lydia's elopement. Elizabeth and Darcy have come far in their mutual mortifications but they have further to go, to bear the effects of their past, the old self, and respond with the liberal conquest of the new. To Elizabeth the elopement is "humiliation" and misery. It justifies Darcy in the two chief offenses she had laid to his charge—his offenses against Wickham and against her family— and it brings those two things together in such a way as to sink Elizabeth's power over him. She believes that he has now made a self-conquest, is no longer subject to his feelings for her, and the belief is exactly calculated to make her understand her own wishes, that she could have loved him (III, iv, 278). After Lydia's marriage is assured, Elizabeth is heartily sorry that she had not concealed from him her initial fears for Lydia: there was no one whose knowledge of her sister's frailty could have "mortified her so much" (III, viii, 311). What she does not know is that Darcy has been stronger, in a more difficult self-conquest, than she could have known. Lydia, who is incapable of understanding the meaning of her affair with Wickham, can't understand why Elizabeth doesn't share her delight and isn't curious to hear all the details of the marriage. "La! you are so strange!" But it is stranger than that. Irrepressible Lydia must tell her how it went off and, in her way, reveals to the utterly amazed Elizabeth that Mr. Darcy was at the wedding. It was exactly a scene, and exactly among people, where, as Elizabeth sees it, he had apparently least to do or temptation to go: how could a man unconnected with any of her family, comparatively speaking "a stranger to our family," be amongst them at such a time? (III, ix, 318–20). But he has seen the connection (III, x, 321–22), takes responsibility for Wickham's act. Elizabeth had thought such an exertion of goodness "too great to be probable," and painful to her in the obligation, but it is proved "beyond . . . greatest extent to be true!" He has "taken on himself all the trouble and mortification" of searching out and supplicating and bribing those he had most reason to abominate, despise, avoid (326). When she finally has the opportunity she thanks

him for the compassion that enabled him to "bear so many mortifications" (III, xvi, 366) and he has done it in his affection. They have
both learned how to perform to strangers.

It has not been an easy course for her. When Mr. Bennet receives
the last of his diverting letters from Mr. Collins, this one with the
idle report, and the warning, that Elizabeth may marry Darcy, he
shares the surprise with his daughter. Mr. Darcy, who never looks at
any woman but to see a blemish, he says, "and who probably never
looked at *you* in his life! It is admirable!" Elizabeth tries to join in
her father's pleasantry, "but could only force one most reluctant
smile. Never had his wit been directed in a manner so little agreeable to her." He won't let go of the sport. "Are you not diverted?"
"Oh! yes, Pray read on." He, as always, lives "but to make sport for
our neighbours, and laugh at them in our turn," and knows his favorite daughter ought share his amusement. "'Oh!' cried Elizabeth, 'I
am excessively diverted. But it is so strange!'" "Yes—*that* is what
makes it amusing." If it is not that for her it is because at that point
she is not certain that she really understands the relations of strange
and true. "It was necessary to laugh, when she would rather have
cried. Her father had most cruelly mortified her," for what he has
said of Darcy's indifference may be true (III, xv, 363–64).

It is only after that last deserved stroke that Elizabeth is allowed
her return to laughter. The Mr. Darcy who was not to be laughed at
is to be educated, by a wife who now understands better how to
laugh. As they compare notes at the end he explains how he arranged Bingley's love, first interfering in the match and then assur-
ing happiness. "Elizabeth could not help smiling at his easy manner
of directing his friend." He certainly has been the superior director
of the loves of foolish mortals who, in that tradition, has made a small
mistake and now repairs it easily. Did he speak from his own observation, Elizabeth asks, or merely from her information about Jane?
(sounding a bit like Mr. Bennet drawing out Mr. Collins). "I had nar-
rowly observed her," he reports. And that assurance, Elizabeth
supposes, carried immediate conviction to Bingley? Elizabeth sees
how well Darcy still plays that role of instant power and she longs to
observe that Mr. Bingley had been a most delightful friend, so easily
guided, but she checks herself. "She remembered that he had yet to
learn to be laught at, and it was rather too early to begin" (III, xvi,

88 What are men to rocks and mountains?

371). Darcy, it would seem, in his aristocratic line, has been taught, like Lord Chesterfield's son perhaps, that the vulgar laugh, whereas well-bred people smile but seldom or never laugh; but we can be confident he will have a better tutor now, one who has herself earned the right. "I am happier even than Jane," Elizabeth confides to Mrs. Gardiner; "she only smiles, I laugh" (III, xviii, 383).

The text for *Pride and Prejudice* is Vol. II of *The Novels of Jane Austen*, ed. R. W. Chapman, 3rd ed. (Oxford 1932), and for *Emma* Vol. IV of the same edition (1933). References are to volume, chapter and page numbers; where successive quotations in the same paragraph are from the same chapter the volume and chapter numbers are not repeated. (In reprints which number the chapters continuously Vol. II of *Pride and Prejudice* is chaps. 24–42, Vol. III is 43–61; Vol. II of *Emma* is chaps. 19–36, Vol. III is 37–55.) The chapter has drawn much upon my own book, listed below, the parts on *Emma* and *Pride and Prejudice*.

Babb, Howard S., *Jane Austen's Novels: The Fabric of Dialogue* (Columbus, 1962)

Brower, Reuben Arthur, *The Fields of Light: An Experiment in Critical Reading* (New York, 1951)

Butler, Marilyn, *Jane Austen and the War of Ideas* (Oxford, 1975)

Chandler, Alice, "'A Pair of Fine Eyes': Jane Austen's Treatment of Sex," *Studies in the Novel*, VII (1975), 88–103

Duckworth, Alistair M., *The Improvement of the Estate: A Study of Jane Austen's Novels* (Baltimore, 1971)

Dussinger, John A., *In the Pride of the Moment: Encounters in Jane Austen's World* (Columbus, 1990)

Fergus, Jan, *Jane Austen and the Didactic Novel* (Totowa, N. J., 1983)

Hardy, Barbara, *A Reading of Jane Austen* (London, 1975)

Harris, Jocelyn, *Jane Austen's Art of Memory* (Cambridge, 1989)

Krieger, Murray, *The Classic Vision* (Baltimore, 1971)

Lascelles, Mary, *Jane Austen and Her Art* (Oxford, 1939)

Mansell, Darrel, *The Novels of Jane Austen: An Interpretation* (London, 1973)

Moler, Kenneth L., *Pride and Prejudice: A Study in Artistic Economy* (Boston, 1989)

Monaghan, David, *Jane Austen: Structure and Social Vision* (London, 1980)

Morgan, Susan, *In the Meantime: Character and Perception in Jane Austen's Fiction* (Chicago, 1980)

Mudrick, Marvin, *Jane Austen: Irony as Defense and Discovery* (Princeton, 1952)

Page, Norman, *The Language of Jane Austen* (Oxford, 1972)

Polhemus, Robert M., "Jane Austen's Comedy," in *The Jane Austen Companion*, ed. J. David Grey, A. Walton Litz and Brian Southam (New York, 1986)

Sacks, Sheldon, "Golden Birds and Dying Generations," *Comparative Literature Studies*, VI (1969), 274–91

Spacks, Patricia Meyer, "Austen's Laughter," *Women's Studies*, XV (1988), 71–85

Tanner, Tony, *Jane Austen* (Cambridge, Mass., 1986)

Tave, Stuart M., *Some Words of Jane Austen* (Chicago, 1973)

Trickett, Rachel, "Jane Austen's Comedy and the Nineteenth Century," in *Critical Essays on Jane Austen*, ed. B. C. Southam (London, 1968)

Wright, Andrew H., *Jane Austen's Novels: A Study in Structure* (New ed., London, 1961)

Chapter Four

All beyond High Park's a desert
The Man of Mode

For a man of mode time is, as we can say with gratifying precision, of the essence. He cannot measure it with the year's development of Elizabeth Bennet, month by month, for pressing as her calendar is it has the time necessary to think and re-think, feel and feel again, period sufficient to grow from witty girl to mature woman. But in the mode the bound of time closes in and in its speed very little human change is possible. If Dorimant speaks lightly, deceptively, of waiting for rich men or beautiful women to be willing to do us good "some time or other," Harriet is not fooled. Men who have fared in this town like Dorimant do not live on hope for many days. "Could you keep a Lent for a mistress?" "In expectation of a happy Easter; and though time be very precious, think forty days well lost to gain your favor." Harriet knows he will not for a minute mean to lose forty days and he is playing his game: "'tis time to leave him. Men grow dull when they begin to be particular" (III, iii, 73). She knows time and she will play the game. But neither of them has many seasons, she as a beautiful and very young woman, he as a man who fares so well in town. ". . . a woman's past her prime at twenty, decayed at four-and-twenty, old and insufferable at thirty," he says to Harriet's mother, playing in his disguised role of "Mr. Courtage," pretending to be repeating the cry of "the young men of this age," of whom he is certainly the leading example. How old is Harriet's mother? Mother protests that at five-and-thirty there are living proofs enough to convince these young men that they are wrong (IV, i, 86–87), so it seems a fair guess that this old and insufferable Lady Woodvill can't be much more than five-and-thirty herself. "See, see," says the loving daughter of his poor mother's convulsions of civility, "her head tottering, her eyes staring, her underlip trembling" (IV, i, 100).

Harriet, in her first season in town, is perhaps what? fifteen?—
remarkably mature and self-possessed for one with presumably no
experience; evidently some have it, whatever it takes, already, and
some don't. There's no mercy for them that don't; and for them that
do there's almost never a second chance. In this town time waits for
no man, and certainly not for woman.

Dorimant must move fast because the clock is that tight, a threat;
and within the play he must keep things moving hour by hour of the
day and night, never sleeping (in or out of bed, but never sleeping).
The sense of time is very much a part of, a sense of, the present age
in which one is living. There is a contempt for the previous generation, its restrictions, both social and moral. Lady Woodvill is said to
be, and she is, "a great admirer of the forms and civilities of the last
age," a defect which Dorimant excuses, in his mode: "An antiquated
beauty may be allowed to be out of humor at the freedoms of the
present" (I, 13). Her mother's "reverend acquaintance" is, Harriet
says, "A fellow beauty of the last king's time, though by the ruins you
would hardly guess it" (III, iii, 70), which does seem to be a youthful
exaggeration. "Mr. Courtage" protests that "Forms and ceremonies,
the only things that uphold quality and greatness, are now shamefully laid aside and neglected" (IV, i, 86), and Lady Woodvill admires
him because he is not a Dorimant, a wild extravagant fellow of the
times; but to Harriet "Mr. Courtage" is "a man made up of forms and
commonplaces, sucked out of the remaining lees of the last age" (IV,
i, 100). It is, then, a new age of freedoms, free of forms and ceremonies. It would certainly seem to be free of religion. The parson is
Mr. Smirk, my Lady Biggot's chaplain, and she is a wise woman:
"the man will serve for the flesh as well as the spirit." In his brief
appearance on stage he is kept in a closet until let out to dispatch the
sacramental question of "Please you, sir, to commission a young
couple to go to bed together a God's name?" (V, ii, 135). Religion, for
other purposes, is tossed to the "fanatic," evidently the dissenting
relic of the previous age dismissed in a simile in the first speech of
the play.

The limits within which life is possible are restricted to the
young, we see, and that is a common enough, often essential, need
in the promotion of the happiness of lovers of many plays. But this is
one play in which that requirement is met with a biting pleasure.

Old Bellair, at five-and-fifty, an age not altogether insensible, he says, seems to be "a mighty good-humored old man," but his sister, Lady Townley, disposes of that gentle assessment: "He ever had a notable smirking way with him" (II, i, 30). The limits extend, of course, only to a certain class, which again is to be expected, though here the abuse of servants as we see it at the start in Dorimant's language has a supererogatory delight in its violence. And the lower classes try to pick up the mode. The Shoemaker, by repute an atheist himself, has brought the envy of the world upon him by whoring and swearing, such vices, he is told, too genteel for his kind; but he won't allow the quality to engross the sins of the nation, having his own pretensions to an aggressive wit and to a gentlemanly relation with his wife: speaking to one another civilly, hating one another heartily (I, 18, 19–20). And he and the Orange-woman have at one another with a scurrility encouraged by their appreciative betters. Citizens, the middle class, do not even enter the play to be made fools and we only hear about them with short dismissal, as they are imagined on a holiday in their walk to Totnam (I, 9), as contemptibly unfashionable Inns of Court men (III, iii, 65), as women with a Holborn equipage who trig to Gray's Inn Walks and now and then travel to the Mail on a Sunday (81). The action is in the town, High Park (Hyde Park), the Mail (Mall), Lady Townley's house. As Harriet says to Dorimant, to him "all beyond High Park's a desert" (V, ii, 133), and so it is to her too. She has deceived her mother with a show of obedience to a proposed marriage "to get her up to London. Nothing else, I assure thee" (III, i, 50).

Then, most importantly, within the town there are levels of distinction: those who are the fools excluded from the inner circle of this tight society; those who are tolerated; those who are in it; and, in effect, that one who is at the center. It is a merciless world. One of the scenes at Lady Townley's, as she enters with Emilia and Medley and continues an offstage conversation, begins with this: "I pity the young lovers we last talked of, though to say truth, their conduct has been so indiscreet they deserve to be unfortunate." We have no idea who these young lovers may be, or what they have done, or what has been done to them, and we never hear of them again—but they are gone. Medley has delivered an exact account, from the great lady in the box down to the little orange wench, but the details are unimportant; Medley is a living libel, a breathing lampoon, Emilia says, and "I wonder you are not torn in pieces" (III, ii, 57). She and Lady Townley are both good-natured and pleasant ladies, but they participate in the pleasures Medley brings with his news service. It is a world in continual movement, not progression, not stability, with no security, short-lived. The Prologue, by the very satirical Sir Car Scroope, Baronet, picks up this uncertainty and threat, as it picks up many of the images in the play, applying them to the playwrights, who share the fate:

> Like dancers on the ropes poor poets fare:
> Most perish young, the rest in danger are.

That dangerous dance is a gamble, the play of chance, irresistible.

> This, one would think, should make our authors wary,
> But, gamester-like, the giddy fools miscarry;
> A lucky hand or two so tempts 'em on,
> They cannot leave off play till they're undone.

And it is sexual play:

> With modest fears a muse does first begin,
> Like a young wench newly enticed to sin;
> But tickled once with praise, by her good will,
> The wanton fool would never more lie still.

"Play" here is not free, not for fun, but a game with big winners and big losers. It is one of Dorimant's figures for love: women commonly are "as unreasonable in that as you are at play: without the advantage be on your side, a man can never quietly give over when he's weary." If he would play without being obliged to complaisance, he is told, he should play in public places; but gentlemen, he replies, do not of late frequent ordinaries. "The deep play is now in private houses" (III, ii, 61–62). And deep play, in both senses, it is. Harriet is using the same figure in conversation with Young Bellair when Dorimant first approaches her and takes his cue. Bellair has warned her pleasantly that the conversations she likes in the Mail have been fatal to some of her sex. "It may be so," she agrees. "Because some who want temper have been undone by gaming, must others who have it wholly deny themselves the pleasure of play?" Dorimant comes up and she feels a change within. "You were talking of play, madam. Pray what may be your stint?" that is, how much will you bet, what's your limit? A little harmless discourse in public walks, at most an appointment in a box barefaced, at the playhouse, she says (as witty in word and able as he); but he, she hears, is for masks and private meetings, "where women engage for all they are worth . . ." "I have been used to deep play," he tells her, which we know is true, but he can make one at a small game when he likes his gamester well. But, says she, with her precocious knowledge of the game, he'll be so unconcerned he'll have no pleasure in it. He knows a bit more than she, knows that where there is a considerable sum to be won the hope of drawing people in makes every trifle considerable (III, iii, 71–73).

It is all very beautifully carried out, with an implied menace. And below that surface there is more, there is dirt. That unblushing Prologue hides nothing. The play of this night is offered as an old mistress, the sort of entertainment whose charms the audience once have looked on with delight,

> But now, of late, such dirty drabs have known ye,
> A muse o'th' better sort's ashamed to own ye.

There are a variety of insults for such a fallen audience and no need to look elsewhere, France of course, for material.

> Of foreign wares why should we fetch the scum
> When we can be so richly served at home?

Nor is there any fear that the soil should grow barren by being plowed too often, while at your door there are daily "Such loads of dunghill to manure the ground." More than that, there is disease:

> 'Tis by your follies that we players thrive,
> As the physicians by diseases live;

and as each year there is "a new distemper" with a friendly poison to increase the gains of physicians, so among you there starts up a new unheard-of fool to play. The diseases and distemperatures of *A Midsummer Night's Dream*, which were a significant but passing affliction in a world that had fallen into lovers' quarrels and which were eminently curable, are here an endemic condition. Love in this play is rather the disease, like religion, an end of freedom.

Etherege is not so coarse as Car Scroope but Dorimant lets us know in his opening scene, as he dresses so handsomely, that the underclass of his servants are dogs, poaching after whores, that if any servant is wanting in his duty the next clap he gets he shall rot for an example. Tradespeople wait upon him: "What vermin are those chattering without?" One is Foggy (fat, gross) Nan the Orange-woman, so "Go, call in that overgrown jade with the flasket of guts before her." This language is alternating with verses he recites of his favorite Waller. Then, "How now, double-tripe, what news do you bring?" She brings fruit and she is a news-carrying bawd, and it is from her that he hears his first report of Harriet, as Foggy Nan offers him the best fruit that has come to town this year—"Here, eat this peach"—and he understands fruit (I, 8–9). She brings notice of a fresh peach, as he is throwing away the old, decayed Mrs. Loveit.

To be a fool in this town is a hard fate, to be excluded, cut off dead with no pity, though offering others some good amusement; and it is a fate not easily avoidable, so small is the center of town. Mrs. Loveit is an unlovely sight to see, at her first appearance or her last, from her opening self-contempt as she looks in her pocket glass, "I hate myself, I look so ill today" (II, ii, 37), to Harriet's triumphant insult—Harriet has never spoken to her or seen her till this moment—that drives her offstage forever: "Mr. Dorimant has been your God almighty long enough. 'Tis time to think of another." 'Tis time indeed and time has left Mrs. Loveit behind and with no place to go. "Jeered by her! I will lock myself up in my house and never see the world again." Harriet, not yet content, suggests a nunnery as the more fashionable retreat, the fatal consequence of many a *belle passion* (V, ii, 143). She deserves it all, Mrs. Loveit, properly jeered, no quarter given. Loveit has loved it and now she's had it, for she has lived in an illusion. For one thing she is passionate, naked and undisguised and therefore totally vulnerable. For another, she expects, demands, that the response to this feeling must be constant, untouched by time. It is to her unbearable, maddening, that Dorimant should be false to his vows of constancy. "Constancy at my years?" he asks, this easy connoisseur of fruit, " 'Tis not a virtue in season; you might as well expect the fruit the autumn ripens i' the spring." It is a doubly unpleasant rebuke, disowning not only her and his vows but claiming a natural virtue of timely, fruitful, growth away from her, when in fact *not* growing to a ripe constancy is what he sees as natural virtue. "Monstrous principle!" she says, speaking as she often does a truth that does her no good. "Youth has a long journey to go, madam," and she is "a lady a little in years." The oaths, vows, protestations of the perjured man whom she, hopelessly self-contradictory, excoriates and appeals to, were made when he was in love and do not bind. To her it is "Oh, impious!" No, he says, swearing may be a certain proof of a present passion, "but to say truth, in love there is no security to be given for the future" (II, ii, 44–45). The sensible women in town, we have seen and will see again, do not want vows. Young Bellair protests, "My constancy! I vow—" Emilia stops him: "Do not vow. Our love is as frail as is our life, and full as little in our power; and are you sure you shall outlive this day?" His reply is sensible too: "I am not, but when we are in perfect health, 'twere an idle thing to fright ourselves with the thoughts of sudden death" (II, 1, 31), and that is only slightly blasphemous, Good Lord deliver us. Those two will do well together, a healthy couple. Dorimant declares to Harriet he will renounce all joys he has in friendship, and in wine, sacrifice to her all the interest he has in other women—but she too stops him: "Hold! Though I wish you devout, I would not have you turn fanatic" (V, ii, 133). But Loveit's is a hopeless case, the only something of great constancy in this town, and she cannot talk this language of those who understand the unstable reality of the center. Her inflated language is the fixed art of the tragedy-queen's "daggers, darts, or poisoned arrows in my breast," a taste for passions that eternally rage in the soul, "Plague, war, famine, fire" (II, ii, 41–42, 48). "Fie, fie, your transports are too violent, my dear," Bellinda mocks her in false friendship as she supplants her (41).

The matching of Loveit with Fopling, which Dorimant concocts for his own purposes, and which she tries to use for her purposes, has its appropriate quality. As she lives in illusion so Fopling in affectation, both at a fool's remove from reality, unable to control the life that flows around them and uses them and discards them. He thinks himself the pattern of modern gallantry, his language a pretty lisp that he affects in imitation of the people of quality in France, the complete gentleman who dresses well, dances well, fences well, has a genius for love letters, is very amorous, but not overconstant (I, 23). In fact he is the pattern of modern foppery, missing the reality every time. He dances by himself (IV, ii, 108). He is hardly aware, complacently assuming his success at the center and recovering quickly from and untouched by any temporary setback. He is, he says, "one of us," as easily known from English clumsiness by his French equipage "as an Inns of Court man is from one of us" (III, ii, 65). He laughs at all the town; "I know you are malicious to your power," the powerful, malicious Dorimant quietly laughs at him with a precise irony (IV, i, 96–97). He allies himself with Dorimant as the arbiters of wit, understanding the town, the fashion, gallantry, "the whole sex" (V, ii, 142). This is a precious commodity, saved for his first appearance until well into Act III for our delight and the skill of the company at Lady Townley's. Emilia wonders why Lady Townley does not love company a little more chosen. "'Tis good to have an universal taste," is the pleasantly sententious response. "We should love wit, but for variety be able to divert ourselves with the extravagancies of those who want it." Fools will make you laugh, Emilia agrees, but only once or twice and the repetition of their folly grows tedious and insufferable. "You are a little too delicate, Emilia." Sir Fopling is announced, to make the point. "Here's the freshest fool in town, and one who has not cloyed you yet." Dorimant, with excellent taste in handling fools and enjoying them, counsels Medley not to fall on the man and snub him, that is, not repress or mortify him, but let him play his role. "Soothe him up in his extravagance. He will show the better" (III, ii, 62–63).

He shows wonderfully and they bring him out. The use of fools, as Dorimant says later of Fopling, is that they are designed for properties (V, i, 120–21). If Fopling uses his affected French gallantry and diction—"the *éclat* of so much beauty, I confess, ought to have charmed me sooner"—Emilia, still delicate but in on the laugh, mimics him like a mirror: "The *brillant* of so much good language, sir, has much more power than the little beauty I can boast." He has never seen anything prettier than her lace, *"point d'Espagne"*; she says it is not so rich as his *"point de Venise."* He is flattered as being a delicate observer, with his knowledge of things French, and he agrees that in England "The world is generally very *grossier* here, indeed." His own clothes, as all take turns in noting details, are very fine. "I was always eminent for being *bien ganté*," an immortal line sealing at once a glorious achievement in triviality and vanity and in absurdity of language. And so they dance him through the gracefully choreographed catechism of his mode.

> LADY TOWNLEY: The suit?
> SIR FOPLING: Barroy.
> EMILIA: The garniture?
> SIR FOPLING: Le Gras.
> MEDLEY: The shoes?
> SIR FOPLING: Piccar.
> DORIMANT: The periwig?
> SIR FOPLING: Chedreux.
> LADY TOWNLEY, EMILIA: The gloves?
> SIR FOPLING: Orangerie. You know the smell, ladies.

Each age will recognize the universal style and supply its own immediate designer labels and smells. The clothes are the man and there is nothing in them. Well, not quite true. Medley notices one slight fault: "Your breech, though, is a handful too high, in my eye, Sir Fopling." In my eye indeed. "Peace, Medley," Sir Fopling frets, "I have wished it lower a thousand times; but a pox on't, 'twill not be" (III, ii, 64–67). Under the coat designed to show him long-waisted and, he thinks, slender, he has a fat ass and nothing can disguise that. He is never successful in disguising himself from the discerning eye; when he later turns up at Lady Townley's, uninvited, and inappropriately in a mask, he asks Harriet archly, "Do you know me?" "Ten to one but I guess at you," says she (IV, i, 93). But this fine-mettled coxcomb, brisk and insipid, pert and dull, as he is analyzed in his oxymoronic parts, and despised by those who have the eye, passes for a wit with many. That may very well be, Dorimant agrees; sophisticate dullness is often put on the tasteless multitude for true wit and good humor (III, ii, 68–69). In this judgment Sir Fopling attained a celebrity in dramatic criticism, following the lead of Dryden in the Epilogue.

Fopling is not one of the "monstrous fools" which most modern writers have shown on the stage, Dryden says, those fools not of

heaven's making but the writers' own. Fopling is different, made
with a fine precision; in the lines that became noted,

> Sir Fopling is a fool so nicely writ,
> The ladies would mistake him for a wit,

pretty company, so brisk, gay, traveled,

> so refined,
> As he took pains to graft upon his kind.

He has done that sort of grafting, Dorimant pointed out: "He went
to Paris a plain, bashful English blockhead and is returned a fine un-
dertaking [bold, enterprising] French fop" (IV, i, 98). In Dryden's
general application,

> True fops help nature's work, and go to school
> To file and finish God a'mighty's fool.

He is the self-made fool of affectation, attempting a role which
he can't carry off before the knowing. He is thoroughly blind to
himself, a man who loves mirrors in which he can never see himself. Mrs. Loveit has enough self-knowledge to see at least the appearance of the self she hates, if but little understanding of what
lies below the appearance. Sir Fopling cannot understand why
Dorimant has not a glass hung up in his lodgings, for a room is the
dullest thing without one. "In a glass a man may entertain himself—"
"The shadow of himself, indeed," Dorimant says, the closest
Fopling will come. Fopling remembers the saying of the wise man,
Medley tells him, and studies himself (IV, ii, 108–09). The Prologue
will not allow the audience that easy superiority or dissociation from
the fool it sees on the stage; he is their truth-telling mirror.

> Then, for your own sakes, be not severe,
> Nor what you all admire at home, damn here.
> Since each is fond of his own ugly face,
> Why should you, when we hold it, break the glass?

No one fool is hunted from the herd, the Epilogue reassures, but
that is small politic comfort: "He's knight o' th' shire and represents
ye all."

It is a rich selection of types who are self-deceived, and thereby easily made fools by illusion, or affectation, or, in a special and interesting case, by an eye that in fact sees much: Bellinda, the present love, between Loveit and Harriet. Bellinda, we hear before we see her or even know her name, is a mask, a spark, working with Dorimant in managing his break with Mrs. Loveit; the break must be carried out before Bellinda's face to prove his present love for her. She has the necessary malice and she loves the mischief. Is this unidentified vizard a friend of Loveit's, Medley asks Dorimant. "Oh, an intimate friend!" "Better and better!" Medley approves; he sees she has a genius that makes her worthy of Dorimant (I, 16–17). She herself evidently thinks she is the clever Puck in league with him, but she will be the fool in his employ. We find out who she is in the second act as she enters Mrs. Loveit's room and greets affectionately the unhappy friend who runs to her: "My dear!" She makes up a story to account to Loveit for an absence of two days and then lets us know she must now carry on her plot. Nothing but love could make her capable of so much falsehood but she must begin, lest Dorimant should come before Loveit's jealousy has stung. That passion which Bellinda will rouse is essential to the scheme in forcing the quarrel; she is cleverly manipulating Loveit's love for Dorimant, while he is manipulating hers. She does her part, laughing and actually reporting Dorimant's entertainment of herself at the playhouse as though it were a tale of another; she even pretends at first that she thought it was Loveit, this unknown mask, tall and slender, with motions very genteel, certainly some person of condition, and brings Loveit to characteristic violence of passion and language and manner. Loveit is walking up and down with a distracted air as Dorimant enters and he completes, masterfully, the destruction, produces the weeping, and wittily continues his affair with Bellinda even in the presence of the unperceiving Loveit as Loveit's thunder turns to rain (II, ii, 39–44). Alone at the end of the scene Bellinda realizes that the promise she demanded has been redeemed and that she has seen before her own face more than she wanted to see. "H'as given me the proof which I desired of his love; but 'tis proof of his ill nature too. I wish I had not seen him use her so." And the couplet ends the act:

> I sigh to think that Dorimant may be
> One day as faithless and unkind to me." (48)

At Lady Townley's Bellinda speaks, with what is intended to be
conscious deception, unpleasant truths of Dorimant to which she
does not herself listen, with a fine irony: "Well, were I minded to
play the fool, he should be the last man I'd think of." When he arrives she whispers to him that he has made her hate him, which she
thought he could never have done. "'Twas a cruel part you played.
How could you act it?" He reminds her of their assignation, five
o'clock tomorrow morning (he doesn't waste any hours in a close
schedule). She trembles, will not come. "Swear you will." "I dare
not." "Swear I say!" (he may not keep vows himself but he knows
their uses). "By my life, by all the happiness I hope for—" she begins. "You will," he closes. "I will." And then, confirming his knowledge, she adds, "I am glad I've sworn. I vow I think I should have
failed you else" (III, ii, 59–61). She exits: Fopling enters. And at five
o'clock she fulfills her vow and plays the fool. We have no need to
wait in doubt, for when we next see her it is already after the fact and
the scene begins in Dorimant's lodgings with his man Handy tying
up linen (bed-linen). She has a thousand fears she may be discovered. She sighs, but he will not allow it. "What does that sigh
mean?" "Can you be so unkind to ask me? Well (*sighs*), were it to do
again—" "We should do it, should we not?" He will allow no sentimentality, will not let her now play the repentant maiden that was.
And, to her credit, she will not do that. Were it to do again we
should do it, should we not, says he, and she—"I think we should."
She asks for his discretion in keeping her secret, but she doesn't expect it, and if he starts an unindented Alexandrine in the midst of
this prose affair she can complete it.

> DORIMANT: By all the joys I have had and those you keep in
>   store—
> BELLINDA: —You'll do for my sake what you never did before.

She is more concerned for another promise, that he will swear he
will never see Loveit more. He will swear, a thousand oaths. "Hold!
Ye shall not, now I think on't better," coming closer to the wisdom of

the women who are not fooled, but she cannot, finally, think on't better. "When will you promise me again?" he asks at parting. "Not this fortnight." "You will be better than your word." "I think I shall. Will it not make you love me less?" (IV, ii, 104–07). She has that much knowledge and that much self-knowledge and it does her no good. Having left him she finds him again, immediately, at Loveit's, and knows she is betrayed "and I love a man that does not care for me." She turns faint for she has eaten too much fruit, as Pert the waiting woman says, and 'tis that lies heavy on her stomach (V, i, 118). Seeing and knowing what she saw and knew, eyes open, unillusioned, so much more clever and better than Loveit, Bellinda was a fool, self-deceived against the obvious. "I knew him false and helped to make him so." Was not the ruin of Loveit enough to frighten her from danger? "It should have been, but love can take no warning." "*Exit* Bellinda" (127). She is not an old stager like Loveit, not about to become like her, in the fate Dorimant predicts for Loveit, the game-mistress of the town (II, ii, 47); but, once entered, "to come off, I must on," she says; "'Twere hard to be found out in the first theft" (IV, iii, 114). It is not a moral question but a matter of survival in just about the only game in town. At the end of the play it is true that Dorimant does keep her secret, tender of her honor, though cruel to her love, she notes, so she will have a second chance—a rare favor in this town. He is immediately ready to use the favor for his own end. "We must meet again." "Never." "Never?" (V, ii, 140). We've heard that dialogue before, though she seems more determined now and we can hope she plays better next time.

Her foolishness was in thinking she could play Dorimant's game. She is not in that league, and who is? Not even Young Bellair and Emilia. They are the attractive young couple, in love, desiring to marry, prevented only by his father, who wants him to marry another young woman, and finally successful in circumventing the old man: they present the pattern of the secondary pair of lovers we are familiar with and we are ready to sympathize. The competition of father and son is not unusual in the history of young lovers and it makes us wish well for this pair, even more than usually; the quality of the old man, not only the oppressive father but rather a lecher in his gross language and his own fumbling designs on Emilia, adds a certain odor of its own. Young Bellair, further, understands the mockery of such a sophisticated well-wisher as Medley, the hope that his marriage will give him "all the joys happy lovers have shared ever since the world began." "You wish me in heaven," the young man replies, "but you believe me on my journey to hell." He knows the reversal in this town of the convention of the lover's journey. He knows that here marriage is a loss of freedom, a loss of a free mind, as institutionalizing as religion. "You have a good strong faith, and that may contribute much towards your salvation," Medley concedes lightly, but Medley himself has doubts and scruples, "and in love they are no less distracting than in religion":

> Were I so near marriage, I should cry out by fits as I ride in my coach, "Cuckold, cuckold!" with no less fury than the mad fanatic does "Glory!" in Bethlem.

(That specific allusion may be to Oliver Cromwell's mad porter, as in Prior's poem). But Bellair is a reasonable young man. "Because religion makes some run mad, must I live an atheist? . . . Preach no more on this text; I am determined, and there is no hope of my conversion" (I, 21–22). But even this pleasing youth is not at the center of the play or where Dorimant stands. Bellair is handsome, well-dressed, complaisant, seldom impertinent, as Dorimant and Medley agree, and by the evidence we see he is effectively witty too; but he is not up to what Dorimant thinks of as wit, only "by much the most tolerable of all the young men that do not abound in wit." The standards are high. Dorimant tolerates him because Dorimant sees a mutual interest, though it is doubtful Bellair would be flattered by seeing it in the same way. For Dorimant their intimacy makes the women think better of Bellair's understanding and judge more favorably of his own reputation; Bellair can pass upon some for a man of very good sense and he himself upon others for a very civil person. It is an amusing deception for which Bellair serves his purpose, and Dorimant has another thing in mind which would please Bellair even less. Emilia, whom Dorimant's intimate friend loves and has honorable intentions of marrying, is a rather special woman: she has, as Medley says, the best reputation of any young woman about town who has beauty enough to provoke detraction; her conduct and manner are unaffected, her discourse modest, not at all like the counterfeits of the age; and what we later see of her and the counterfeits bears out his judgment. Dorimant thinks so well of her, a discreet maid, that he believes nothing can corrupt her but a husband. Even Medley is not up to this wit. Dorimant must explain that he has known many women make a difficulty of losing a maidenhead who have afterwards made none of making a cuckold and Medley is quick enough to understand now how this prudent consideration has made Dorimant confirm poor Bellair in his desperate resolution to marry. Yes, the little hope Dorimant has found there was of Emilia, in her present condition, has made him by his advice to Bellair contribute something towards the changing of her condition. His intimate friend re-enters at that moment and Dorimant greets him again—"Dear Bellair . . ." (25–26). That's as close as anyone comes to intimacy with Dorimant, and certainly in this play Bellair and Emilia are less interesting, the secondary couple with the smaller and more easily disposable obstacle in the course of their love.

Dorimant stands alone, with a self-sufficiency, no woman he loves, no friend he shares with, no father to balk or even annoy him, or any family at all other than the servants he abuses. He stands above the condition of all others, controlling and using them, invulnerable. Medley, the miscellaneous news-gatherer and reporter, who hears and spreads everyone's secrets, fancies he himself is a clever Puck. "I love mischief," and he is eager to forward it. He will volunteer to flit quickly to Loveit to help Dorimant in his scheme of driving her to distraction, heighten the truth with invention, leave her in a fit of the mother and be here again before Dorimant is ready to go. Dorimant tells him to stay and save himself the labor, because he already has an agent (Bellinda) who will manage the business with as much address and more malice than Medley can. Dorimant is well ahead of any minor pretender to cleverness. He has the superior ability to move people around. He has the finer mischief, the malice; like Puck he does "love a quarrel," he can always play a "new prank," he can promise to stir up "good sport," and he does it all with style, as the "unlucky look" (the mischievous, malicious look) becomes him (I, 16; III, ii, 58; III, iii, 76–77). Mrs. Loveit is the victim of all this and he does enjoy producing the tormenting love, that power. But she is not the only one who feels his force and there is general agreement that he is a devil. A goodly grave gentlewoman knows him by reputation to be an "arrant devil," the Orange-woman reports, and if the gentlewoman should see him she would look for the cloven foot; he knows that must be Lady Woodvill (I, 12). If not much talent is required to impress Lady Woodvill even a connoisseur like Medley can testify that there is not a "devil upon earth so proper" to produce torment (II, i, 35). But, more than this, he captivates his fools. Loveit knows he is a devil, as she says; "but he has something of the angel yet undefaced in him" (she seems to have been reading, not profitably, a recent poem by a Puritan), which makes him "so charming and agreeable that I must love him, be he never so wicked" (II, ii, 37–38). Bellinda agrees "he has a way so bewitching" (41). "He is the prince of all the devils in the town . . . Oh, he has a tongue, they say, would tempt the angels to a second fall," Lady Woodvill declares, continuing the allusion, as she is speaking to him in his disguised role of the "Mr. Courtage" who so pleases her (III, iii, 74–75). He has "charms for the whole family" (IV, i, 89). The spell is there, diabolical ("Would I had made a contract to be a witch when first I entertained this greater devil," Loveit cries, ready to tear herself in pieces, II, ii, 48), destructive, irresistible in its appeal, its tongue, its charm, the magic.

There is hardly a man he sees he does not understand and use as far as he wants to. He understands and makes a play for almost every woman, simultaneously; "a man of great employment—has more mistresses now depending than the most eminent lawyer has causes" (II, i, 35). He has now depending Loveit, Bellinda, Harriet, past, present, future; he can win even Lady Woodvill, fits her humor so well "a little more and she'll dance a kissing dance with him anon" (IV, i, 87); and he has Emilia in mind as a speculation; to say nothing of odds and ends of correspondence, like an offstage whore. His favorite target for display is Loveit, who cooperates so well. If, as we start, there has been such a calm in his affairs that he has not had the pleasure of making a woman so much as break her fan, be sullen or forswear herself these three days, we see him attain these accustomed successes very quickly. When Bellinda has worked Loveit to the proper pitch he enters Loveit's chamber with a pretty, flattering couplet from Waller's "Of her Chamber," then catches at her as she walks up and down in her distraction with the calming inquiry, "What, dancing the galloping nag without a fiddle?" then pursues her with "I fear this restlessness of the body, madam . . . proceeds from an unquietness of the mind." He gets his anticipated response from the clock he has wound: "Faithless, inhuman, barbarous man—" "Good," he says to himself, "Now the alarm strikes." And so to her "Hell and furies!" and she tears her fan to pieces. "Spare your fan, madam. You are growing hot and will want it to cool you." Having got the tears he goes on in the most restrained, polite and candid words and manner with the most lacerating insults, to the truth he wants. "False man!" "True woman" (II, ii, 42–45). He must penetrate, finger the soul. If Loveit later seems to be slipping from his control, in her show of toying with Fopling, he cannot allow that but must make her "pluck off this mask and show the passion that lies panting under." The business must not end so, with her seeming triumph, and before tomorrow sun is set he will have his revenge and clear his name before Medley's witness.

> And you and Loveit, to her cost, shall find
> I fathom all the depths of womankind (III, iii, 84–85).

She cannot keep anything under the dress. He takes a pride in using her, she says, "that the town may know the power you have over me . . ." (V, i, 121).

He meets his match in Harriet, a girl who has little to learn and will not be anybody's fool. As a girl she has less freedom than he and she is quite proper. Neither she nor her money are to be had without marriage—there is no taking up there without church security (IV, ii, 113). She arranges her own affairs without allowing any effective interference from her mother, will not accept her mother's match-making and will marry no man but the one she wants: but she will never do anything against "the rules of decency and honor," never anything against "my duty" and will never marry against her mother's will, which of course is the way to melt her mother's heart (V, ii, 134, 138, 141). Playing within those rules, which do not hamper but meet her purposes, she gets what she wants. She wants the town, obviously the habitat in which her nature flourishes. Like

Dorimant she is contemptuous of, allows no life to, those who
haven't the gifts of nature for life in town. "That women should set
up for beauty as much in spite of nature as some men have done for
wit!" Women for whom it is impossible to make themselves agreeable "ought to be no more fond of dressing than fools should be of
talking. Hoods and modesty, masks and silence, things that shadow
and conceal—they should think of nothing else." As for the man
proposed for her, young Bellair, he appears well enough to this
young proto-Millamant—"I think I might be brought to endure him
and that is all a reasonable woman should expect in a husband"—but
that's not free and interesting enough for her. "Are you in love?"
"Yes—with this dear town, to that degree I can scarce endure the
country in landscapes and in hangings," pictures and tapestries (III,
i, 49–51, 53). The thought of being carried back and "mewed up in
the country again" is dreadful, second only to being married to a
man she does not care for (V, ii, 129).

She is vastly rich, the beautifulest creature he ever saw, Medley
says, in his rapturous account (itself quite beautiful); but Dorimant
already had determined she was beautiful. His question now is "Has
she wit?" "More than is usual in her sex, and as much malice. Then,
she's as wild as you would wish her, and has a demureness in her
looks that makes it so surprising." It is then that Dorimant's flesh
and blood cannot hear this and not long to know her (I, 13–14). She
is of his kind, with the wit and the malice, well demonstrated as we
see more of her; as he with his pranks and his sports, she has "so
many fetches" (III, i, 50); and, in her demureness, she has the feminine equivalent of his controlled manner that makes them effective
in bewitching others. Like him she is "wild." We first see her dressing, as we have first seen him; both love to be well-dressed and know
the value of dress, both are irritably impatient with the servant who
fiddles about them with officious fingers, as though they were beholden to art. "Will you never leave off this wildness?" asks her
woman Busy (I, 22; III, i, 49). Dorimant recognizes her style, "wild,
witty, lovesome, beautiful and young" (III, iii, 85). And she is smart
enough not to change that. No, she says later to Dorimant when he
asks for sweetness and calm, as she catches him. "My eyes are wild
and wand'ring like my passions, and cannot yet be tied to rules of

charming." She, like him, has the conscious art beyond art, the freedom above the rules, that appears as nature. Her looks are "From
nature, sir; pardon my want of art." She charms (IV, i, 90).

Their superior skill, the skill that enables them to control others,
the fools of illusion or affectation, or even the open-eyed Bellinda, is
the art of dissembling, of acting. The spirit who knows how to dissemble, to mimic when useful, is powerful because he has the secret, the essential secret of others, knows how to present the play
that will move them because knowing what and how they think.
Those who are so moved, understood in their limits, suffer a loss of
freedom, as the superior wits enlarge their own freedom. It has an
intrinsic pleasure, this ability, as Puck knew, as well as a profit. When
Harriet and Bellair agree that they will not accept the present ar-
rangements of their parents and will never marry one another—"A
match!" "And no match!"—they agree to "do something to deceive
the grave people!" and to delay those proceedings by pretending to
be in love with one another. "Let us do 't," she says, "if it be but for
the dear pleasure of dissembling." Dorimant is the master dissembler, but Harriet is the mistress and gives her preliminary credentials in cooperation with Bellair. She and Bellair know the accepted
signs of this town that will convey the feeling to be dissembled.
They can act. "Can you play your part?" Bellair asks and off they go
(III, i, 52–54). "Now for a look and gestures that may persuade 'em I
am saying all the passionate things imaginable." She directs:

> HARRIET: Your head a little more on one side. Ease yourself on
>   your left leg and play with your right hand.
> YOUNG BELLAIR: Thus, is it not?
> HARRIET: Now set your right leg firm on the ground, adjust
>   your belt, then look about you.
> YOUNG BELLAIR: A little exercising will make me perfect.

She takes her turn to be instructed, with all her heart.

> YOUNG BELLAIR: At one motion play your fan, roll your eyes,
>   and then settle a kind look upon me.
> HARRIET: So.
> YOUNG BELLAIR: Now spread your fan, look down upon it, and
>   tell the sticks with a finger.
> HARRIET: Very modish.

Very, and certainly not innocent:

> YOUNG BELLAIR: Clap your hand up to your bosom, hold down
> your gown. Shrug a little, draw up your breasts and let 'em
> fall again, gently with a sigh or two, *etc.*

Harriet sees how his good instructions grow from good observations, one of those "malicious observers who watch people's eyes"
and can draw even from innocent looks scandalous conclusions. He
knows some who "out of mere love to mischief" can give an account
of every glance that passes at a play and in the Circle (in Hyde Park).
These two are not looking for scandal but to dissemble as a means to
their desire. "Admirably well acted!" he compliments her after she
achieves a complicated look and gesture. "I think I am pretty apt at
these matters," she says, and she is, and not only before the immediate and easy audience of the grave people (55–56).

Dorimant is the master of the art. "Dissembler, damned dissembler!" Loveit cries, knowing well the truth she has no power to cope
or meet with, and he is in such easy command of his art that he can
play with it in a devastating irony. "I am so, I confess," and he turns
that again coolly to a deeper thrust: that his good nature and good
manners corrupt him, for he is so honest in his inclinations it is only
to avoid offense that he makes her believe he does not think her now
old, artful and wearisome (II, ii, 45). He is an actor, quick study of all
roles, can mimic Fopling, is ready to take on the disguise of
Courtage—"You know the character you are to act, I see" (III, iii,
85)—play his cruel part with Loveit, play a different part with
everyone to get what he wants from each. But Harriet can act
Dorimant. It is one of the first things he learns of her when the
Orange-woman reports Harriet's arrival in town: she could repeat
the twenty things he said, "and acted with her head and with her
body so like you—" (I, 10). In their first meeting and passage at
arms, on matters of gambling and of time, they move quickly to mutual mimicry. Their play is sexual, gambling, and acting. He begins
this act, thinking he will win this event handily:

> As I followed you, I observed how you were pleased when the
> fops cried "She's handsome, very handsome, by God she is!"
> and whispered aloud your name—the thousand several forms
> you put your face into; then, to make yourself more agreeable,

how wantonly you played with your head, flung back your
locks, and looked smilingly over your shoulder at 'em.

But he has mistaken his opponent:

I do not go begging the men's, as you do the ladies' good liking,
with a sly softness in your looks and a gentle slowness in your
bows as you pass by 'em. As thus, sir. (*Acts him.*) Is not this like
you? (III, iii, 73–74)

She is his equal in discerning secrets, has an eye for the inner
truth of those she sees. What Harriet knows, and none other has
seen before—the shadow in the glass, the knight o' th' shire—is that
Fopling is not the only modish man who is affected. She knows the
book, of men as well as women, *The Art of Affectation* (II, i, 36),
better than anyone. Her mother dreads Dorimant, by reputation,
but Harriet does not apprehend him so much. "I never saw anything
in him that was frightful." "On the contrary," Bellair agrees, "have
you not observed something extreme delightful in his wit and person?" She has observed more than that: "He's agreeable and pleasant, I must own, but he does so much affect being so, he displeases
me." Bellair is surprised: "Lord, madam, all he does and says is so
easy and natural," but she knows more of Bellair's friend than he
does and more of the "natural": "Some men's verses seem so to the
unskillful; but labor i' the one, and affectation in the other to the
judicious plainly appear." Bellair, her clever and instructive partner
in dissembling, has never seen that, or heard that, before: "I never
heard him accused of affectation before" (III, iii, 70–71). She has no
hesitation in repeating her original observation to Dorimant himself. When they exchange bow and curtsy he tells her, pointedly,
"That demure curtsy is not amiss in jest, but do not think in earnest
it becomes you." She understands that as well as he. "Affectation is
catching, I find. From your grave bow I got it," and she goes on to
her little lecture on art and nature, her wildness and the rules of
charming (IV, i, 90). He is quite accurate in what he says of her demureness, which she has brought to town with her, and her act and
her art are as mannered as his, and as good as his. She knows him.
She speaks of him to Emilia, near the end, as she did to Bellair at
first. "Mr. Dorimant has a great deal of wit," Emilia says. "And takes

a great deal of pains to show it," she replies. "He's extremely well-fashioned," Emilia tries agains. "Affectedly grave, or ridiculously wild and apish" (V, ii, 129–30). As she loves him she can see into the truth about him, how the wild freedoms of the present live only in the restrictions of their own forms and ceremonies; and that means she can laugh at him.

There is nothing Dorimant fears more than being laughed at; it means his reputation, because in the town to be laughed at is to be a fool, to be exposed as less than appears, to have lost power. It is, with some justice, Mrs. Loveit who first opens that possibility for him when Dorimant confidently promises Medley he shall see good sport between her and this Fopling. In a pleasant trick Dorimant has encouraged Fopling to talk to her, reporting to the fool falsely that she is interested in his attentions, to make good Dorimant's pretended jealousy: in the humor she will be in, after his own provocations, her love will make her do some very extravagant thing, doubtless, when Fopling sets upon her. But Loveit is determined Dorimant shall no more find her "the loving fool" he has known (III, iii, 78). She will make all advances to Fopling and make Dorimant jealous in fact, a revenge he little thinks on. She is able to predict better than he this time, knows she will make him uneasy, though he does not care for her, because she knows the effects of jealousy on men of his proud temper. Bellinda wants to dissuade her because it may make him fond of Loveit again, but Loveit, using Fopling, carries off her "counterfeit." "Dorimant, you look a little bashful on the matter," Medley observes. Loveit has surprised Dorimant: "She dissembles better than I thought she could have done." It is her one temporarily successful play, foiling the prediction of the part he had planned for her. "She cannot fall from loving me to that?" an intolerable thought (as we too may think). Medley thinks jealousy may produce a dangerous relapse in a fit which Dorimant says has long been over and Dorimant has an audience of two keen observers on him. Medley, he says to himself, "guesses the secret of my heart," a sure sign of loss of power; and also "I am concerned but dare not show it, lest Bellinda should mistrust all I have done to gain her." Bellinda is the less perceptive of the spectators: "I have watched his look and find no alteration there. Did he love her, some signs of jealousy would have appeared," so his own dissembling manages that. But the ironic Medley is amused: "Would you had brought some more of your friends, Dorimant, to have been witnesses of Sir Fopling's disgrace and your triumph!" and Dorimant cannot escape that easily:

> 'Twere unreasonable to desire you not to laugh at me; but pray
> do not expose me to the town this day or two.

With that respite which he needs to complete the bedding of Bellinda, he will then show both Medley and Loveit how deep his power is over womankind (III, iii, 82–85). He attacks Loveit again. For her to be seen publicly transported with the vain follies of a notorious fop, he says, is to him an infamy below the sin of prostitution with another man. It will be "a commonplace for all the town to laugh at me." He must consult his reputation, it is a necessity, and she must justify his love to the world, must make a public spectacle of her spurning of Fopling. But Loveit will not do it, in her one moment of, or at least as close as she comes to, a certain nobility or self-respect. She would die to satisfy his love, "but I will not, to save you from a thousand racks, do a shameless thing to please your vanity" (V, i, 122–24).

Dorimant's power with women is therefore in difficulties before Harriet completes her capture and those difficulties are inevitable. If it is only the fools of the town who expect stability to stand then Dorimant's maintenance of his position is bound to shake. He has so many threads of control extended that cross-purposes if nothing else will at last trip him. The narrow escapes, which have always been adroitly handled, begin to fail, and as he is pressing Loveit here, at his most shameless and devilish and losing control, Bellinda enters. She has come to Loveit's a few moments earlier, after leaving her five o'clock assignation, because the chairmen, following their routine, have carried the lady leaving Dorimant's lodgings to Loveit's. He has promised Bellinda never to see Loveit again and now, immediately, he has come to Loveit, betrayed his promised love. He is caught by Bellinda, who this time sees him start and look pale: "I am confounded," he says, "and cannot guess how she came hither." She attacks him, pretending, to protect her name, that she is speaking on behalf of Loveit. "Here is a fine work towards!" Dorimant continues his internal monologue; "I never was at such a loss before."

But he has no remedy and must submit to the women's tongues now and some other time bring himself off as well as he can. He has three women at him including even Pert, Loveit's serving woman, which is rather pleasant to see since Pert has always scolded against him, to Loveit's annoyance. "Nay, if she begins too," he realizes, "'tis time to fly. I shall be scolded to death, else." He will seek a more convenient time to clear himself, he declares, but the women will not accept his "weak pretenses." He exits with "You were never more mistaken in your life; and so farewell," and *"flings off"* in a lame escape (V, i, 125–26). In the next, and final, scene, Loveit and Bellinda together make an unexpected entrance upon him and he feels the reversal. "The devil owes me a shame today, and I think never will have done paying it" (V, ii, 137). It is not quite what that never bewitched little Pert had once hoped—"The devil should carry him away first, were it my concern" (II, ii, 47)—but it is a fair enough end for this kind of Don Juan.

Harriet has already known—what does she not know?—how to handle Dorimant without the adventitious aid of the farcical entrances and exits to which he is liable; she is another kind of woman. She has begun by a bit of the mortification she will apply effectively. When he makes his first play for her by letting her know that "some time or other" she may be willing, she is not impressed. "To men who have fared in this town like you, 'twould be a great mortification to live on hope," and puts him on a probationary diet, which does not, for the moment, disturb his confidence (III, iii, 73). But she can do better than that in her administering of the corrective humiliation we recognize. When he begins his serious wooing he is in a weak position, loving her but not daring to let her know it. That is a reciprocal weakness, each in love with the other, neither daring to admit it because to do so would be to surrender the ascendant. He speaks of love, which, she says, makes her start, for she did not expect to hear of love from him.

> DORIMANT: Is the name of love so frightful that you dare not stand it?
> HARRIET: 'Twill do little execution out of your mouth on me, I am sure.
> DORIMANT: It has been fatal—

She will not allow him, this hitherto witty, triumphant, speaker, to finish his commonplace sentence and turns it to her use:

> HARRIET: To some easy women, but we are not all born to one destiny. I was informed you use to laugh at love, and not make it.
>
> DORIMANT: The time has been, but now I must speak—

And again she cuts him off, cuts him down, because time is now hers:

> HARRIET: If it be on that idle subject, I will put on my serious look, turn my head carelessly from you, drop my lip, let my eyelids fall and hang half o'er my eyes—thus, while you buzz a speech of an hour long in my ear and I answer never a word. Why do you not begin?

She has the act pat and directs the scene. It would take a more than ordinarily potent man, which he has always assumed he was, to begin at that point and he is not now up to it. He can't, he says, allow the company to take notice of how passionately he makes advances of love and how disdainfully she receives them.

> HARRIET: When your love's grown strong enough to make you bear being laughed at, I'll give you leave to trouble me with it. Till when, pray forbear, sir. (IV, i, 91–93)

She is not one more woman, born to the one destiny he assumes, but his match, and she demands the unique response which is love. For him the time has been when he laughed at that, but she has his secret and she can silence and laugh at him. She forces him out of his act. He is not above the human condition.

Dorimant does save his reputation, clear himself, and the town sees only success once more. Loveit, when she finds he is to be a bridesman, and there is no point to continuing her act with Fopling, in her own fury makes the public spectacle of that fool which Dorimant had required and predicted. "Dorimant, I pronounce thy reputation clear," Medley announces, "and henceforward, when I would know anything of woman, I will consult no other oracle" (V, ii, 143), though we know more. In his own terms, reversing the common feeling of the freedom and the restoration to health that the course of true love brings with its happy conclusion, Dorimant has

caught the sickness. From the start he has been the master diag-
nostician and manager of disease, passing off his own decay of passion (I, 8) on Mrs. Loveit:

> DORIMANT: When love grows diseased, the best thing we can
>   do is to put it to a violent death. I cannot endure the torture
>   of a ling'ring and consumptive passion.
> MRS. LOVEIT: Can you think mine sickly?
> DORIMANT: Oh, 'tis desperately ill! What worse symptoms are
>   there than . . .

and he puts upon her just those distempers he has been concocting
for her (II, ii, 46). She is clever enough to turn her own distemper of
jealousy (III, ii, 58) upon him, as a dangerous and uncertain remedy,
"the strongest cordial we can give to dying love. It often brings it
back when there's no sign of life remaining" (III, iii, 78–79); and in
fact it partly works, for though Dorimant thinks his "fit" of love for
her has been long over Medley notices that men "fall into dangerous
relapses" when they find a woman inclining to another (83). His
symptomatic problem here is the preparatory sign for his new experience with Harriet, who, she says to his advances, did not think to
have heard of love from him.

> DORIMANT: I never knew what 'twas to have a settled ague yet,
>   but now and then have had irregular fits.
> HARRIET: Take heed; sickness after long health is commonly
>   more violent and dangerous.
> DORIMANT (*aside*): I have took the infection from her and feel
>   the disease now spreading in me. (IV, i, 92)

She cools him with laughter.

If he has declared he will open his heart and receive her where
none yet did ever enter—"You have filled it with a secret might I but
let you know it"—she knows his secret and she won't believe him.
She knows his record in falsehood and he himself has said to her that
women nowadays put on their emotions with the same ease as their
paint and patches. "Are they the only counterfeits?" she asks. The
inimitable color in her cheeks, he pleads, is not more free from art
than the sighs he offers. She won't trust in a hardened sinner the
first signs of repentance, so he picks up her figure and strains it, for

the prospect of such a heaven will make him persevere and give marks that are infallible, renounce all his joys in friendship, wine, other women. But fanaticism, that sort of fixed feeling and language, certainly isn't what she wants and she has a better, more appropriate and more sensible test. "Could you neglect these a while and make a journey into the country?" To be with her, says he, he could live there and never send a thought to London. That's just talk, she knows, as well as we. "Whate'er you say, I know all beyond High Park's a desert to you, and that no gallantry can draw you farther." "Youth has a long journey to go, madam," he had mocked Loveit, but now Dorimant must make his journey to find a new love and life—to the desert. It seems a fitter place for the truly isolated Alceste, but we may hope that for Dorimant it will be an opening to a better country and emotion than he has known. He tries to talk of it that way: High Park as been "the utmost limit of my love; but now my passion knows no bounds . . ." "When I hear you talk thus in Hampshire, I shall begin to think there may be some little truth enlarged upon." Is that all she will say? "Will you not promise me—," he tries to ask. "I hate to promise." May he not hope? "That depends on you and not on me . . ." (V, ii, 143–34). And there she leaves it for now. He's been well-matched.

She must now return, to that great, rambling, lone house that looks as if it were not inhabited, with her mother, an old lame aunt and herself "perched up on chairs at a distance in a large parlor, sitting moping like three or four melancholy birds in a spacious volary": a place obviously empty, crippled, sadly less than human, unspeaking. Does that not stagger his resolution? she asks. Not at all, he says, for she has left him with "the pangs of love" upon him, "and this day my soul has quite given up her liberty." She has an ear for false notes and better resolutions and these sounds of his do not impress her. "This is more dismal than the country." Pity me, she says to Emilia, who am going to that sad place, hearing already the hateful noise of rooks, "—kaw, kaw, kaw. There's music in the worst cry in London. 'My dill and cucumbers to pickle'" (V, ii, 144–45). It is a discerning choice of that London cry with an air that was still pleasing to Addison, and alas! like the song of the nightingale not heard above two months (*Spectator* No. 251).

"The young lady shall have a dance before she departs" (V, ii, 145).

The text is George Etherege, *The Man of Mode*, ed. W. B. Carnochan (Lincoln, Nebr., 1966). References are to act, scene and page number (Act I is a single scene); where successive quotations in the same paragraph are from the same scene the act and scene numbers are not repeated.

Barnard, John, "Point of view in *The Man of Mode*," *Essays in Criticism*, XXXIV (1984), 285–308

Berglund, Lisa, "The Language of the Libertines: Subversive Morality in *The Man of Mode*," *Studies in English Literature*, XXX (1990), 369–86

Corman, Brian, "Interpreting and Misinterpreting *The Man of Mode*," *Papers on Language and Literature*, XIII (1977), 35–53

Davies, Paul C., "The State of Nature and the State of War: A Reconsideration of *The Man of Mode*," *University of Toronto Quarterly*, XXXIX (1961), 53–62

Hawkins, Harriett, *Likenesses of Truth in Elizabethan and Restoration Drama* (Oxford, 1972)

Hayman, John G., "Dorimant and the Comedy of A Man of Mode," *Modern Language Quarterly*, XXX (1969), 183–97

Holland, Norman, *The First Modern Comedies: The Significance of Etherege, Wycherley and Congreve* (Cambridge, Mass., 1959)

Hughes, Derek, "Play and Passion in *The Man of Mode*," *Comparative Drama*, XV (1981), 231–57

Hume, Robert D., *The Development of English Drama in the Late Seventeenth Century* (Oxford, 1976)

Krause, David, "'The Defaced Angel': A Concept of Satanic Grace in Etherege's *The Man of Mode*," *Drama Survey*, VII (1968–69), 87–103

Markley, Robert, *Two-Edg'd Weapons: Style and Ideology in the Comedies of Etherege, Wycherley and Congreve* (Oxford, 1988)

Powell, Jocelyn, "George Etherege and the Form of Comedy," *Restoration Theatre*, edd. J. R. Brown and Bernard Harris, "Stratford-upon-Avon Studies" 6 (1965)

Traugott, John, "The Rake's Progress from Court to Comedy: A Study in Comic Form," *Studies in English Literature*, VI (1966), 381–407

Underwood, Dale, *Etherege and the Seventeenth-Century Comedy of Manners* (New Haven, 1957)

Weber, Harold, "Charles II, George Pines, and Mr. Dorimant: The Politics of Sexual Power in Restoration England," *Criticism*, XXXII (1990), 193–219

Zimbardo, Rose A., "Of Women, Comic Imitation of Nature, and Etherege's *The Man of Mode*," *Studies in English Literature*, XXI (1981), 373–87.

Chapter Five

Bevil Junior's lodgings

The Conscious Lovers

The Man of Mode is certainly a play that can offend the moral senses and it certainly did that. It had a significant afterlife as a bad example, corrupting influence, and it seriously exercised Steele as a continuing present danger over a period of years and up to half a century after it had first appeared in 1676. It was, in an early stroke of his campaign, the subject of *Spectator* No. 65 (1711), which he presented as a useful application of Addison's preceding papers on wit and false wit. The seat of wit, when one speaks as a man of the town and the world, Steele says, is the playhouse and he will in this paper reflect on its uses in that place. Wit in the theater has a strong effect on the manners of our gentlemen and, though it may seem to be presumptuous to tax the writings of such as have long had the general applause of the nation, his standards will be reason, truth and nature. He will look into some of the most applauded plays to see if they deserve the figure they at present bear in the imaginations of men, and the present paper reflecting on such works will be on *Sir Fopling Flutter*. In fact it is not the first of a series but the whole of it; and he returns to that play (in *Spectator* No. 75) in response to the raillery of a fine lady who did not like what he had said of Dorimant.

The received character of the play, he begins in No. 65, is that it is the pattern of genteel comedy, but if Dorimant and Harriet, the characters of greatest consequence, are low and mean the reputation of the play is very unjust. He takes it for granted, he says, that a fine gentleman should be "honest in his actions, and refined in his language. Instead of this, our hero, in this piece, is a direct knave in his designs, and a clown in his language." If Dorimant is now a clown, we note, a different notion of comic characters is at work. An

example of Dorimant's actions is his design to persuade Young
Bellair, his admiring friend, to marry a young lady whose virtue, he
thinks, will then fall to his share as an irresistible fine gentleman;
and his falsehood to Mrs. Loveit "and the barbarity of triumphing
over her anguish for losing him" is another instance of "his honesty,
as well as his good nature." We hear this gentleman's language in the
way he calls the Orange-woman, "who, it seems, is inclined to grow
fat," an overgrown jade with a flasket of guts before her and salutes
her with the pretty phrase of Double Tripe; or we hear it in the in-
sulting of a country gentlewoman, whom he knows nothing of, an
unnatural mixture of senseless commonplace. The generosity of
his temper is in his insolent treatment of his poor footman. As for
Harriet, she laughs at obedience to an absent mother whose tenderness is described "to be very exquisite"; this witty and fine young
lady has so little respect for the good mother that she ridicules her
seeming infirmities. But all this is atoned for, in this play, because
she has wit and malice, is wild but demure in looks. It seems unnatural (Steele piles on the irony), for we don't understand how she
should have been bred under "a silly pious old mother" and yet came
to be so polite. The negligence of everything which engages the
attention of the "sober and valuable part of mankind" is very well
drawn in this play, but it is denied that a fine gentleman is someone who should in that manner "trample upon all order and decency." The character of Dorimant is more of a coxcomb than that of
Fopling. And so to the conclusion,

> This whole celebrated piece is a perfect contradiction to
> good manners, good sense, and common honesty . . . there is
> nothing in it but what is built upon the ruin of virtue and inno-
> cence . . .

That should make the Shoemaker in reality the fine gentleman, as
he is an atheist, as the Orange-woman says, and he lives with his
wife, by his own description, like a gentleman of the town, speaking
civilly and hating one another heartily; his pretense at superior language is as good as if Dorimant had spoken it himself. And since the
Shoemaker "puts human nature in as ugly a form as the circumstance
will bear, and is a staunch unbeliever, he is very much wronged in
having no part of the good fortune bestowed in the last act."

> To speak plainly of this whole work, I think nothing but be-
> ing lost to a sense of innocence and virtue can make any one see
> this comedy, without observing more frequent occasion to
> move sorrow and indignation, than mirth and laughter. At the
> same time I allow it to be nature, but it is nature in its utmost
> corruption and degeneracy.

A severe indictment, and not foolish. If Dorimant is intended to
be the fine gentleman and he has a strong effect upon the manners of
our gentlemen we are in trouble. (Evidently Harriet, though no
better example for the ladies, is not likely to be a threat.) Dorimant
is indeed a knave in his designs, as he is here declared to be, and to
call him a clown in his language, even if one thinks it is not true, is
itself a witty stroke in rearranging his role in the cast. If he is not
really more of a coxcomb than Fopling, to say so is at least a revealing insight worthy of Harriet, who, for other reasons, noted the affectation in both men. But Mr. Spectator is not a wholly accurate
reporter. The triumph over Mrs. Loveit is, with just sarcasm, said to
be an instance of Dorimant's honesty, but it is not just to add "as well
as his good nature," because Bellinda is explicit in seeing it as proof
of his ill nature. Dorimant is not a moral man, but there is no pretense that he is: he is "a man of no principles," as Bellinda says ("Your
man of principles is a very fine thing, indeed!" the cynical Medley
replies, *Man of Mode* II, ii, 48; III, ii, 58–59). But more important,
and more interesting, are the ways in which, in Steele's reading and
writing, the hard and harsh focus of some of the details of the play
softens to another diction: to the "anguish" of Mrs. Loveit, or the
"very exquisite" tenderness of Lady Woodvill, or the finer language
for the Orange-woman, "who, it seems, is inclined to grow fat." That
last unoffending phrase does take us to the important difference in
the concerns and the audience he assumes: to "everything which
engages the sober and valuable part of mankind," who want "order
and decency" and are indignant with the wild or the heathen. Their
values are "virtue and innocence," "innocence and virtue," twice,
and in the joining and the casual reordering of those words, evidently a close pair. The objection is not to the truth of what is shown
but to the showing, putting human nature in an ugly form. "I allow it

to be nature, but it is nature in its utmost corruption and degeneracy."

The full response, on which Steele worked for many years, was his own play *The Conscious Lovers*, finally produced in 1722 (published 1723) and a great success. There were at least forty-seven editions before the end of the century, including Italian, French and German. In its first season it brought in more money than any play previously performed by the Drury Lane Theater, it was one of the most frequently performed comedies for fifty years and it was on the stage into the nineteenth century. Steele's "fine gentleman," and that was an earlier working title, is close to a point-by-point reversal of Dorimant. Bevil Junior is the chaste lover of a virtuous lady. He is a good friend, dedicated and active in his friend's behalf. He treats his one servant with an insistence on moral behavior, addressing him with a casual manner and a proper decency. He has a father whom he respects as he should; they live as well together as possible and fear only to give each other any pain; and since the son has an independent fortune from his deceased mother there is no cause for that filial regard other than what he owes the goodness of that father. For purposes of the plot young Bevil must exercise some temporary and uncharacteristic dissimulation on his father but he is uncomfortable with that. If it is said that a man of his figure and fortune can but "make himself the jest of the town" by marrying not for money and only for love, the reply is a sharp and clear defense by the lady who loves him:

> The town! I must tell you, madam, the fools that laugh at Mr.
> Bevil will but make themselves more ridiculous. His actions
> are the result of thinking, and he has sense enough to make
> even virtue fashionable. (II, ii, 40)

A new fashion, already well in favor, one guesses, is in town. We know when we meet him in his proper lodgings that Mr. Bevil is a virtuous man, for his taste in literature is not the verses of the Waller Dorimant loves to quote, and to which when appropriate Harriet can offer an antiphonal response (*Man of Mode*, V, ii, 131); it is, in Steele's graceful tribute to his recently deceased colleague, Addison's vision of Mirza, a moral allegory (*Spectator* No. 159).

"These moral writers practice virtue after death. This charming Vision of Mirza! Such an author consulted in a morning sets the spirit for the vicissitudes of the day better than the glass does a man's person" (I, ii, 23).

Where has Dorimant gone? The way of all old fashions, to the lower class, the servant clowns. Bevil's man Tom, in the description by Humphrey, the old family servant, is "the prince of poor coxcombs," gay and airy, with follies and vices enough for a man of ten thousand a year. He started, rather like Fopling, a bashful great awkward cub and booby, his oaken cudgel becoming him much better than that dangling stick at his button now he is a fop. But he is, in his own estimation, loftier than that, like Dorimant contemptuous of the previous generation, aspiring to be the "wild rogue" he is called. He speaks disrespectfully of those of Humphrey's generation, who could not fall to their dinner till a formal fellow in a black gown said something. "Despising men of sacred characters!" says the shocked Humphrey, "I hope you never heard my good young master talk so like a profligate!" This foolish profligate frequents a gang of similar servants who cut a figure, think they lead a fine life and are very pretty fellows who are kept only to be looked at. The rebuke of old Humphrey is prompt in its historical analysis.

> Very well, sir. I hope the fashion of being lewd and extrava-
> gant, despising of decency and order, is almost at an end, since
> it is arrived at persons of your quality.

But these words are wasted because to Tom, in effect happily agreeing, "the lackeys are the men of pleasure of the age . . ."

> We are false lovers, have a taste of music, poetry, billet-doux,
> dress, politics, ruin damsels, and when we are weary of this
> lewd town and have a mind to take up, whip into our masters'
> wigs and linen and marry fortunes. (I, i, 14–16)

It is the Dorimant-catalogue, the false lover, the taste for music, poetry, billet-doux, dress, ruining damsels, marrying a fortune. Even the politics is there in Dorimant's intentionally ambiguous pretense that he had neglected Loveit for "business" (i.e., public business). Tom's lady counterpart, the maid Phillis, is his match. "Lard!" says she to Tom, "You are so wild—but you have a world of humor—" She has her ideas of the town and the fashion and dress and how to go through the motions. "Oh Tom! Tom! Is it not a pity that you should be so great a coxcomb and I so great a coquette and yet be such poor devils as we are?" (17, 19). Things are rather lively when Tom and Phillis are on stage and one would like to see them there more often.

But the play is Bevil Junior's. His problem is familiar but, since the play is not, the story will require several pages of telling and some patience. He is in love with one young lady, Indiana, but his father, Sir John Bevil, wants him to marry another young lady, Lucinda. He has a friend named Mr. Myrtle, who, it happens, is in love with Lucinda and she with him, while her father of course is arranging the marriage with Bevil; Lucinda's foolish mother is trying to arrange another marriage for her, with the foolish Cimberton. So we have a pair of young lovers, tangled, and they must travel the course of true love and work out their fates. Bevil Junior has a particular problem because he is a virtuous lover and a dutiful son. If he were not a virtuous lover (and she the same) he might be able to have his Indiana; indeed some others suspect he has done, or plans to do, just that, but we soon learn that he has rescued this unfortunate and penniless orphan from a villain's persecution and he has been charitably supporting her, untouched. If he were not a dutiful son he might ignore his father's wishes and marry her, needing neither the father's nor Lucinda's fortune. But he must attain his happiness in a virtuous way.

He cannot engage in the trickery or in the escape to another and freer realm that may fool or circumvent his father. All he can do is pretend to agree to his father's commands, with the security gained from the confidential information of Humphrey that his father is having problems of his own in his relations with Lucinda's father. That father, Mr. Sealand, has seen, by an accident at a recent masquerade, that Bevil Junior seems to have a serious interest in a lady other than Lucinda, a discovery which has disturbed Sir John Bevil too, and Sealand has now told Sir John that the match is broken. Sir John will have to provide a satisfactory explanation of this seeming defection by Bevil Junior and therefore he presses the marriage on his son to see if the young man, having an offensive reason, is unwilling. So there is some inconclusive jousting here but there is nothing much Bevil Junior can do except delay, having no way to act effectively to help himself and with nothing anyone else can do. All we can do is listen to him as he explains to Humphrey the history of Indiana, so that we learn of his goodness (I, ii): how she lost her father, younger brother of an ancient family and an eminent merchant of Bristol, who went to the Indies to repair his fortunes; how that was accomplished in six years and how the father then sent for his wife, sister and at that time seven-year-old daughter to join him; how the plan was interrupted by a French privateer which took the ship and the ladies to Toulon, where the mother pined and died. The sister and daughter were well treated for some years until they passed to the hands of a villain who found "this blooming virgin, at his mercy" and firing his blood. Failing in persuasion this wretch then seized her little fortune and was dragging her by violence to prison when Bevil Junior, on his travels and happening to be present, relieved her, secretly paid off the villain and took her safe to England. He has never told Indiana of his love for her, though he believes she loves him too, because tender obligations to his father have laid an inviolable restraint on his conduct. He will never marry without his father's consent, though he will not marry whomsoever his father pleases. And that leaves us at an impasse.

We are turned to the affairs of Mr. Myrtle, that sad man, and the second pair of lovers. He and Lucinda are in love but then both her father and mother want her to marry another, and each is promoting a different other. So, like his friend Bevil Junior, he has old folks in his way, but, rather more interestingly, the two young men have different kinds of obstacles. The candidate of Lucinda's mother is Cimberton, not really a major problem because neither Lucinda nor her father, Mr. Sealand, has any inclination to that coxcomb. Still there is the possibility that when Bevil's match with Lucinda comes to an open rupture Mr. Sealand may be tempted by Cimberton's fortune; so at Bevil's suggestion Myrtle will try to delay and confound matters a little and gain some information by a trick. Mrs. Sealand is now about to draw up the articles for the marriage she is pushing and her counsel, a couple of legal characters whom she has never seen, will appear. Myrtle can put on the wig and gown and pretend to be one of them and Tom—"The rogue's intelligent and is a good mimic"—can be the other. Fortunately Tom will not have to say too much but only stutter heartily, for that is the old lawyer's case. The scene Mr. Myrtle and Tom play in the following act has its amusement, mildly satirical on lawyers, though that has no relevance to anything, and with easy laughs certainly provided by the mimic stuttering, though that too has no relevance. The mocking of the defect does seem to run counter to the humane standard Steele had asked for; and in fact Bevil says in advance, "Nay, it would be an immoral thing to mock him, were it not that his impertinence is the occasion of its breaking out to that degree" (II, ii, 36), a disingenuousness and an ineffective prophylactic which did not save Steele from the attack of unfriendly critics. But the scene does not have any effect in advancing or retarding the action. Similarly, there is a late scene in which Myrtle disguises himself as Cimberton's old uncle and that leads to some farcical by-play, but with equal inconsequence.

The other problem in Myrtle's love life is the sort that resides within himself, that lack of self-understanding which must be cured to clarify his distorted vision. He is terribly, foolishly jealous, necessarily relying on Bevil's fidelity but always fearful that Bevil really will marry Lucinda. It comes to the awful point where, in his misunderstanding, he challenges Bevil to a duel on supposed artificial dealing while Bevil was proposing to be a friend. Lucinda too finds the jealousy in Myrtle's temper a thing that gives her terrors and she writes to Bevil of her concern. Her esteem for Myrtle leads her to hope that this fault is only an ill effect of a tender love and "what may be cured." Bevil cannot tell his friend of the lady's letter, written in confidence, unless he can "cure him of the violent and intractable passion . . ." He refuses to accept the duel, abhorring it as an offense against the Author of Life, until the hot Myrtle insults the name of Bevil's love, calling her the convenient, the ready Indiana. But fortunately Bevil, having shown that he is of course courageous, then recollects himself and, rather than following his friend's rash behavior and entering upon the duel, must show Lucinda's letter to Myrtle. "When he is thoroughly mortified" and shame conquers his jealousy, Bevil thinks, he will deserve to be assisted to Lucinda. The cure and the mortification work and Myrtle, a changed man, is "beholden to that superior spirit you have subdued me with." They now agree also on the general opinion of how ridiculous it is to duel. The lesson stays with Myrtle and he reports later how "mortified" he has been at this conduct of his (IV, i, 68, 72; IV, iii, 81). Myrtle, then, has the role we have seen before, the primary blind lover who must be mortified, endure the eye-opening counter-charm, to be cured of his internal fault. But in this play he is the secondary young lover. It is Bevil, the lead, who administers the lesson, for Bevil is identified explicitly as the superior spirit, the more than mortal figure who controls the lives of others and is himself exempt from human foolishness. Even as the Puck, though, Bevil cannot provide much action; he cannot stir up mischief, still less provoke a duel like Puck, and he certainly cannot be like Dorimant and love a quarrel. In his main deed (and the whole play, Steele says, was writ for the sake of that scene) he "evades the quarrel" (Preface, 5). He has little to do, nothing to learn, no need to move or be moved. "The chief design of this," Steele says of his play in the Preface, "was to be an innocent performance" (5); that would seem to fulfill the attack on *The Man of Mode* in the *Spectator* by providing a counter-example.

The spectators whose hearts and praise comic-writers strive to win have been told that the present poet has resolved to write in a new way, to please by wit that scorns the aid of vice. In praising him, they will be happy to know (like the readers of the *Spectator* in this age and nation), they will bring praise to themselves:

> Your aid, most humbly sought, then, Britons, lend,
> And lib'ral mirth like lib'ral men defend:
> No more let ribaldry, with license writ,
> Usurp the name of eloquence or wit . . .
> 'Tis yours with breeding to refine the age,
> To chasten wit, and moralize the stage.
>   (Prologue, by Steele's friend, Leonard Welsted)

Bevil Junior, then, will show us this chastened wit, innocent and virtuous. Tom, as fashionable servant-fop at Bevil's lodgings, does not admit Sir John Bevil directly but announces the arrival to his son: "I thought you had known, sir," says Bevil, "it was my duty to see my father anywhere." "The Devil's in my master!" Tom confides to himself; "He always has more wit than I have" (I, ii, 24). Tom's notion of the wit as Devil is out of date and "wit" has a sober and valuable meaning now. Where we see Bevil's wit on display in conversation with his lady it is an exchange of mutual compliment. In their previous meeting, Bevil begins,

> . . . I never saw you in such agreeable humor.
> INDIANA: I am extremely glad we were both pleased, for I thought I never saw you better company.
> BEVIL JUNIOR: Me, madam! You rally. I said very little.

This "rallying" continues, to a discussion of esteem, which is the result of reason and which Indiana therefore prefers to love.

> BEVIL JUNIOR: You certainly distinguish right, madam; love often kindles from external merit only—
> INDIANA: But esteem arises from a higher source, the merit of the soul—
> BEVIL JUNIOR: True. And great souls only can deserve it.
> *Bowing respectfully* (II, ii, 42–43)

This is rather depressing language for what is given as the best language, both in its substance and its deadness of style. Unlike Dorimant and Harriet these people are never going to learn anything from one another, but then they have no need. They have no need to expose themselves to the chances of a lively discovery of self, are carefully protected from that.

It is not that there is no laughter in *The Conscious Lovers*, for Steele does want "lib'ral mirth" in it. There are the two extended scenes of disguise. There is the scene in which the two pretentious fools, Cimberton and Mrs. Sealand, compare notes and Cimberton then runs over Lucinda's fine points as though he were buying a horse, exasperating the girl to the point where we get this bit:

> CIMBERTON: What an elasticity in her veins and arteries!
> LUCINDA: I have no veins, no arteries.
> MRS. SEALAND: Oh, child, hear him, he talks finely, he's a scholar, he knows what you have. (III, 60)

And, best, it has Tom and Phillis, Tom who will play tricks, who can mimic, as we have been told (I, i, 14; II, i, 36), and who can play with Phillis their own version of the lower-class Pyramus and Thisbe. He recalls his first meeting with Phillis, when he had been ordered to get out of the window, upstairs, to rub the sashes clean, while she

was employed on the inner side, her charming self whom he had
never seen before. He almost fell into the street, he says,

> when you immediately grew wanton in your conquest and put
> your lips close and breathed upon the glass, and when my lips
> approached, a dirty cloth you rubbed against my face and hid
> your beauteous form; when I again drew near, you spit and
> rubbed and smiled at my undoing.

What silly thoughts you men have, says she.

> TOM: We were Pyramus and Thisbe. But ten times harder was
>   my fate. Pyramus could peep only through a wall; I saw her,
>   saw my Thisbe in all her beauty but as much kept from her
>   as if a hundred walls between, for there was more, there was
>   her will against me. Would she but yet relent! Oh, Phillis!
>   Phillis! Shorten my torment and declare you pity me.
> PHILLIS: I believe it's very sufferable; the pain is not so exqui-
>   site but that you may bear it a little longer. (III, 51–52)

It is a pretty game they play, and this Pyramus and Thisbe pair do
see through the wall of pretenses and keep up a mutual instruction.
As Tom had said, "we shall never be dull in marriage when we come
together" (I, i, 21). A current story was that Colley Cibber (that experienced playwright and actor, who played Tom) had warned
Steele the play needed more amusement and that Cibber wrote this
scene in. Steele's originality is vindicated because he had written
such a scene earlier (*Guardian* No. 87); but the story is still instructive, because it could not have been invented if the scene were not
detachable or insertable, whoever wrote it in. The laughter in *The
Conscious Lovers* is in the minor characters and the minor plot,
which is not a unique shape in the history of the drama, but here the
main characters and their plot must be walled off, insulated, from
the laughter.

Tricks and disguises, modes of misleading, are important, but in
this play they are without meaning. Tricks can be fun and ebullience
and high spirits, or may be cruel, or plain stupid. But the good ones,
even the simple or the lightly mischievous, are a way of probing and
revealing truths, small or great. There is a delight on the part of the
trickster who has had the superior wit to understand the mind of the
fooled victim; and even if we don't share the delight, or withdraw in

pain, we must share the knowledge. (Black humor may make us uncomfortable by drawing us in to acknowledge a complicity we want
to disown.) Sometimes the target is the general mind of man, when
the trick is played on unknown victims (the wallet on the sidewalk is
pulled by the thread to catch out the greedy passerby); but a trick is
finer when it is calibrated for the particular fool and works upon particular points. What was done to Malvolio gained him pity in later
centuries but it was certainly a campaign well planned to expose
publicly the inward parts of that man. Clever tricks are significant
revelations, of correlative delightful power and self-blinded foolishness, because the fool always cooperates with the trickster, and thus
tricks advance knowledge and often action. But in *The Conscious
Lovers* the trickery and the disguising become a kind of tired
formula, subordinate in the play and detached pieces, insignificant,
revealing nothing, solving nothing.

There is a reason for that. Bevil Junior must be above laughter.
The problem he had, between his duty to his father and his love for
Indiana, was not something that could be soled by a trick, or any sort
of ingenuity of a lively mind. He could not fool his father, not circumvent him in any way, because Sir John is a good and loving father
and neither needs nor deserves such treatment. Bevil is virtuous
and must solve his problem virtuously and, we are given to understand, that is what he does, receives his love because he has been
virtuous: "Tell him the reward of all his virtues waits on his acceptance." Sir John, in the benediction of the final speech presents the
moral conclusion:

> Now, ladies and gentlemen, you have set the world a fair ex-
> ample. Your happiness is owing to your constancy and merit,
> and the several difficulties you have struggled with evidently
> show
> > Whate'er the generous mind itself denies
> > The secret care of Providence supplies. *Exeunt.*
> >   (V, III, 95, 98).

In fact all has been resolved not by anything generous Bevil has
achieved, in denial or in doing, and not by Providence, but by a fantastic coincidence in which Indiana turns out to be a long-lost
daughter of Mr. Sealand (who had of course changed his original

name), so that the marriage is happily approved by both fathers. That does mean Mr. Myrtle will now receive a smaller fortune with Lucinda, since the sisters must now split the Sealand money; but Myrtle's readiness to accept that (it made Cimberton duck out) increases his virtue and Lucinda's love for him; the sum is evidently such that it doesn't seem to require much of a sacrifice on his part ("We have much more than we want . . .").

The matter of the coincidence is no shock, because many authors, such as Sophocles and Dickens, if one may pick at random, have used extraordinary coincidences; and in such works as we have already looked at, in Shakespeare, Shaw and Jane Austen, coincidences have played a part. Of course there are coincidences of various kinds, and if Mr. Collins's patroness turns out to be Mr. Darcy's aunt that is mildly surprising, and not obtruded on our notice to solve a large problem Jane Austen could not have managed otherwise; it allows her a convenient economy in bringing Elizabeth and Darcy to a second set of meetings, closer to his home turf, where, among other things, he can blush for an ill-bred relative of his own. Shaw announces a coincidence in Mendoza's delight to find that Straker is Louisa's favorite brother Enry. "A dramatic coincidence!" It is exactly the sort of thing that should happen to confirm Mendoza's yearning for the romantic literature in which he is happy to play a role. In Dickens, where the coincidences are often wonderful and tie things by main force, they often seem so right because they reveal again what we have already learned in other ways in the action—that lives, and inanimate objects for that matter, are always more closely bound to one another than we thought and even if the wicked have tried to deny that truth. When, a small example from *Dombey and Son,* high Edith Dombey and low Alice Marwood turn out to be cousins, the several significant parallels in the courses of their lives have already been established and the discovery of their cousinship simply confirms them as relations. In a tighter instance, from those incredible predictions which Oedipus doesn't want to believe there is absolutely no escape: and run as he will he can only run to the coincidences which fulfill his fate; and he certainly cooperates, doing it his way but never leaving the basic pattern long set by the gods. To come closer to *The Conscious Lovers,* coincidences are plentiful and pleasing in the traditional plot Steele uses. Specifically, the coincidence of the identity of the beloved and the long-lost daughter is here taken from Terence's *Andria*, Steele's source for his play, a "translation" which he valued himself so much upon (Preface, 7); and Molière uses it in his *Fourberies de Scapin* (twice, in a rapid succession). But in those plays there is a great deal of trickery as the participants in the action work madly at their job of reaching their desires by whatever, often wildly ingenious, means they can invent; and, when they've done their exhausted best to deserve success, fortunate chance steps in with the last and best trick of all. So comic coincidence can be not only acceptable but wonderful. It can also be a wonder in a religious tale where Providence sets the stage and favors the faithful. But that's not how *The Conscious Lovers* works.

Here the coincidence is a fake, even pernicious, end to the play, because it is a lie. It is false because the problem is set as though it were real, in the given reality of the play, and solved ideally with the pretense that no shift has occurred. No dream, no journey is needed for the young man because in his double capacity of young lover and superior spirit Bevil Junior has arrived at his perfection already, is in his lodgings. The trick is a pretense that heaven is on earth. Bevil can describe himself readily and he does that for Indian's benefit and ours. In response to her aunt, who has cynical and sensible doubts of Bevil's motives and plans in keeping the young lady, Indiana tests him by what she presents as a hypothetical case; this requires several pages of dialogue. The aunt has said that no man ever does any extraordinary kindness or service for a woman except for his own sake: to Indiana's surprise Bevil agrees with that. Though the man maintains and supports the woman without demanding anything? Yes, Bevil says, an expense in supporting a valuable woman, even if she never knows who does her the service, is not such a mighty heroic business. Well, the man certainly must be of an uncommon mold. No, for the man it is just a better taste in expense to be conscious that from his superfluity an innocent, virtuous spirit is supported above temptations and sorrows; and if he delights in that prospect then there is no mighty matter in all this. No mighty matter in so disinterested a friendship? No, "Your hero, madam, is no more than what every gentleman ought to be, and I believe very many are." This goes on as she finds in more detail how sincere Bevil is in this analysis of a gentleman, a gentleman who doesn't love dogs or cards or dice or bottle companions or loose women and has rather a taste for this other way of spending "a bit of ore which is superfluous" (II, ii, 45–48). The point is made and made as explicitly as it can be: Bevil Junior as modest hero is both the gentleman that ought to be and the gentleman that is, the ideal and the reality, the perfection of the dream and the man in his lodgings in the town, at once. That move, that slipping of levels, in the identification of real and ideal, is one definition of the sentimental. Providence simply confirms when it suddenly appears on earth and by its more than human stroke turns all earthly problems to perfect happiness, as a reward for virtue. Steele is skillful because Providence has been planted early in the play, in Act I, before it returns in the last scene and in the last line, and is associated with the beginning as well as the end of Bevil's connection with Indiana. In his account to old Humphrey of his meeting with her Bevil told how she was being dragged wickedly and by violence to prison, "when Providence at the instant interposed and sent me, by miracle, to relieve her"; and Humphrey agreed, "'Twas Providence indeed" (I, ii, 30). So the miracle, the supernatural, was their normal mode of relationship, we are given to understand. But in fact that intervention by Bevil had nothing in it of "Providence." He and she had no prior connection and he happened to be a bystander; it was a random chance, as one crosses paths with a thousand strangers every day, and once in a while one may establish a connection. The use of the same word to describe what is in fact another species of thing, that convenient solution of Act V—which is such a statistically astonishing connection that it seems to defy the laws of natural probability and therefore must be credited to a heavenly intervention and reward—that resolution is, to be kind, not quite honest. The fault of sentimental comedy is not that it is too moral but that it is immoral.

This sort of play works hard at being instructive, pushes that, but it also works hard at being delightful, goes out of its way to work in the laughs. The fault of sentimental comedy is not that it tried to eliminate laughter or that it tried to make comedy instructive but that it separated the instruction from the laughter. It must keep the laughter away from the main plot and its hero, because if any occasion of laughter may be the perception of a gap between the offer of the *ought to be* and the demand of the *is*, then that hole must be hidden. Bevil Junior cannot risk, must be protected from, the danger of such a moment. It is the danger that Dorimant most feared and which, luckily for him, he was made to bear, by the woman who caught him in love. Mr. Darcy was not to be laughed at, Miss Bingley knew, but, luckily for him, Elizabeth Bennet knew better; and if he has not yet learned to be laughed at, even in the last pages, he will learn it after he marries the woman he loves. But the fools that laugh at Mr. Bevil will but make themselves ridiculous, as his loving Indiana has said (II, ii, 40). He is above laughter and must never learn. He is in that special place where, as Don Juan says, sentiments are called heroism and aspirations virtue, with no facts to contradict, no ironic contrasts; he is out of the human comedy on earth where Jack Tanner, luckily for him, learning from the woman he loves, ended in universal laughter.

Steele is not obliged to write another man's kind of play (though I do think a man who insists on virtue and innocence is obliged to be honest) but it is a question why he would want to write this kind. It is clear that he had an audience in mind, "the sober and valuable part of mankind" offended by *The Man of Mode* and its mode. The best representative in the play of that part of mankind would seem to be Mr. Sealand, the once eminent merchant of Bristol, subject to the ups and downs of that life and now in his second fortune as a great India merchant. He has been prepared to offer his only daughter and sole heiress of a vast estate as a wife to Bevil Junior. It seems to be a social step up for Mr. Sealand; and the landed Cimberton, his daughter's other suitor, and the snobbish Mrs. Sealand have made much of their own planned match for Lucinda as an advancement for a merchant's family: but Mr. Sealand has a higher pride in his own class. He has been attracted to Bevil because Bevil's reputation has been so fair in the world (I, i, 12), an early indication to us that virtue will indeed find its reward in this world, from the rich as well as from Providence. When Mr. Sealand, who evidently has so renamed himself to signalize his honorable occupation, finds that Bevil's fair reputation may not be deserved, he sensibly backs off, to protect his daughter. Sir John Bevil, who does not want to lose this money for his honored family, and knows it is not easy to deal with such rich old fellows, goes to Sealand to talk over the question. Sir John doesn't help himself by beginning with his point that, as they are on a treaty for uniting their families, a value he and his family bring to the union is genealogy and descent. Mr. Sealand responds with a list of names in his own family, such as Ptolemy, Crassus, Earl this, Marquis that, Duke etc., which astonishes Sir John, until he finds that these were famous fighting cocks in the domestic establishment. Sir John the gentleman realizes that Mr. Sealand is laughing at this stress on descent, and for us bluff old Sealand, practical and sharp-tongued, is a likeable fellow. If Sir John never knew anyone but the man who lacked the advantage of descent turn it to ridicule, Mr. Sealand the merchant never knew anyone who had many better advantages put that in his account. But it is not the son's family he objects to, Mr. Sealand says, it is the young man's morals; so we get this bit of exchange on class moralities.

> SIR JOHN BEVIL: Sir, I can't help saying that what might injure
> a citizen's credit may be no stain to a gentleman's honor.

Sir John's point is not foolish because a citizen's credit, his sound financial reliability, may be injured by a course of immorality in his leisure hours, but Mr. Sealand will have none of that distinction which allows the gentleman a license. Mr. Sealand is talking of a marriage and the father of a daughter may not think it is an addition to the "honor or credit" of her lover that he is a keeper. Sir John fires up at that and insists, with justice, that his son is a discreet and sober gentleman. Shrewd Sealand—we can believe in him as a successful trader—who has the experience and insight, says that he never saw a man that wenched soberly and discreetly that ever left it off, that the decency observed in the practice hides even from the sinner the iniquity, that such men pursue it not that their appetites hurry them away but because it is their opinon that they may do it. This is good stuff, much better than Sir John's gentlemanly "do you design to keep your daughter a virgin till you find a man unblemished that way?" which gives Mr. Sealand his opening for his big speech:

> Sir, as much a cit as you take me for, I know the town and the
> world. And give me leave to say that we merchants are a spe-
> cies of gentry that have grown into the world this last century,
> and are as honorable, and almost as useful, as you landed folks

that have always thought yourselves so much above us. For
your trading, forsooth, is extended no farther than a load of hay
or a fat ox. You are pleasant people, indeed, because you are
generally bred up to be lazy; therefore, I warrant you, industry
is dishonorable.

That does seem rather more than the occasion calls for and when
Sir John asks him not to be offended and to go back to the point,
Sealand, in character, declares he is not at all offended, "but I don't
like to leave any part of the account unclosed" (IV, ii, 73–75).

The cit has had his full say and even if this difference of class has
little to do with the plot, neither advancing nor retarding it, the cit
establishes himself as an important spokesman. He speaks to the
audience, is probably in the audience. Unlike the audience of
Dorimant's town Mr. Sealand's hearers would seem to be the citizens who never made it into that town except as absent contempt-
ibles. This audience insists on its sober and valuable daily reality as
the realm of interest and of morality, and it certainly has earned its
right to do so; but evidently it must have its romance too; or rather it
wants its sober daily life to be rewarded romantically, supremely,
recognized as the worthiest, wants to identify its sober reality with
the blessed ideal. And sentimental literature is its art. *The Conscious Lovers* lasted for a century and if it creaks some today its kind
was still recognizable to Don Juan at the beginning of this century as
the literature of his notion of hell, and at the end of this century we
can buy its literature in the family magazines at the check-out counter every day and watch it on our screens several times every night.

The problem with sentimental comedy is not that it is moral and
sententious, or emotional and draws tears, or that it believes in the
goodness of human nature and exemplary characters, or that it turns
on improbable resolutions. Any one of these parts may be and has
been in works of a literary art we find admirable. And even the combination and prolongation of such parts, which certainly can become
wearisome, become important only as they raise questions of why
they are needed, questions of what kind of feeling needs this shape.
The art becomes false because the morality is false. Goldsmith's
"Comparison between Laughing and Sentimental Comedy," not
otherwise a good essay, makes its point when he says of the good and

the exceedingly generous characters of the sentimental that "they are lavish enough of their *tin* money on the stage"; or if they happen to have faults the spectator is taught not only to pardon but to applaud them "in consideration of the goodness of their hearts; so that folly, instead of being ridiculed is commended" (1773). This is a morality that makes virtue cheap, purchaseable with tin money, or not a hard deed but an easy feeling. It makes this sort of separation because it has something to defend. What is sentimental is a fearful protection of what is felt to be a necessary illusion. We all have something to protect. Goldsmith is terribly snobbish about tradesmen. What is *he* hiding? Or why am I so exercised about this whole thing?

The text is Richard Steele, *The Conscious Lovers,* ed. Shirley Strum Kenny (Lincoln, Nebr., 1968). References are to act, scene and page number (Act III has only one scene); where successive quotations in the same paragraph are from the same scene the act and scene numbers are not repeated.

Bevis, Richard, *The Laughing Tradition: Stage Comedy in Garrick's Day* (Athens, Ga., 1980)

Cohen, Michael M., "Reclamation, Revulsion, and Steele's *The Conscious Lovers,*" *Restoration and 18th Century Theatre Research*, XIV, No. 1 (1975), 23–30

Ellis, Frank H., *Sentimental Comedy: Theory & Practice* (Cambridge, 1991)

Friedman, Arthur, "Aspects of Sentimentalism in Eighteenth-Century Literature," in *The Augustan Milieu*, edd. Henry Knight Miller, Eric Rothstein and G. S. Rousseau (Oxford, 1970)

Hume, Robert D., *The Rakish Stage: Studies in English Drama, 1660–1800* (Carbondale, 1983)

Kenny, Shirley Strum, "Humane Comedy," *Modern Philology*, LXXV (1977), 29–43

———, Introduction to the 1968 edition of the text and to the material in her edition of *The Plays of Richard Steele* (Oxford, 1971)

Krutch, Joseph Wood, *Comedy and Conscience after the Restoration* (New York, 1924)

Loftis, John, *Steele at Drury Lane* (Berkeley, 1952)

———, *Comedy and Society from Congreve to Fielding* (Stanford, 1959)

Marshall, W. Gerald, "'Joy too exquisite for laughter': A Re-Evaluation of Steele's *The Conscious Lovers,*" *Literature and Belief*, IV (1984), 33–48

Novak, Maximillian E., "The Sentimentality of *The Conscious Lovers* Revisited and Reasserted," *Modern Language Studies*, IX (1979), 48–59

Parnell, Paul E., "The Sentimental Mask," *PMLA*, LXXVIII (1963), 529–35

Sherbo, Arthur, *English Sentimental Drama* (East Lansing, 1957)

Traugott, John, "Heart and Mask and Genre in Sentimental Comedy," *Eighteenth-Century Life*, X, No. 3 (1986), 122–44

Zimbardo, Rose A., *A Mirror to Nature: Transformations in Drama and Aesthetics, 1660–1732* (Lexington, 1986)

Chapter Six

A league below the city

Measure for Measure

If plays that end in marriage are usually said to be comedies, and those works we have looked at have ended with a pair of marriages by way of reinforcing the general happiness in several forms, *Measure for Measure* does seem to be overqualified. It has a quadruple set, a number something like the deaths in a real good tragedy when in the fifth act players have to stagger off into the wings to keep the stage from getting cluttered—perhaps to keep the sad audience from embarrassed laughter, because too much of a good thing can reverse its intended effect. Even in *As You Like It* four marriages ask for a saving melancholy wit. "There is, sure, another flood toward, and these couples are coming to the ark" (V, iv, 35–36). But nobody in the present play is amused by the spectacle of this conclusion. The rapid coupling in the last bit of *Measure for Measure* comes as rather a surprise to us and to some of the participants as rather more than that. The main female character is so stunned at the proposal she receives she never says a word after. One of the lesser males, who is ordered to prison for the execution of his nuptials, in place of whipping and hanging, beseeches to be let off from that merciful reduction of sentence, seeing the new punishment as much worse, as pressing to death, whipping and hanging. There is no dancing to celebrate the end of these somber affairs. The only young couple in this concluding scene who can rejoice in marrying, in the fulfillment of a desire long delayed on their course of true love, have good reason to be relieved (apart from the fact that she and almost everyone has assumed his head had been cut off by law): by Act II she was already groaning, near her hour of producing their baby. But then that marriage ceremony, in limping after the fact, is but one among three of these four affairs, for a civic statistic of 75 percent. If freedom from a strict and frustrating law was a desired end in the Athens of *A Midsummer Night's Dream,* and if a similar escape from a restraining local condition seemed to be an attractive hope in the London of *Man and Superman* and the Longbourn of *Pride and Prejudice,* the characters in Vienna have long had the liberty to do what pleases them; and they do fornicate readily and generally.

It is a serious problem. The law of the land set the initial bounds in *A Midsummer Night's Dream,* but the authority of Theseus is never challenged within Athens, so that he can graciously suspend the law's threatening force to meet the loving need of his young subjects. In *Man and Superman* and *Pride and Prejudice* the stability of the state is hardly an issue, though Jack Tanner likes to think it is. But in *Measure for Measure* the polity of Vienna is in question. It is a sick city, so fevered that it appears the dissolution of it must cure it. The Duke begins the action with a pretense that governing is a simple matter which he can hand over to his appointed deputies, while he must go off on his travels. His commission of power, he explains to Escalus, unexpectedly sudden as it may be, requires no special instruction, since that deputy knows more of the "properties" of government than he does. Escalus, he says, with unqualified confidence, understands well

> The nature of our people,
> Our city's institutions, and the terms
> For common justice,

is as pregnant in these as "art and practice" have enriched any he remembers. But Angelo will be the primary deputy: "What figure of us think you he will bear?" given the deputation of "all the organs / Of our own power. What think you of it?" Escalus has no doubt that if any in Vienna be of worth to undergo such ample grace and honor it is Lord Angelo, as we, from the name alone, might expect to be the case (I, i, 1–24). The Duke addresses Angelo as a man of such virtues that they are not to be his alone but used by Heaven: "Spirits are not finely touched but to fine issues . . . " So Angelo's spirit will be touched, as by a touchstone, and Nature, having lent him excellence will have her repayment. But Angelo knows all this, the Duke adds, and in the Duke's absence "be thou at full ourself":

> Mortality and mercy in Vienna
> Live in thy tongue, and heart.

Angelo is thereby the designated controlling figure in this city, presumably with even more knowledge of how to govern and of the nature of the people than Escalus. With the modesty we might expect he says he may not be ready for so great a test but the Duke will allow no evasion. The Duke is off in haste and privily: he loves the people but he does not like to "stage" himself to their eyes. The puzzled Escalus, who has been credited with so much understanding, does not yet know what to do: "A power I have, but of what strength and nature / I am not yet instructed" (25–80). Angelo, it turns out, has more certainty of instruction in what to do when he is the man with the organs of power, of mortality and mercy.

It seems the Duke has changed dramatic roles, given to Angelo the control in order to take a different one for himself, and it is evidently a natural doubt of the Friar Thomas, with whom he then confers privately, that the Duke is off to be a lover. "No," the Duke says,

> Holy father, throw away that thought.
> Believe not that the dribbling dart of love
> Can pierce a complete bosom.

Our suspicions may well be with Friar Thomas when we hear that declaration of a complete bosom safe from the dribbling dart: we know that a man who makes that boast in the first act speaks like a lover in a comedy who is sure to be married by the last act. But law and not love is the Duke's present purpose. The strict statutes and most biting laws, to curb headstrong wills, he has for fourteen years let sleep, bound up (nineteen years, Claudio says, in any case an awful lot of time to have been sleeping), so that the decrees are dead and liberty plucks justice by the nose. Friar Thomas says, justly enough, that the Duke himself could have unloosed this justice and in him it would have seemed more dreadful than in the Lord Angelo. Too dreadful, is the answer, since it had been the Duke's fault to give the people scope it would be tyranny to punish them for the evil deeds he permitted. He has therefore imposed the office on Angelo, who may in the ambush of the Duke's name strike home, with the Duke's name never involved in "slander," which is good statecraft but doesn't seem quite fair to Angelo—except that the Duke doesn't quite believe that Angelo is for real: he is a precise Puritanical sort, "scarce confesses / That his blood flows, or that his appetite / Is more to bread than stone" (I, iii, 1–54). That certainly alerts us to the more than possibility that this deputy with pretension to be more than human will be something less than fully human, or may develop another human flow and appetite, or both. Lucio shortly after confirms this diagnosis of the blood, "a man whose blood / Is very snow-broth" (I, iv, 57–58), and later adds his own doubts—"when he makes water, his urine is congealed ice" (III, ii, 96–97)—so we have very different authorities agreeing on his deficiencies in the fluids of a normal life. The Duke is interested in a test: "Hence shall we see, / If power change purpose, what our seemers be" (I, iii, 54–55). All this may be disturbing to a later audience and with many commentators the devious Duke has not been popular; but if we accept the premise that he has a problem, for which he bears responsibility and which requires an extraordinary response, and that he is going to try a political and moral experiment of unknown result, he becomes too interesting to judge readily before we see how he will do. If he does not like to stage himself he has a director's imagination and his art and practice will attempt a play with a large cast and a strange tale. He knows that the properties of government, the nature of his people, his city's institutions, the terms for common justice, are a good deal more complicated than they seem, and that a man named Angelo may be more human than he seems, and that power can change purposes. If he knows that he has been at fault in too fondly giving the people scope, that it is time to end a sleep, he will find too that his exchange of power teaches him a necessary lesson about staying free of slander, about how to govern, and something about his complete bosom.

We have begun to understand the desperate current state of Vienna, in the immediately preceding scene (I, ii), when we have gone into the street and heard the language there. Lucio and two gentlemen talk of Heaven granting us its peace, as a formula and nothing more, for these are not gentlemen who accept all Ten Commandments when one or another may interfere with their functions. Grace with them is a matter for witty jest, in any proportion or in any language, or in any religion. "Ay? Why not? Grace is grace, despite of all controversy: as, for example, thou thyself art a wicked villain, despite of all grace." Nor is there anything to choose between these gentlemen, cut from the same cloth. The use of words here becomes even sharper as they speak "feelingly" of one another's venereal diseases, which bring "painful feeling" of speech, in the mouth. Now we see approaching the immediate provider for their feelings, Madam Mitigation, Mistress Overdone the bawd. (She has been done by many men; and married nine times, Overdone by the last.) Lucio has purchased many diseases under her roof, as come to three thousand dolours a year, and more; for one of the gentlemen, Lucio says, it has been a French crown more (a venereal souvenir). The gentleman is annoyed, for this joke seems to have no end, and we may agree. "Thou art always figuring diseases in me, but thou art full of error: I am sound." No, there is no bottom to this wit: "Nay, not, as one would say, healthy, but so sound as things that are hollow. Thy bones are hollow. Impiety has made a feast of three" (1–46). The clever and handsome surface and the clap below that surface in Dorimant's town do not go so deep as this graceless, hollow, syphilitic, impiety that has eaten Vienna.

But something is being done, as Mistress Overdone tells them. Claudio is being carried to prison and within these three days his head is to be chopped off, for getting Juliet with child. Angelo is in power. These are bad days for Mistress Overdone, what with the war, the sweat, the gallows, poverty, she is custom-shrunk, and worse is in store because there is now a proclamation that all houses of resort in the suburbs are to be pulled down. "Why, here's a change indeed in the commonwealth," she says truly and weeps (I, ii, 49–88). In Angelo's commonwealth even the young lovers, both of them, are in custody and Claudio is being shown to the world, as example, on the way to prison, by order of "the demi-god, Authority." Claudio, as he says this, is not a neutral party, but he does not appear to have done terrible wrong; he and Juliet love one another and he is contracted to her, his wife in all but outward order; and they are not in that order only because, in a familiar difficulty in the course of true love, there is some money with her friends, from whom they have hidden their love till time makes the friends more friendly. But now the stealth of their mutual entertainment is grossly apparent and so they have another legal problem in Angelo. We might expect this sort of thing standing between two young lovers to be amenable to ingenuity or chance, and even the threat of death (we've seen that in *Midsummer Night's Dream*) ought not be taken too seriously. But Claudio is serious, takes his own act seriously, and when the trivial Lucio asks the origin of this legal restrain on him Claudio delivers a homily: "From too much liberty, my Lucio, liberty." Every scope by immoderate use turns to restraint and he improves the occasion of his own case to a general moral pronouncement on humankind.

> Our natures do pursue
> Like rats that ravin down their proper bane
> A thirsty evil, and when we drink, we die.   (102–12)

The surprised and admiring Lucio says that if he could speak so wisely under an arrest he would send for certain of his creditors, though on second thought he'd rather have the foppery of freedom as the morality of imprisonment. But that view of a young lover that the fault is in having too much of liberty, in a flaw of nature that pursues an evil which leads to death, does give us pause. We've not before heard that sort of thing as youthful wisdom. By this reasoning, Lucio sees, freedom is foppery, the way of the fool, and if he prefers such freedom that is no endorsement. It does not follow that Claudio is content with his proposed punishment; he doubts the motives of Angelo, who may be a new ruler looking for a name, putting the drowsy and neglected law on him, and since the Duke is gone Claudio has no appeal above the law. His one hope is to send Lucio to a sister Claudio has, this day entering a cloister, to have her make friends with the strict deputy; this is a sister, he says, who knows how to play with reason and discourse. The rather high level at which the young lover has conducted his thought is degraded by Lucio, who sees that he himself has a general and personal interest in circumventing such a sentence, as well as being sorry to see Claudio's life "foolishly lost at a game of tick-tack" (a game in which one puts pegs into holes) (113–71). It is not a clear situation here, how a governor ought to deal with a city that has a Claudio and a Lucio. The Duke doesn't know what will happen but he proposes to see.

When Lucio goes to visit the sister at her nunnery it appears that Angelo is not the only strict character in the city. Isabella is disap-

pointed in the menu of privileges available to the nuns and says she
had been "rather wishing a more strict restraint." Lucio, in his way,
says he speaks to her differently from the way he speaks to other
virgins, holding her as a thing enskied and sainted, an immortal
spirit. Isabella finds this extravagance repellent, but she is certainly
on the side of the law of strict restraint, the saints above mortal fault.
He says all hope is gone for her brother unless she has the grace to
soften Angelo. What poor ability is in her? "Assay the power you
have." "My power? Alas, I doubt" (I, iv, 1–76). Her grace and power
are put to the test, for her and for Angelo.

Angelo will not be easy. Other good people, not the Lucio-type
but Escalus, and the gentle Provost with whom the hidden Duke
works and comes to respect and promote, plead for Claudio. They
do not approve what Claudio has done but there is a fellow-feeling in
judging it. "Alas," the Provost soliloquizes,

> He hath but as offended in a dream.
> All sects, all ages smack of this vice, and he
> To die for't? (II, ii, 3–6)

(As Jack Tanner said to Roebuck Ramsden in a similar event, "this is
an act of which every man is capable," *Man and Superman,* I, 28).
Escalus, addressing Angelo, "most strait in virtue," tries to put the
act in a human context of feelings and circumstances and blood and
tries to ask Angelo to see himself in that: let but his honor know that
in the working of his own affections, "Had time cohered with place,
or place with wishing, / Or that the resolute acting of your blood"
could have attained his purpose, whether he had not sometime in
his life erred in the same point and pulled the law on him. It is no
good appealing to blood in Angelo, but apart from that Angelo understands law better than Escalus, who misses the point. Of course a
jury may have, unknown, a thief or two guiltier than him they try,
but justice must act where it can; and if it does not see all things that
does not mean it cannot take what it sees. Besides, the question is
not whether Angelo might do what Claudio has done but whether
he does, and if he does then he is willing to let his own judgment
pattern out his death too. Which is fair enough, though Angelo sees
no risk in his offer, for as he has said, "'Tis one thing to be tempted,

Escalus, / Another thing to fall" (II, i, 1–31). This is another man confident in his complete bosom.

Now comes another enforcer of the law, the Duke's constable Elbow, who leans upon justice, who cannot distinguish the meanings of benefactor and malefactor, with his much more clever-talking prisoner Pompey, who can erase the seeming differences of true and false. Angelo, seeing no distinction here, leaves them to Escalus, hoping there will be cause to whip them all (II, i, 41–121). With this officer and offender before him, "Which is the wiser here?" Escalus wonders, "Justice or Iniquity? Is this true?" It is a real question and Escalus certainly doesn't know the answer. Different people have different ideas about law in Vienna and Pompey Bum, partly a bawd, thinks he has a case to plead. "Truly, sir, I am a poor fellow that would live." Escalus has a simple question: "What do you think of the trade, Pompey? Is it a lawful trade?" and Pompey has a less simple answer: "If the law would allow, it, sir." That does seem to remove the legal question from the moral and Escalus's response, "But the law will not allow it, Pompey," isn't fully responsive. Pompey thinks it is unnatural. "Does your worship mean to geld and splay all the youth in the city?" and since he does not, "Truly, sir, in my poor opinion they will to't then." If there is to be heading and hanging that way authority will run out of heads and if the law hold in Vienna ten years the real estate market will collapse. How much more of the law Pompey knows than Escalus—you do what you can get away with in life, for pleasure or profit—is clear when the good Escalus lets him off with a warning and good counsel; Pompey thanks him for that and confides to us that he will follow the advice "as the flesh and fortune shall better determine" (122–219). Having disposed of Pompey Escalus then tells a Justice that Angelo's severity is needful, that

> Mercy is not itself, that oft looks so,
> Pardon is still the nurse of second woe,

good counsel which he has not himself listened to. "But yet, poor Claudio; there is no remedy" (240–46). That's not right either, but finding a remedy for Vienna, a remedy for these confusions in truth and in law, is extraordinarily difficult and it will now develop a shocking complication.

Isabella makes her call on Angelo, but they are on the same side of the law: her brother's vice is one "that most I do abhor, / And most desire should meet the blow of justice." She does not want to plead but must, must not plead but that she is "At war 'twixt will and will not." She is wasting everyone's time and Angelo wants to know what she is talking about. "Well; the matter?" She makes a feeble gesture to get out of her dilemma—let it be her brother's fault that dies and not her brother—but Angelo puts up with no nonsense: every fault is condemned before it is done; to punish the fault and not the actor is to make a cipher of the judge's function. And she agrees. "Oh just but severe law: / I had a brother then. Heaven keep your honor. [*Going*]" (II, ii, 27–43). Fortunately for her Lucio, about as free and dirty as she is strict and saintly, is there to put a little human feeling into her, send her back. "Kneel," "You are too cold"; if she needed a pin she could not with more tame a tongue desire it. She tries again, still a weak sister at this sort of thing. "Must he needs die?" But Angelo makes his first mistake. "Maiden, no remedy." Not only is he wrong in his superior certainty but he is moving into a territory where she is now more comfortable. "Yes," she says, because he might pardon Claudio and neither heaven nor man grieve at the mercy. "I will not do't." She sees an opening. "But can you if you would?" He refuses the distinction, not being troubled by a divided mind like her in her unaccustomed moment 'twixt will and will not. "Look what I will not, that I cannot do." He will not allow the possibility of a distinction between his will and his power, what he ought to do and what he does. In every sense this is a man with a working complete bosom. But now she sees that this is an issue not simply of a just but severe law but of person, too, of heart and remorse (pity). She will not let Angelo keep it comfortably impersonal, with his "He's sentenced, 'tis too late," and with the repeated urgency of Lucio's "You are too cold" she herself warms. Not too late, and Angelo can move from his dress of power to mercy. She tries what Escalus had tried only to be rebuked, but with an added element now:

> If he had been as you, and you as he,
> You would have slipped like him, but he like you
> Would not have been so stern.

She has got to move him to change roles, not only to think that he in Claudio's place might have been as bad as Claudio, but that Claudio in his place might have been better than he. Angelo does not want to go on with this. "Pray you be gone," which may be his dismissal of a meaningless appeal, though given the direction of the dialogue before and after, it may be a new uneasiness (44–67).

Isabella turns it up and makes the exchange of roles more personal, he and she: if she had his power and he were Isabel, "No. I would tell what 'twere to be a judge, / And what a prisoner." It earns her first compliment from Lucio: "Ay, touch him, there's the vein." Angelo's spirit would be touched, the Duke promised, and by what fine issue and in what sense was to be seen. Angelo continues to insist it is a matter of law only, her brother is a forfeit of the law, it is the law not he who condemns, but she has the touch now and she has the vein. There is nothing he can say now that she cannot use, and if he says her brother is a forfeit of the law she is ready with the remedy he said did not exist.

> Why all the souls that were, were forfeit once,
> And he that might the vantage best have took
> Found out the remedy. How would you be,
> If he, which is the top of judgement, should
> But judge you as you are? Oh, think on that,
> And mercy then will breathe within your lips,
> Like man new made. (II, ii, 68–81)

The stage is now both personal and heavenly and He has a remedy, which Angelo, like all of us, needs, needs to be man new made. Angelo can only repeat himself but she, with approving interjections from Lucio, goes from strength to strength against this proud man in his power. Heaven is merciful

> but man, proud man,
> Dressed in a little brief authority,
> Most ignorant of what he's most assured,
> His glassy essence, like an angry ape,
> Plays such fantastic tricks before high heaven
> As makes the angels weep; who, with our spleens,
> Would all themselves laugh mortal. (81–127)

And now she has him as a character in a comedy, the character who thinks he has control and is ignorant of himself, thinks he stands above human imperfection and is thereby not more but less than what a human being should be, thinks he has the authority of real power when he is only playing foolish, apish tricks. Angels, with whom Angelo thought he stood, judge these things by a heavenly standard of perfection and they weep. But to human organs he is a clown for our laughter, on earth, where the human comedy is acted. Lucio, himself a fantastic and lover of tricks, sees how effectively this works and cheers her on. "Oh, to him, to him, wench, he will relent. He's coming: I perceive't." The gentle Provost has his stance: "Pray heaven, she win him!" She begins to challenge our ability to weigh our brother ("our" brother now) with ourself, makes pointed comparisons of how those in power have license, how "Great men may jest with saints: 'tis wit in them," while in the less it is foul profanation. More of that, Lucio says, knowing something of the license of jest and superior wit (though, like his kind, not as much as he thinks). Then a rather surprising analogy, not in her field, where one would not expect her to have knowledge. A captain gets away with a choleric word, which in the soldier is flat blasphemy. Lucio is surprised and delighted, "Art avised o' that? More on't," because Angelo is taken aback: "Why do you put these sayings upon me?" (128–37). And then she really makes him go into himself.

Authority has its private remedy; though it err like others it has yet "a kind of medicine in itself" that skins over the vice:

> Go to your bosom,
> Knock there, and ask your heart what it doth know
> That's like my brother's fault. If it confess
> A natural guiltiness, such as is his,
> Let it not sound a thought upon your tongue
> Against my brother's life.

And with that demand for confession of natural guiltiness—Claudio's confession of our natures that do pursue a thirsty evil—we hear, in Angelo's private thought, for the first time, that he has been made to recognize the truth of what she says.

> She speaks, and 'tis such sense
> That my sense breeds with it. (II, ii, 138–47)

But we do not yet know why, why this breeding of the senses, and she does not know what a terrible success she has had. He will see her again tomorrow. "Heaven keep your honour safe," an irony only he understands, that man of strict and single, angelic mind, for he is now going that way to temptation "Where prayers cross." " 'Save your honour." Save from Isabella, because what Angelo has just found in himself is a natural guiltiness which brings revulsion, not the desire of Claudio for the woman he loves and wants to honor and marry but the desire of a man who is tempted by virtue, as carrion corrupts in the sun. With waste ground enough he desires to raze the sanctuary and pitch his evils there. "Oh fie, fie, fie," that exclamation of men who have had sudden sight, in a purity unsuspected, of a depth of sexual foulness they had not before imagined, and here not in a woman but in himself. So certain was his knowledge of himself and his acts, but now, "What dost thou or what art thou, Angelo?" He desires her foully for those things that make her good, to defile her a saint, he a saint. He enters the dream—"What is't I dream on?"—this one a nightmare (162–91). Good Angelo will see himself becoming devil.

We could have anticipated Angelo's fall—some girl would tempt him and he would tumble and it would be good for him, both as a fit return for thinking himself above human flaw and as humanizing him. But this is a startling turn. Now that he has become a lover ("What, do I love her . . . ?" II, ii, 181) he is worse than ever, more human in his baseness. And he is the deputy, in command of others if no longer of himself, so that the disease of Vienna runs from top to bottom; again no remedy, after Isabella has offered one way. Angelo's self-knowledge does not improve life for him or for Vienna but pushes us further down. To turn this dark power around, find the cure for this disease, end this dream, is going to require some enormous controlling director, both more dark and more powerful, someone who can work still deeper. We do not have to wait to see what this will be, for it is there in the immediately following scene. The Duke is there, has never left, and the Duke can step in at any moment and stop Angelo, so we probably don't have to worry greatly about Claudio or Isabella; but that intervention would not take us very far because we would still have the Vienna we have seen. And we still do not know what it is the Duke will or can do, because we still don't have the Duke's credentials as effective power, and what we have seen so far, in his previous record and in his present choice of deputy, may not give assurance. We are given the assurance we need before Angelo can do much, between his discovery of his guilty desire and his attempt to put it into action, between his first and second scenes with Isabella, before he makes his proposition. We see not only that the Duke is indeed there but that he is at work, and what that work is.

He visits Juliet. She is one of those wonderful Shakespearean characters who has half-a-dozen little speeches, one of them only a word, none of them much more, and then is heard no more, who lives and loves and makes us fall in love with her. We see now that the power of the Duke is not only supremely temporal but supremely spiritual, because he has taken upon his hidden self the role of the holy father who can learn the inmost thoughts of others, both as the Duke invisible, that fairy privilege, and the hooded confessor. He puts his questions to Juliet to see and to direct her state of mind.

> DUKE: Repent you, fair one, of the sin you carry?
> JULIET: I do; and bear the shame most patiently.

A good answer, but we don't know if it has the right meaning.

> DUKE: I'll teach you how you shall arraign your conscience
> And try your penitence if it be sound
> Or hollowly put on.

Another kind of sound and hollow wit from what we heard in the street with Lucio, and Juliet is sound: "I'll gladly learn." A good pupil and the next question will test her.

> DUKE: Love you the man that wronged you?

Tough question, for what is she to say? Yes, madly, passionately? Then her repentance is false and she is still in sin. No, I hate him, look what he did to me? Then she is hollow in another self-regarding sin, putting the blame on him and his wronging of her. What does she say?

> JULIET: Yes, as I love the woman that wronged him.

Beautiful answer, true to him and to herself, true to her feelings, in her integrity sharing the wrong and sharing the love. Mutually committed act, then? the confessor asks. "Mutually." Of course the woman's sin is of heavier kind, he says, and since that is a premise not to be argued at the moment, "I do confess it, and repent it, father." He is persistent and because there are different kinds of repentance, one as that the sin has brought her shame and she is sorry toward herself, not heaven, not as she loves heaven but in fear—. She is already there and can interrupt:

> JULIET: I do repent me as it is an evil
> And take the shame with joy.

The Duke-Friar knows she is where she should be. "There rest . . . Grace go with you, *Benedicite*." There was really nothing he had to do for her for she was already resting in grace, but we have seen his mode, in his easiest case, and wait to see his work with his people of more difficult nature. How he will proceed with them is pointed in his last words to Juliet even as he blesses her, by making her face the imminent death of Claudio for their mutually committed offenseful act; she has been respited, she says, "a life whose very comfort / Is still a dying horror!" (II, iii, 19–42).

We return to Angelo, still struggling with this unaccustomed division within, thinking and praying "To several subjects," heaven in his mouth, in his heart strong and swelling evil. "Blood, thou art blood," he finds now, and it musters to his heart (II, iv, 1–30). And in this vein he now begins to put Isabella to the test by dividing her mind, turning his inner disgust to a purpose. "Ha! Fie, these filthy vices!" he says to her of her brother; it were as good to pardon him that has "from nature stolen / A man already made" as those that "do coin heaven's image, / In stamps that are forbid," the thief of life or its counterfeiter, murderer of man or maker of illegitimate child. It is a specious argument but well directed at its audience—a sin's a sin and she of all people should understand that. She, who abhors the vice, who thought the law just, who even now, in her second visit, was prepared to accept the law, backs off. "'Tis set down so in heaven, but not in earth." We don't in fact judge all sins by one heavenly standard, not on earth. In the language of her previous encounter with Angelo, presumably for murder we weep with the angels in heaven, for Claudio's sin we might laugh with the mortals on earth; in any case she has made a distinction that puts her in a trap he has set. "Say you so? Then I shall pose you quickly." If such choice between heavenly and earthly judgments are allowed, would she rather that the law took her brother's life or that she redeem him by giving up her body to such "sweet uncleanness" as the woman her brother stained? He himself is getting confused and can, he knows, speak against his own arguments, and she of course doesn't know where he is going. He proposes "a charity in sin," or "equal poise of sin and charity." She can't follow him and he's getting annoyed at this lack of cooperation in moral confusion. "Your sense pursues not mine: either you are ignorant / Or seem so crafty, and that's not good." So he tries to make it clearer, but still as a general proposition, and she understands that and is herself clear that it is better for a brother to die than that a sister, by redeeming him this way, die forever. That makes her as cruel as the law, says he, but she is clear on the distinction that the "lawful mercy" she has been pleading for is "nothing kin to foul redemption." But she, he says, has of late been making the law a tyrant and rather proved the sliding of her brother a "merriment than a vice." That is not true and it is of course Angelo who is doing the sliding, but it is true that the heaven-and-earth distinction she has used pushes her brother, and Angelo, of different sorts but both mortals on earth, in the direction of laughter. That bothers her, because she has always been uncomfortable with having to plead with two minds. She needs a pardon, she thinks:

> Oh, pardon me my lord, it oft falls out
> To have what we would have, we speak not what we mean.
> I something do excuse the thing I hate
> For his advantage that I dearly love.

It has not in fact oft fallen out that she has spoken not what she means, but it has happened in this difficult mixed problem of hate and love she has been made to enter. And Angelo is working well with this human weakness she has been made to recognize. "We are all frail," he offers. She still cannot make the application to herself and takes him, quickly, as offering an excuse for her brother as one among other men. Angelo pushes her to make the application he wants: "Nay, women are frail too." It is something she can admit readily, doctrinal truth, but he tries to be more bold in authority ("I do arrest your words") and wants her to show now that she is a woman "By putting on the destined livery": still a confusing language for one who is about to take the veil. Ambiguities have been distracting her:

> I have no tongue but one. Gentle my lord,
> Let me entreat you speak the former language. (41–141)

So it must be "Plainly conceive, I love you," and your brother will not die "if you give me love." She says she knows his virtue "hath a license in't" to seem a little fouler than it is to pluck on others, but no, he assures her, "Believe me on mine honour, / My words express my purpose." It is a rich perversion of words which she now understands—"Seeming, seeming"—which she still thinks that she can proclaim with "an outstretched throat." He makes it clear that no one will believe and she will stifle in her own report (142–71).

She is at the end of the line of power, with none higher to appeal to: the last authority of the state has done worse than reject her appeal, has revealed in himself the deepest corruption; with "one and the self-same tongue" he can condemn and approve, bidding the law make curtsy to his will. In this confounding of right and wrong she has only one certainty left, that her brother, though he fell by prompture of the blood yet has in him such a mind of honor he would tender down twenty heads on twenty bloody blocks before his sister should her body stoop (II, iv, 172–88). We have been given cause to think well of Claudio but expecting him to yield twenty heads is rather much; one is a lot and Isabella's absolute assurance that it carries an undivided mind of honor doesn't seem to give enough consideration to the fact that he does have in him blood, too, and that it has already prompted him to life on at least one occasion. We have seen her require urgent prompting in learning how to kneel and she is not likely to stoop.

What gives us more hope is that we know the hidden Duke is there, and we want to see what he may have in mind. Happily the next scene and act begins with him, having attended previously to Juliet, now questioning Claudio's mind, a more difficult case. But

Claudio too, Juliet's love, is an attractive youth. He has high hope of
pardon from Lord Angelo? the Duke-Friar asks. "The miserable
have no other medicine / But only hope," he answers, a resigned
attitude for someone in what seems to be a desperate condition with
no cure at hand to make him whole. "I have hope to live, and am
prepared to die," a noble response and what more could we ask of
him? The Duke-Friar wants more. He wants no division. "Be absolute for death," and that absolute—the certainty that one will die
and the ordering of one's life by that—is the one undivided truth of
this Vienna, which makes death or life thereby the sweeter. Claudio
must reason thus with life:

> If I do lose thee I do lose a thing
> That none but fools would keep: a breath thou art,
> Servile to all the skyey influences
> That dost this habitation where thou keepst
> Hourly afflict. Merely, thou art death's fool,
> For him thou labour'st by thy flight to shun
> And yet runn'st toward him still.

In Vienna, it seems, the charm that blinds, that makes fools of those
who think that they are free, that they are successful lovers or superior spirits, is death. Merely—entirely, fully—thou art death's fool.
There is no other identity, as the Duke-Friar displays with his many
examples of the illusions of being noble, valiant.

> Thou art not thyself,
> For thou exists on many a thousand grains
> That issue out of dust.

Happiness is not real—"Happy thou art not," striving for what you
have not, forgetting what you have. You are not certain, stable, but
shifting "to strange effects / After the moon." All realities are the
reverse of your illusions. If you are rich you are poor, not more but
less than a man,

> For like an ass whose back with ingots bows
> Thou bear'st thy heavy riches but a journey
> And death unloads thee.

The journey here, the journey of life, is to death. And life is

> as it were an after-dinner's sleep,
> Dreaming on both . . .

The terms are by now familiar to us from our previous works, but the foolish illusion, strange effects after the moon, the journey, the dream, all seem to be final here with no egress for the fool, for life is the illusion, the reality is death. "He hath but as offended in a dream," the Provost had said in Claudio's excuse, but here the dream is life itself that leads to death. But then that is the knowledge that liberates, the real liberty:

> What's yet in this
> That bears the name of life? Yet in this life
> Lie hid moe thousand deaths; yet death we fear,
> That makes these odds all even.

Claudio, an impressive and intelligent young man, understands the paradox:

> I humbly thank you.
> To sue to live, I find I seek to die,
> And seeking death, find life: let it come on. (III, i, 1–43)

If ignorance of death is the charm, knowledge of death is the counter-charm, the eye-opener: it makes odds even, gives order to desires, sets free from fear. The Duke-Friar will not cut off anyone's head by way of improving an errant subject's condition, will not allow anyone to die, will try, so far as he can, to bring each to a better life; but he will do that by bringing each to the face and acceptance of death. He will administer where it is needed, at the moment it is needed, in the form it is needed, the mortification which opens that better life. For those who have learned to see that truth about themselves either death or life is thereby the sweeter. The Duke-Friar who knows how to apply that medicine to the eye is the superior administrator. Once again it seems to have been easy for him.

Claudio accepts and is ready to let it come on. And then it comes on, with Isabella, who brings her news of death. For all her asserted confidence in Claudio it takes her a while to get to the point, as it had with her plea to Angelo. "Is there no remedy?" Claudio asks. "None, but such remedy as, to save a head, / To cleave a heart in twain." This fencing goes on for a bit until Claudio, with justice, has to say, "Let me know the point," and we see that she is not so certain of his integrity. "Oh, I do fear thee Claudio," who may still prefer a "feverous life" to perpetual honor, and who may not have to die. Claudio is rather indignant that she gives him this shame: "I will encounter darkness as a bride / And hug it in mine arms," he says, the pupil of the hidden Duke-Friar, though given his peculiar circumstances not with a simile that inspires full confidence. But it is a great relief to Isabella, who hears the brother she wants, the voice of her father's grave. When she gives him the details he is again indignant and he is firm: "Thou shalt not do't." If it were but her life, she adds, she'd throw it down for him as frankly as a pin. "Thanks, dear Isabel." Lucio has already indicated that she is not a great picker up of pins and Claudio may not know how good she is at throwing them down, but he is grateful. She tells him to be ready for death tomorrow and he says "Yes," but presumably with a certain abstraction, because his mind is beginning to wander (III, i, 60–107). He is astonished at Angelo—can he have affections in him that make him bite the law by the nose? Angelo's example is now raising a question in Claudio's absolute mind. "Sure it is no sin, / Or of the deadly seven it is the least." And now Isabel is worried about the precise direction of his reference. "Which is the least?" He'll stay with the pronoun:

> If it were damnable, he being so wise,
> Why would he for the momentary trick
> Be perdurably fined? Oh Isabel!

Death is a fearful thing, he says, and her counter, that shamed life a hateful, is no longer above that thought. Claudio's imagination works on what it is to lie in cold obstruction and to rot, this sensible warm motion (which he has known with love), to bathe in fiery floods, in thick-ribbed ice, to be imprisoned in the winds and blown with violence (the imprisoning sin he has given himself to); and, beyond bounds of the lawless mind,

> to be worse than worst
> Of those that lawless and incertain thought
> Imagine howling; 'tis too horrible.

He has reversed the lesson of the Duke-Friar and now the weariest and most loathed worldly life, imprisoned, is a "paradise"—that fool's paradise—to what we fear of death. The appeal is now to Isabella, "Sweet sister, let me live," the sin he asks of her will become a virtue (107–36).

That sweet sister's "prone and speechless dialect / Such as move men" (I, ii, 164–65), on which he had placed his dependence, has another sound now, putting him outside human kind, and certainly not her kind, in a series of startling imaginations of foulness in the family.

> O, you beast!
> Oh faithless coward, oh dishonest wretch!
> Wilt thou be made a man out of my vice?
> Is't not a kind of incest to take life
> From thine own sister's shame? What should I think?
> Heaven shield my mother played my father fair,
> For such a warped slip of wilderness
> Ne'er issued from his blood.

He is disowned, a beast condemned to death with no forgiveness, and there is no pin she will bend for now.

> Take my defiance,
> Die, perish. Might but my bending down
> Reprieve thee from thy fate, it should proceed.

She will listen to no word of "Nay hear me, Isabel," for to her it is "fie, fie, fie!" seeing in her brother, as Angelo in himself, the abyss. "O hear me, Isabella" (what does he want to say?) (III, i, 136–51).

It is a shocking, frightening scene, but it has a saving grace, one that is always present and keeps our expectations within the bounds of good hope, because we have seen the invisible Duke-Friar overhearing everything, all through the scene. Few characters in Shakespeare have more to say, his task is so great, but he dominates the stage, he is the stager, even more than he dominates the text. As she leaves, in a hurry, he delays Isabella and takes Claudio aside, tells him that Angelo has only been testing Isabella, that therefore he must prepare for death, putting aside hopes that are fallible, and go to his knees and make ready. Claudio, with his first opportunity to speak, wants to ask pardon of his sister; presumably that was what he had wanted to say when she would not listen. Now "I am so out of love with life that I will sue to be rid of it." We have heard him say that sort of thing already, but this time the words have another meaning which we can believe, because this time, after suing shamefully for life, he has been forced through the experience of what that means and has found he seeks to die. Certainly the Duke-Friar believes him: "Hold you there. Farewell" (III, i, 152–70), the words he had left with Juliet when he knew her mind was whole. He then turns to Isabella, who wishes the good Duke were there to speak to, and it seems she would test him if she had the chance, and he had better watch out—"I will open my lips in vain or discover his government." But he is there and his government will work. To the love he has in doing good a "remedy presents itself," and he will tell her of the Angelo-Mariana broken engagement; she can easily heal that rupture and the cure of it will save her brother and not dishonor her. "Show me how, good father," and before the end of the scene which had been so disastrous for her she has content already and expects a most prosperous perfection: "I thank you for this comfort" (176–250). It is going to be much more surprising than she thinks, as we know these things always will be, and she will not come so easily, by external arrangement, to perfection.

The Duke-Friar himself is going to find his problems less responsive to his power than he had thought, some subjects showing themselves intractable, with lessons of the limits of power. In the street there is Pompey, who is not easily amenable to advice that he should mend, an ingenious fellow, as we have seen, who is prepared to argue on behalf of his vocation ("it does stink in some sort, sir, but yet, sir, I would prove—") and there is little to be done for one to whom the devil has given proofs for sin. "Correction and instruction must both work / Ere this rude beast will profit," the Duke-Friar says, though recognizing that, unlike Angelo, Pompey is free of seeming (III, ii, 25–35). Lucio adds himself and his voice to the scene, witty, degrading, enjoying the customary "trick of it." "Still thus, and thus:

still worse," says the Duke-Friar (39–47), and still worse in this
seemer who invents for that Friar he has never seen before gratu-
itous lies of the Duke of whom he knows nothing. "It was a mad fantastical trick of him to steal from the state . . . " These words may hit
us rather more than the Duke, if we recall Isabella on the man of
authority playing fantastic tricks before high heaven, as they de-
grade the Duke to a fool. What particularly shakes the Duke in this
moment of the state is Lucio's insistence that, unlike Angelo, the
Duke "had some feeling of the sport, he knew the service, and that
instructed him to mercy," which is not quite the Duke's notion of
mercy; and then to make his report the more specifically convincing
Lucio credits the Duke with, to say the least, unsavory tastes ("he
would mouth with a beggar though she smelt brown bread and garlic . . . "). There is an artistry in this, an assumption of the superior
spirit and his insight, the trick, a light freedom with a dark mali-
ciousness from which, the Duke sees, no mortal can escape. "What
king so strong / Can tie the gall up in the slanderous tongue?" (82–
161). We learn immediately, from Mistress Overdone, of the treach-
erous license of Lucio at every level; she is being hauled to prison
because of Lucio's information against her, she who has cared for his
bastard child by Mistress Kate Keepdown, to whom he falsely promised marriage. It is a wretched city the Duke sees, as he pursues his
role of a visitor from another country, a brother of a gracious order
from the See, in special business from his Holiness. "What news
abroad i'th' world?" Escalus asks this delegate. "None but that there
is so great a fever on goodness that the dissolution of it must cure it,"
a desperate prognosis for which his special business will be a better
medicine. What dispositions and knowledge must he bring to his
task? The Duke was, Escalus tells the Friar, "One that above all
other strifes contended especially to know himself." That is the sort
of strife he has been proposing to those of his subjects he has so far
questioned, and he will now begin on the others. Claudio now willingly humbles himself to justice and, by the Friar's instruction of his
frailty, no longer frames "many deceiving promises of life"; he is "resolved to die" (170–212). But we know already that the hard cases
are to come, and they will test too the Duke's knowledge of himself,
of what he can do.

He plays his trick on Angelo, casting Mariana as Isabella, expecting that Angelo's vice will make mercy for Claudio, the wrong sort of mercy, and he will proceed from that to deal with Angelo. But Angelo surprises him and presses on with the order for the execution of Claudio, a worse depth of vice which the Duke had not imagined. He must improvise now to find a way of deceiving Angelo a second time, to make him think he has seen the head of the executed Claudio; and for that he turns to another man who is to be executed the same day, of whom he knows nothing, one Barnardine. Has this available substitute borne himself patiently, seems he to be touched? He is, says the Provost,

> A man that apprehends death no more dreadfully but as a drunken sleep: careless, reckless, and fearless of what's past, present, or to come: insensible of mortality, and desperately mortal.

Just the sort of case the Duke-Friar can deal with: "He wants advice." This man will hear none, the Provost reports, has no desire even to escape, forever drunk; even when told, by experiment, that he is about to be executed "It hath not moved him at all" (IV, ii, 123–34) But the Duke-Friar wants that head. "I will give him a present shrift, and advise him for a better place," and he must work rapidly because, as these things go with spirits, "it is almost clear dawn" (180–83). But no, it will not yet be clear dawn for him. Barnardine will not be moved to a journey, will not listen either to the clever cajolery of Pompey (now promoted to the moral level of the hangman's helper—that's the best we can do for him), or to the Friar's attempt at comfort, prayer.

> BARNARDINE: Friar, not I. I have been drinking hard all night, and I will have more time to prepare me, or they shall beat out my brains with billets. I will not consent to die this day, that's certain.
> DUKE: Oh, sir, you must; and therefore I beseech you
> Look forward on the journey you shall go.
> BARNARDINE: I swear I will not die today for any man's persuasion.
> DUKE: But hear you—
> BARNARDINE: Not a word.

Sleepy Barnardine who will not awake to die has a certainty about death as strong as the Duke-Friar's and he will not go *that* journey, not he. "Unfit to live or die," and his advisor is exasperated. Here is a man he can't prepare, who refuses to have his eyes opened, a man "unmeet for death" and to transport him in the mind he is would be damnable (IV, iii, 45–60). No remedy.

At this most critical moment, with his most difficult subject yet, who is refusing to play patient, who will not be touched, the Duke-Friar is stopped. This mind-doctor from Vienna, a looker-on who undertakes his cure of the psyche, by role-playing, by asking questions and listening to confessions, by analyzing the stories he hears and giving advice, has reached the limits of his practice. He could now simply reveal himself, give up the disguise and resume his deputized authority, but he would have failed to cure his city. Barnardine, with his gravel heart, has set a term to the Duke-Friar's ability to move. At this moment, this morning, the Provost tells him, there died of a cruel fever one Ragozine, a most notorious pirate and, even more fortunately, a man of Claudio's age, with beard and head just of Claudio's color, so his head will be an even better substitute to deceive Angelo. "Oh, 'tis an accident that heaven provides," the Duke-Friar declares (IV, iii, 60–68). That is convenient, as he says (94), and yet, accident that it is, and attributed to heaven as it is, it is not offensive. It seems very close to a sentimental solution, to the ending of *The Conscious Lovers*, as our nearest example, where an accident credited to Providence ended all problems in reward for virtue. But this heavenly accident I think we are willing to accept; for one thing because it is not the happy end but only enables the Duke to continue and because it is quickly dispatched, not dwelt on like a sweet dessert; but more importantly because it is not false. Death has been and will be a continual presence in the fevered life of this city, held off only by the Duke-Friar, who has used and will continue to use the figure of death and its moving sight to remedy the city's threatened dissolution. He cannot in fact control death's motions; he cannot stop it from looming when he does not want it, cannot make it come when he wants it. Suddenly it appears, from an unknown source and with an unexpected effect for good. In this play heaven, heavenly power and its examples of powers, its justice and its mercy, its tears and the correlative mortal laughter, have been always present. It has been essential that there is a great gap between an angelic heaven and a sick and naturally guilty earth and that no man, not even the Duke-Friar in his double power, can control or solve that problem. Only He found out the remedy, and all the Duke-Friar can do is, above all other strifes, contend especially to know himself and find his limits in governing on earth. He cannot claim heaven's reward but he can do all that is possible for a Duke-Friar; and at that point he may be helped. The Duke has never left Vienna but it has been a long and hard journey he has made, down and back. When he re-enters his city he will come from

> the consecrated fount
> A league below the city,

and there he will meet and proceed with Angelo (89–90). It will be a cleansed and remade city because he has worked from below, invisible in his disguise, in darkness, in the streets, and within the nature of his people, seeing and helping where none think he is.

With Isabella now, who has expected a ready perfection presented by the Friar—and "Peace, ho, be here" she calls as she enters to hear of her brother's pardon—the Duke will present an unimagined evil demanding much more from her unbending certainty. He will deliberately keep her ignorant of her good, that her brother has been saved by him, "To make her heavenly comforts of despair / When it is least expected." It is a painful way to teach, and it may make us uncomfortable too, but it was (for a friar) good Protestant theology, a deep instruction that she needs. She wants to deny, as who would not, that her brother's head is off and sent to Angelo. "Nay, but it is not so!" "It is no other. / Show your wisdom, daughter, / In your close patience." Not she. She has always had her own ideas about making men respond to the vision of death. "Oh, I will to him and pluck out his eyes!" She will not be admitted to his sight, she is told, the short truth. And from that explosive, passionate violence she breaks down, with no place she can go, nothing she can do.

> Unhappy Claudio, wretched Isabel,
> Injurious world, most damned Angelo!

Poor her and hers, rotten world and worse villain. She has cause enough to weep but this is as futile as her projected eager eye-scratching.

> This nor hurts him nor profits you a jot.
> Forbear it therefore, give your cause to heaven.
>
> (IV, iii, 97–116)

She must accept the death. If she can pace her wisdom in that good path he would wish it to go she will have her revenge. He brings her to the point now of accepting at least that much patience. That Duke is, says Lucio, like so many fools confidently speaking truth in the underground sense he does not understand, "the fantastical Duke of dark corners . . . " (147–48).

Angelo now has been quite unshaped by his deed, not knowing what to do (and not, in fact, knowing what he has done). In this ignorant and confused mind with its contrary impulses—

> Alack, when once our grace we have forgot,
> Nothing goes right: we would, and we would not
>
> (V, iv, 31–32)

—he must be made again, and the Duke is waiting for him at the fount a league below. Isabella is schooled now to expect that her advisor may speak against her on the adverse side, but she "should not think it strange," for "'tis a physic / That's bitter to a sweet end" (IV, vi, 5–8). That strange experience, in a realm beyond what one can understand, the truth beyond the truth that one can imagine, is something we have met before in our other works. It can be disconcerting or wonderful or both. It can work a restorative magic. Here too it will be curative but it will be fiercely bitter, and that is new.

Neither of them, Angelo nor Isabella, knows what has happened, though both think they know the hidden truth, and neither knows what will happen. Angelo thinks he has known Isabella and killed Claudio; Isabella knows he has not known her but she too thinks he has killed Claudio. (Some others have their partial knowledge, but most others know nothing.) She is prepared for some sort of surprise but with the confidence that things will go well for her. But when the great Duke, who is unknown to her, returns and she cries for "justice, justice, justice, justice!" the astonishing reply is "Here is Lord

Angelo shall give you justice; / Reveal yourself to him." The Duke,
she says, is bidding her "seek redemption of the devil." Angelo,
forced now to sink deeper, from sin to sin, says her wits are not firm:
"she will speak most bitterly and strange." She will do that, as the
irony holds the knife to him.

> ISABELLA: Most strange, but yet most truly will I speak.
>   That Angelo's forsworn, is it not strange?
>   That Angelo's a murderer, is't not strange?
>   That Angelo is an adulterous thief,
>   An hypocrite, a virgin-violator,
>   Is it not strange, and strange?
> DUKE: Nay, it is ten times strange.
> ISABELLA: It is not truer he is Angelo
>   Than this is all as true as it is strange;
>   Nay, it is ten times true, for truth is truth
>   To th'end of reck'ning.

She hasn't got it right either. It is indeed strange and it is indeed
true that Angelo has played the devil; but it is not as true as it is
strange, since her accusation against Angelo is not true (she thinks it
is a half-truth). The truth is ten times strange, not as simple as she
thinks, and not as near to the end of reckoning. "Away with her,"
says the Duke; "poor soul, / She speaks this in th'infirmity of sense,"
as he seems to accept Angelo's falsified truth but knows that in fact
she does speak in an infirmity of sense. She conjures him, as he
believes there is another comfort than this world, that he not neglect her because she seems touched with madness: "make not
impossible /That which but seems unlike"; it is not impossible that
the wickedest caitiff on the ground may seem as just, as absolute as
Angelo, and even so may Angelo in all his dressings, forms, be an
arch-villain. Her madness, the Duke notes, has "the oddest form of
sense." She appeals to him,

>   let your reason serve
>   To make the truth appear where it seems hid,
>   And hide the false seems true.

That is better, and he is more ready to continue with her: "Many
that are not mad, / Have sure more lack of reason" (V, i, 20–68). It is

better because to make the hidden truth appear, hide the false seems true, will require both the touch of madness and the service of reason, the oddest form of sense, the recognition of the strange that transforms.

Now Lucio thrusts his face and mouth into the process, unbidden and unwelcome, to speak against the missing Friar, complicating the tale even more. "This gentleman told somewhat of my tale," Isabella says, not knowing the liability of such an ally. "Right," he says. "It may be right," the irritated Duke responds, "but you are i'th'wrong / To speak before your time" (V, i, 84–87). His time will come and this truth must be made to appear in the right way, the effective way. Isabella proceeds with her unlikely story, the Duke refuses it, orders her to prison, she wishing that her one good help, her Friar, were here. Another friar, Peter, one of the Duke's confidants, steps forward to declare that this woman has wrongfully accused Angelo, free from touch or soil with her, which is perfectly true. Where is that Friar whom both Isabella and the Duke now want to see? ". . . he is sick, my lord," Friar Peter says, "Of a strange fever" (151–52). The critical time of remedy, the truth of the strange tale, is about to break from below.

Mariana appears, a veiled truth who will not show her face until her husband bid her, telling in mysterious words her tale of how Angelo thinks he knows that he ne'er knew her body, but knows, he thinks, that he knows Isabel's. For the first time Angelo, the secure judge in his own cause, hears something he cannot understand: "This is a strange abuse—let's see thy face." Her husband bids her and she now unmasks. "Know you this woman?" the Duke asks. "Carnally, she says"—the answer comes from Lucio. Angelo really thinks there is practice against him, these women set on by some mightier member, as there really is, though of course he does not know who or why (V, i, 169–237). The Duke leaves it to him to find out and departs, returns quickly in his disguise as Friar to make his indictment, and is unhooded by Lucio. The Duke takes Angelo's place, resuming his authority, to see if Angelo now has word or wit or impudence to do him office to rely upon "till my tale be heard" (359). But Angelo does not need to wait for that tale, the fullness of which he does not know, and that readiness does well for him. He will not

be guiltier than his guiltiness to think he can be undiscernible now
when he perceives that the hidden Duke, like power divine, has
looked upon his passes. No longer session need be held upon his
shame, by his own confession, which puts him in the condition in
which the Duke-Friar, by testing, had found Juliet; but Angelo's sin
has been so enormously greater that he knows there is only one end:

> Immediate sentence then, and sequent death,
> Is all the grace I beg. (359–67)

He is now at the point to which the Duke had brought Claudio, absolute for death, that point of mortification, which we have seen in
other forms before this work. Here the eye-opening experience is of
a startling power, a devastating mortification which brings a real desire for an end because the fault has been a mortal guilt, a natural
guiltiness, which Isabella had once asked him to confess, and in his
case far worse than her brother's.

Escalus is more amazed at Angelo's dishonor than at "the strangeness of it." But Escalus has known nothing and he cannot yet have
any imagination of the strangeness of it, nor can Angelo. The Duke's
tale has still not been told. Isabella, learning now something of her
own ignorance, asks pardon of her Duke for having employed and
pained his unknown sovereignty; but she must be as free to pardon
him: her brother's death sits at her heart and she may marvel why
that Duke would not rather use his hidden power than let that
brother be lost. It was the swift celerity of the death, the Duke says,
which he had thought would come with slower foot that brained his
purpose; and that indeed, we know, had been very close to the fact, a
narrow escape from the braining of purpose and with the help of an
accident that Heaven provided. It is the lesson of the death that always waits on human purpose which the Duke has been teaching his
subjects and will continue to teach, in word and practice. What
he tells Isabella now is what he had told Claudio (and what in fact
Claudio now sees in a fuller truth):

> That life is better life, past fearing death,
> Than that which lives to fear: make it your comfort,
> So happy is your brother. (V, i, 373–92)

She does make it her comfort and we may feel that it is easy enough
for her who still lives, but we remember her first response to the
death and her swift eagerness to pluck out eyes, which did not profit
her a jot, as she had been instructed—"Forbear it therefore" (IV, iii,
116) She knows now she has no choice but to forbear and to accept
the death.

But that is not enough and she must do more yet, make a new
conquest. She must pardon Angelo, the new-married man, whose
salt imagination wronged her, must do that for Mariana's sake, the
Duke tells her; but that too, the single pardon for wronging her, will
not be enough. The Duke himself as judge will not pardon that
criminal and that double violation which cost her brother's life.

> The very mercy of the law cries out
> Most audible, even from his proper tongue:
> An Angelo for Claudio, death for death.

Like doth quit like and Angelo is condemned to the very block
where Claudio stooped to death. Death for death, by a just law.
Mariana pleads but the law will not hear. "Never crave him, we are
definitive." Mariana kneels, begs "Sweet Isabel" to take her part,
"Lend me your knees," but the Duke can answer for sweet Isabel,
having some first-hand experience of how unapt she is to kneel in
mercy when she has cause to condemn.

> Against all sense you do importune her.
> Should she kneel down in mercy of this fact,
> Her brother's ghost his paved bed would break,
> And take her hence in horror. (V, i, 393–430)

Mariana will not importune her against the sense of what she knows
to be so hard, to speak for him who unjustly sent her brother to
death:

> Sweet Isabel, do but kneel by me,
> Hold up your hands, say nothing; I'll speak all . . .
> Oh, Isabel! Will you not lend a knee?

The answer, again, is from the Duke. "He dies for Claudio's death."
He is making it as hard as he can for Isabel, for those knees that do

not bend. Three times Mariana pleads, "Lend me your knees . . . do but kneel by me . . . Will you not lend a knee?" The charm is wound and now Isabel bends, gives to death.

> Most bounteous sir,
> Look if it please you on this man condemned
> As if my brother lived . . . (431–38)

The case she offers for Angelo, qualified and unenthusiastic—"I partly think / A due sincerity" governed his deeds until he looked at me (V, i, 438–40)—is not very convincing. Dr. Johnson, in his annotation, is put off by what he sees here as a feminine vanity, that women are ready "to pardon any act which they think incited by their own charms"; but without trying to confront this larger indictment we can say we have seen nothing in Isabella that suggests what she would regard as a contemptible triviality; we might like her better if we could accuse her of charm. She seems rather to be pointing to a defect in Angelo, who for no reason but his proper bane stumbled over what happened to be her: "Is this her fault, or mine?" Angelo had asked himself, and had no doubt of the answer (II, ii, 167). But take her line any which way it is not much of a point in what is nowhere much of an argument. To say her brother had but justice in that he did the thing for which he died, but that Angelo had only bad thoughts without the act, is to say only that the law and its letter seem to have been met even if the defense carries no moral force. In fact, as far as her knowledge goes, her brother did not die justly for what he did but for Angelo's fearful and vicious revocation of the promise to pardon him unjustly; and that hardly excuses Angelo for what he did there. As for the failure of his attempt at a foul rape, he gets no credit for having been unknowingly frustrated in bedding what he thought was the desired victim. There is no case anyone can make for Angelo and the Duke is quite right in what he says to both women: "Your suit's unprofitable. Stand up, I say" (V, i, 441–48). Angelo knows he has no suit. The amazed, good and naive, Escalus says to him

> I am sorry one so learned and so wise
> As you, Lord Angelo, have still appeared,
> Should slip so grossly, both in the heat of blood
> And lack of tempered judgement afterward.

We can imagine the response of the earlier Angelo to an address of this sort from Escalus, because we have heard his brisk contempt for any collegial doubt of his wisdom or the temperature of his blood. It is another Angelo now.

> I am sorry that such sorrow I procure,
> And so deep sticks it in my penitent heart
> That I crave death more willingly than mercy.
> 'Tis my deserving, and I do entreat it. (V, i, 463–70)

That deep penitence, more willing to crave a just death than a mercy, is the only thing that can be said for Angelo and he says it and says it with the right mortification. Mortality and mercy in Vienna live in his tongue and heart.

It is not Isabella's plea that saves him; that has saved her, that bending of the knee, that willingness to say, against all reason, "Look, if it please you, on this man condemned, / As if my brother lived," and to say of this man condemned, "Let him not die" (V, i, 436–41). It does please a most bounteous sir. She can say nothing when she sees the admirable consequence of her act; and we can only say, in words she herself had not understood, and which none of us can ever wholly understand, that it is strange, and strange, nay it is ten times strange, but at last it is true as it is strange, for what she has done is bring her brother back to life. "What muffled fellow's that?" (479). In this play of multiple substitutions and disguises and seeming, seeming, and masks and hoods and dark corners and a league below, those who have gone down to death are so saved for life. Now even Angelo, deserving and entreating his own death, can be granted that mercy.

The never-ending possibility of that remedy has been placed before us when the gentle Provost has produced another fellow with the yet muffled Claudio. "Which is that Barnardine?" This is the stubborn soul the Duke-Friar has been unable to move, who apprehends no further than this world and squares his life according, apprehends no other world so comprehends nothing of this world, and nothing can be done with him. But he cannot be abandoned, forfeit without remedy. He is condemned, but for his earthly faults the Duke will quit them all, "And pray thee take this mercy to provide / For better times to come." When will better times come

to Barnardine? The Duke cannot know, has no indication they will
ever come, leaves him to Friar Peter's hand—"advise him" (V, i,
471–78). Perhaps the extraordinary new circumstances Barnardine
finds himself in, among all these subjects who have been shaken and
moved by death, will have an effect on him. And perhaps not. The
Duke will pardon him but he will not not let him go.

So the Duke finds an apt remission in himself and yet there's one
in place he cannot pardon. It has been disturbing to readers who do
not like him that he should be handing out pardons all round, a
couple to heavy criminals, including the brute who has yet to show
any sign of being touched, and then stick so when he turns to a character whom he accuses only of having offended him personally. But
slander here is not a personal offense (though it is that, too, and at
once), but much more; and this is the third time the matter has come
up in this final scene. The Duke has raised it when he was pretending to believe Isabella and Mariana were falsely injuring his deputy
authority and ordered Angelo to make the proper determination
"Upon these slanderers" (V, i, 257). The Duke himself a moment
later, when in his resumed character of Friar he was denouncing the
unjust Duke, the corruption of Vienna and its laws, has drawn the
only hot words we have heard from Escalus: "to th'rack with
him! . . . Slander to th' state! / Away with him to prison" (295–319).
To Lucio's lament for the punishment that comes upon him the
Duke's response is "Slandering a prince deserves it" (516). Slander
of the prince, the state, undercuts all order of the society, the law.
And why has Lucio done this to the Duke? "Wherein have I deserved so of you . . . ?" "'Faith, my lord, I spoke it but according to
the trick . . . " (495–97). Lucio has always spoken for the trick of it,
as the Duke has heard before, the customary, irresponsible trick of
one who will not hold his tongue. Language has always been a problem of the law in Vienna, the terms for common justice never easier
to understand than the nature of the people, at any level: from the
constable who misplaces; to the parcel-bawd who cleverly confuses
meanings; to the strict deputy who found his tongue and heart,
where mortality and mercy lived, slipping viciously apart; to the
cloistered maid who insisted that she had no tongue but one but indeed had other dialect and art. With these several languages these

subjects have made their own attempts to stage their desired
scenes. It is the unseen Duke who has been working to direct them
within his own staging; and in this last scene he has confounded
them all with the instruction of his strange language. In this setting
Lucio in his slander is at once the wittiest and the most contemptible abuser of language, the false mischief-maker who affects superiority. Lucio is so lively, unstoppable, says such clever, disconcerting, sometimes biting things that we are attracted to him; but we
should understand how much credit he deserves for this wit. And in
our attraction we would do well to have as much self-knowledge as
Elizabeth Bennet, who learned something about being uncommonly clever without any reason, finding in a target such a spur to
one's genius, such an opening for wit: "One may be continually abu-
sive without saying anything just; but one cannot always be laughing
at a man without now and then stumbling on something witty"
(p. 85 above). Lucio is in fact, as the Duke has said, a knave, a sneak
(349–51); at the very moment before his exposure he was attributing
all his actionable slanders to the unknown Friar. Now that Friar is
the Duke this knave has made and who has taught the Duke that
there is no might nor greatness in mortality that can tie the slanderous tongue. There will always be a Lucio, though the Duke can
dispose well of this one. And we need not feel Lucio's punishment is
too great. If the Duke will hang him for the trick, he says, the Duke
may, but he would rather that it please the Duke he might be
whipped, which is evidently as close as a sneak can come to accepting mortification. No, says the Duke, this lewd fellow will have to
marry the Kate Keepdown he got with child, as he has himself sworn
he did; and, as the Duke knows too, he then left the support of the
child to Mistress Overdone, to whose moral level he has never risen
and whom too we have seen him betray to the law. His punishment
is even worse than the death he hoped to escape by a whipping, for
marrying a punk is pressing to death, whipping and hanging (497–
515). So in his last stroke the Duke forgives even him, forgives his
slanders and remits his other forfeits, the whipping and the death,
but not the marrying. All the souls that were were forfeit once, but
in this case the remedy found out, a much more witty trick than any
Lucio has ever imagined, will be his marriage. His only punishment

will be the righting of the one wrong where righting is possible, and for him it is a very appropriate end and the ironic beginning of a new life.

It is for Vienna a profoundly happy but for all its inhabitants a deeply sobering end. It is certainly that for both the Duke and the strangely silent Isabella, she of the sometime outstretched throat. Neither he nor she had thought of being the marrying kind and both had been quite clear that they were above that sort of thing, but both it would seem have been brought to the human condition by the unexpected and never smooth course they have run. Unfolding the properties of government, the dark Duke knew, would be no easy thing, but the nature of his people, the city's institutions and the terms for common justice have proved to be rather more than even he had thought. It has required an extraordinary art and practice. Vienna is not the same city. Almost no inhabitant we have seen has been untouched, most of them shaken to within an inch of their lives, and their lives will never be the same again. Except Barnardine, for there will always be a Barnardine, if not this one then another. Government will never come to an end. The Duke knows how to rule now, each subject, one by one, man new made again and again. It does not seem to be a very practical solution of the problem of government, but in strange truth it is evidently the only practical one.

The text is *Measure for Measure*, ed. Brian Gibbons, "New Cambridge Shakespeare" (Cambridge, 1991). References are to act, scene and line number; where successive quotations in the same paragraph are from the same scene the act and scene numbers are not repeated.

Berry, Ralph, "Language and Structure in *Measure for Measure*," *University of Toronto Quarterly*, XLVI (1976–77), 147–61

Eagleton, Terence, *Shakespeare and Society* (London, 1967)

Evans, Bertrand, *Shakespeare's Comedies* (Oxford, 1960)

Foakes, R. A., *Shakespeare: the Dark Comedies to the Last Plays* (London, 1971)

Frye, Northrop, *The Myth of Deliverance: Reflections on Shakespeare's Problem Comedies* (Toronto, 1963)

Gless, Darryl J., Measure for Measure, *the Law, and the Convent* (Princeton, 1979)

Hammond, Paul, "The Argument of *Measure for Measure*," *English Literary Renaissance*, XVI (1986), 496–519

Hawkins, Hariett, *Measure for Measure* (Brighton, 1987)

Hunt, Maurice, "Comfort in *Measure for Measure*," *Studies in English Literature*, XXVII (1987), 213–32

Ide, Richard S., "Shakespeare's Revisionism: Homiletic Tragicomedy and the Ending of *Measure for Measure*," *Shakespeare Studies*, XX (1988), 105–27

Jensen, Ejner J., *Shakespeare and the Ends of Comedy* (Bloomington, 1991)

Lamb, Mary Ellen, "Shakespeare's 'Theatrics': Ambivalence toward Theater in *Measure for Measure*," *Shakespeare Studies*, XX (1988), 129–46

Lascelles, Mary, *Shakespeare's* Measure for Measure (London, 1953)

Lever, J. W., "Introduction," *Measure for Measure*, "Arden Shakespeare" (London, 1965)

Mansell, Darrel, Jr., "'Seemers' in *Measure for Measure*," *Modern Language Quarterly*, XXVII (1966), 270–84

Pinciss, G. M., "The 'Heavenly Comforts of Despair' and *Measure for Measure*," *Studies in English Literature*, XXX (1990), 303–13

Sale, Roger, "The Comic Mode of *Measure for Measure*," *Shakespeare Quarterly*, XIX (1968), 55–61

Schleiner, Louise, "Providential Improvisation in *Measure for Measure*," *PMLA*, XCVII (1982), 227–36

Stevenson, David Lloyd, *The Achievement of Shakespeare's* Measure for Measure (Ithaca, 1966)

Traversi, Derek, *An Approach to Shakespeare*, 3rd edition (London, 1969), Vol. II; earlier version, "Measure for Measure," *Scrutiny*, XI (1942), 40–58

Trombetta, James, "Versions of Dying in *Measure for Measure*," *English Literary Renaissance*, VI (1976), 60–76

Chapter Seven

To the hospital of the *Incurabili*

Volpone

Jonson was, as always, irritably aware of critics who might not like what he was doing and in *Volpone* the end of his play was an obvious point of attack. If he has taken the office of a comic poet then that end in which all the major and a couple of minor characters are destroyed, socially, morally, financially and physically, permanently, is apparently illegitimate. It is his catastrophe, as he says, in the sense of his play's ending, and as others may say in another sense. ". . . my catastrophe may in the strict rigor of comic law meet with censure, as turning back to my promise." The promise of the joyful "goings out" which the practice of most ancient comedies extends has been withdrawn. But his final aim has been to put the snaffle in their mouths that cry out we never punish vice in our interludes (Epistle, p. 32). He would seem to have silenced those who want punishment of vice but then there remain a number for whom the catastrophe is only too appropriate to such a gang of thoroughly awful, irredeemable, characters for whom one can feel no sympathy. It is a play of such diseases—phthisis, gout, apoplexy, palsy, catarrhs, cramps, convulsions, paralyses, epilepses, stoppings of the liver, strangury, dysentery, torsion of the small guts (that must be very painful). It is wonderfully instructive (what *is* hernia ventosa?), in a kind of fascination with all this which one develops, uneasily, as horrors attract. So much of it is false, feigned sicknesses in design to deceive, to draw in and trap those creatures who are hoping to benefit from approaching dissolution, that it becomes emblematic of inner sicknesses. Yet Jonson insists, with pride, that this is "quick comedy refined, / As best critics have designed," not only because it observes the laws of time and place and persons, swerving from no needful rule, but because

174

  All gall and copperas from his ink he draineth,
   Only a little salt remaineth,
  Wherewith he'll rub your cheeks, till red with laughter,
   They shall look fresh a week after. (Prologue, lines 29–36)

It is a healthy play, he says, nothing bitter or acidic in it, just enough
witty sting to make you laugh vigorously to a therapeutic end, stim-
ulating bright cheeks, restorative. But where shall we find that pleasure if our expectations have been set by the other works we have
been looking at?

Look around for young lovers in this play and it is readily apparent
that there's not much to find. More than that, we seem to be deliberately frustrated by the author (as Coleridge fretted), because the obvious candidates for the roles of that loving pair are Bonario and
Celia, evidently the only young, good-looking, moral residents in
Venice, or visitors for that matter, the only people with any one of
those attractive qualities. With none but appropriately named pred-
atory brutes around them, his good and her heavenly labels do make
them unique. He meets her by performing a heroic rescue, saving
her from rape by a powerful, wicked, ugly old man, so she has reason to be grateful at least; and he might see, as others do, that she
has so rare a face. "O, sir," as Mosca reports,

     the wonder,
  The blazing star of Italy, a wench
  O' the first year! a beauty ripe as harvest!
  Whose skin is whiter than a swan, all over!
  Than silver, snow, or lilies! a soft lip,
  Would tempt you to eternity of kissing!
  And flesh that melteth in the touch to blood! (I, v, 107–13)

Bonario doesn't seem to notice. She is married, to be sure, which
may be an initial difficulty for the young man, but her husband is a
violent wretch who has been abusing her and, in the immediate
scene that introduces her to Bonario, this husband has been trying
to prostitute her to what he thinks is a sick, disgusting, near-corpse
in hope of an inheritance; so at the end of the play she is released by
the law from that terrible bondage, sent home to her father, with
her dowry trebled, and should be a more than eligible candidate for
Bonario and a deserved new life. Bonario himself has been disin-

herited by his foul old father and, for his good deed of rescue, has
been falsely denounced as a villain by that father. The young man
and the young lady as a couple have been publicly and legally vil-
ified, graphically, as lewd, lascivious in secret adulteries, and then
taken into custody separately. Having been through that horror as a
common experience, and then finally cleared and restored to their
rights, both in name and in fortune, these two innocents would
seem to have run a good lap on the course of true love; and one might
think that as sole survivors, if nothing more, they will have to join at
last. But not even the hint of such a possibility is allowed. They have
never met except in those two places of the attempted rape and of
the scenes in court; they have never passed so much as a greeting,
except his two lines of "Lady, let's quit the place" (III, vii, 273–74)
when he helps her away from the attack of the eager old man and
they exit. In their trial scene they never say a word to one another,
have no connection except as a pair accused by the most extraordinary perversions of the truth. As they sit there before the magistrates
of the Scrutineo, with the birds of prey all around them pouring vile
animal names on their heads, if they could only hold hands it would
be something of a relief, for them we would hope, and certainly for
us. But they are hardly acquaintances. At the end of the play, when
every other character of any importance is being thrown out of Venice in deservedly terminal punishments, if these two could come together, just nod, there could be a hope that the city might at some
time be repopulated with a better breed, or at least that in this once
deafening place two decent people could exchange a quiet gesture.
They don't even wave farewell. Jonson didn't want to shift the force
in that direction by so much as a little touch. She has been said by
her filthy slandering husband to be a whore of hot exercise seen by
his own eyes "glued unto" that well-timbered gallant (IV, v, 117–24);
they could hardly in any decency think of touching after that.

Touching is never a pleasant contact in this play and its usual
mode is certainly repellent. There is more kissing, and more invita-
tions to kiss, here than in all the other works together, but it rather
turns the stomach. "Excellent, Mosca," Volpone calls, "Come hither,
let me kiss thee," as the gulled Voltore exits; enter Corbaccio, gulled
too, and at the departure there is a second invitation, "good rascal
let me kiss thee" (I, iii, 78–79; I, iv, 137). Neither the occasion nor

the nature of the giver or the receiver can make it a savory delight. Corvino, who has been threatening his wife with the most frightful and often imaginative forms of destruction for looking out the window to see another human being, suddenly tries to stop her blubbering with a "Come, kiss me," because he now wants to prepare her to enter Volpone's couch (II, vii, 13). When she arrives at those curtains and is told by her husband what to do, and is utterly appalled, he makes the touching as nothing.

> What, is my gold
> The worse for touching? clothes for being looked on?
> Why this 's no more.

When she will not touch, preferring to take down poison or eat burning coals, he says he will grow violent, as one who speaks with a practiced, vivid, authority,

> rip up
> Thy mouth unto thine ears, and slit thy nose,
> Like a raw rotchet! [a fish],

and raises the possibilities from that point. If he then, in desperation at her stubbornness, returns to entreaty it does not appear to be much of an improvement.

> Do, but go kiss him.
> Or touch him, but. For my sake. At my suit.
> (III, vii, 40–42, 97–99, 111–12)

And then, poor creature, handed over to Volpone and his handling she is forced to accept his touch and his attempt to "transfuse our wand'ring souls *[kissing her.]* / Out at our lips . . . " (234–35). The only lady who is attracted to Volpone, for her own mean and foolish motive, is Lady Wouldbe, who bore false witness for him in the court; "Yes," he says,

> And kissed me 'fore the fathers, when my face
> Flowed all with oils—

"And sweat, sir," Mosca adds (V, ii, 96–98), with a happy touch at Volpone.

If young love is excluded, about every other loving human relationship is here, in some perverted form. When Corbaccio is induced to disown his son, to make out his will to give all to Volpone, an enormity in hopes of an enormous gain, Mosca praises his "diverted love,"

> where, without thought
> Or least regard unto your proper issue,
> A son so brave and highly meriting,
> The stream of your diverted love hath thrown you
> Upon my master, and made him your heir . . . (I, iv, 102–06)

Marriage is either the abuse of Celia by Corvino or, presumably more perverse and therefore more amusing, of Sir Politic by Lady Wouldbe. And Volpone has all delights: "I have no wife, no parent, child, ally," but what far transcends all style of joy within; so what should he do but cocker up his genius "and live free" (I, i, 16–17, 70–73). He has a populated household and no family. Has he children? Corvino asks.

> MOSCA: Bastards,
> Some dozen, or more, that he begot on beggars,
> Gypsies, and Jews, and black-moors when he was drunk.
> Know you not that, sir? 'Tis the common fable,
> The dwarf, the fool, the eunuch are all his;
> He's the true father of his family,
> In all save me, but he has given 'em nothing. (I, v, 43–49)

Inventive Mosca often tells brilliant lies which are revealing truths. Volpone is the true father of a monstrous collection held by no emotion but self-interest. That "Loving Mosca!" (I, ii, 122), as Volpone calls him while looking in self-deception into the mirror, exempts himself from this family and will betray the father. As for other loving possibilities, if Volpone is set afire by the thought of Celia, her flesh that melteth at the touch to blood, he enjoys the glorious outcome of that botched affair more than the sexual pleasure he had planned.

Not much successful sex here, even in its modest desires: we have Volpone's unsuccessful attempt at rape, Corvino's unsuccessful attempt at pimping, Lady Wouldbe's unsuccessful attempt at prostitution (with Mosca; V, iii, 40). And then there is that curiously mixed cast with a eunuch and a hermaphrodite, and an amusing mistake when Lady Wouldbe thinks Peregrine is a professional transvestite; Volpone has a fond remembrance, too, of how he played Antinous, but that was long ago (yes, but—). Mosca's is perhaps the ultimate perversion, in the lines of the soliloquy with which he begins Act III:

I fear I shall begin to grow in love
With my dear self and my most prosp'rous parts,
They do so spring and burgeon; I can feel
A whimsy i' my blood.

It is a play with no lovers, all the world divided between only fairies (as we have been calling them) and fools—the most awful fools, who deserve every trick and every disaster and punishment that comes on them, and the most devilish fairies, only destructive in their dealings with others and merciless and utterly successful in that role. There is no one who can stand against Volpone and Mosca, none capable of a counterforce. Bonario and Celia are not only never made a couple, never can combine forces, they are incompetent, useless. What witnesses have you? they are asked in court.

BONARIO: Our consciences.
CELIA: And heaven, that never fails the innocent.
4TH AVOCATORE: These are no testimonies. (IV, vi, 14–17)

Their faith is proven right, but not by any effectiveness of theirs. They are less than useless because they are so colorless and uninteresting that though we may feel some sympathy for them, such helpless nonentities, we never expect or really want them to do anything. The stage is left clear for Volpone and Mosca, who do wonders.

These two are marvelously ingenious. Their mark is not so much in the general scheme of the defrauding, which is not new and has many variants past and future and is plain enough; but that broad outline of a ready convention gives them the scope of simplicity within which great artists delight in displaying, in detailed and fascinating skills, the grand effects they can create. Volpone has an ar-

tist's pride in his workmanship, not in the miser's dull accumulation
of things but in the process of achievement, and what he does bears
out his vaunt of inventive originality.

> I glory
> More in the cunning purchase of my wealth
> Than in the glad possession, since I gain
> No common way:

He has the genius that despises the common way.

> I use no trade, no venture;
> I wound no earth with ploughshares; fat no beasts
> To feed the shambles; have no mills for iron,
> Oil, corn, or men, to grind 'em into powder;
> I blow no subtle glass; expose no ships
> To threat'nings of the furrow-facèd sea;
> I turn no monies in the public bank,
> Nor usure private— (I, i, 30–40)

The common way is the way of the world, the way men earn their
bread and contribute to society, so that there is a deliberate and
immoral inversion here, except that a world that wounds the earth,
sends beasts to the shambles, grinds to powder indifferently oil,
corn or men, turns over its money in public banks or private usury,
is not itself quite right side up, and not so innocent, and may be
ready for the taking. These two characters, the ruling spirit and his
quick agent, know how to be taking and know the minds they capti-
vate. They are masterful producers-directors-writers-actors, setting
the stage with the right props, dress, make-up, working up the
script, composing the music and the lyrics ("Come, my Celia," so
beautiful when taken out of its context), choreographing, casting
with a fine eye the players in the roles best suited to them, coaching
them so as to gain the best effort and effect from them. They have
the lively flexibility of great actors, changing costume, character,
passion, dialect, disguising themselves impenetrably to the other
characters (though *we* always delight in recognizing the mark of the
master), as the moving scene requires, and astonishing us in their
readiness as improvisers: glorying, as Volpone says, in the sheer joy
of the achievement. "I did it well," he exults after his appearance in

the street as the mountebank Scoto of Mantua. He was beaten away
by Corvino, unknowing Corvino, because he has done it so well, a
small pain which is less important to his feelings than the pleasure of
his success in playing. "But were they gulled / With a belief that I
was Scoto?" "Sir, / Scoto himself could hardly have distinguished!"
And as we realize that Mosca is playing his own role in manipulating
Volpone the levels of our pleasure multiply (II, iv, 31–36). Volpone's
great compliment to Celia, as he begins his wooing, is to tell her it
was her beauty's miracle which had raised him "in several shapes"
that morning as a mountebank to see her, and

> Ay, before
> I would have left my practice for thy love,
> In varying figures I would have contended
> With the blue Proteus, or the hornèd flood. (III, vii, 148–53)

The climactic sentiment he can offer her—after what have already seemed to be breath-taking sensual, unheard-of, riches and
delicacies—will be that

> we, in changèd shapes, act Ovid's tales,
> Thou like Europa now, and I like Jove,
> Then I like Mars, and thou like Erycine;
> So of the rest,

until they have quite run through and wearied all the fables of the
gods; and then he will have her "in more modern forms," extensive
varieties of national and racial and hot and cold temperamental em-
bodiments,

> And I will meet thee in as many shapes;
> Where we may, so, transfuse our wand'ring souls,

to that kiss (221–34).

It is at the beginning of that Act that Mosca's moving abilities have
made him begin to grow in love with his dear self and parts, as well
they might:

> I could skip
> Out of my skin, now, like a subtle snake,
> I am so limber. (III, i, 5–7)

Enter Bonario, who hates Mosca's baseness (rather mildly in fact,
knowing so little as he does), for the parasite's sloth and flattery.
Mosca takes this hard, as scorn for a virtuous poverty. " . . . 'tis inhuman. *[He cries]*." And Bonario, "What? does he weep? the sign is
soft and good. / I do repent me that I was so harsh." Bonario is not
great as a reader of signs, and Mosca drives on, admitting that he is
indeed by necessity, not being born to a free fortune, obsequious,
but he hopes to perish if he has done

> Base offices, in rending friends asunder,
> Dividing families, betraying counsels,
> Whispering false lies, or mining men with praises,
> Trained their credulity with perjuries,
> Corrupted chastity, or am in love
> With mine own tender ease,

and so forth, presenting an exact catalogue of what he has been and
will be doing. To Bonario, "This cannot be a personated passion" and
he apologizes for so mistaking Mosca's nature (III, ii, 1–37). It is difficult to maintain one's sympathy for Bonario after that. Mosca is so
much more alive, larger than life. Mosca, so limber, comes from a
world more than human.

> O! your parasite
> Is a most precious thing, dropped from above,
> Not bred 'mongst clods and clodpolls, here on earth.

He muses his mystery has not been made a science, not a mechanical craft but a liberal art, all the wise world professing it; most have a
bare art and a base, but he is

> your fine, elegant rascal, that can rise
> And stoop, almost together, like an arrow;
> Shoot through the air as nimbly as a star;
> Turn short as doth a swallow; and be here,
> And there, and here, and yonder, all at once;
> Present to any humor, all occasion;
> And change a visor swifter than a thought,
> This is the creature had the art born with him:
> Toils not to learn it, but doth practice it
> Out of most excellent nature . . . (III, i, 7–34)

That swift control of time and space and change, born with him, is the genuine Puck.

These rascals create a world. One hears that plastic imaginative remaking of first space and then time as Volpone—playing Scoto, only one of his roles—is presenting one of his cosmetics:

> Here is a poulder concealed in this paper of which, if I should speak to the worth, nine thousand volumes were but as one page, that page as a line, that line as a word: so short is this pilgrimage of man, which some call life, to the expressing of it. Would I reflect on the price? Why, the whole world were but as an empire, that empire as a province, that province as a bank, that bank as a private purse to the purchase of it.

And this same powder has a history, temporal from the gods of ancient myth to this moment, a charm distilled to work the magic of youth and beauty.

> I will, only, tell you: it is the poulder that made Venus a goddess (given her by Apollo), that kept her perpetually young, cleared her wrinkles, firmed her gums, filled her skin, colored her hair. From her derived to Helen, and at the sack of Troy unfortunately lost; till now, in this our age, it was as happily recovered by a studious antiquary out of some ruins of Asia, who sent a moiety of it to the court of France (but much sophisticated), wherewith the ladies there now color their hair. The rest, at this present, remains with me; extracted to a quintessence, so that wherever it but touches in youth it perpetually preserves, in age restores the complexion; seats your teeth, did they dance like virginal jacks, firm as a wall; makes them white as ivory, that were black as— (II, ii, 225–45)

Celia is rather fortunate that Corvino breaks up the spell at that moment (his own spell-bound moment will follow quickly) because it is a language of irresistible power. It has already tempted this heavenly lady above to throw down her handkerchief. It charms. It can speak with extensiveness of reference and loveliness to fascinate the beautiful, it can create its own scabrous diction to annihilate "turdy-facy-nasty-paty-lousy-fartical rouges" (59). It can control the most clever lawyer, Voltore, or the most absurd fool, Sir Politic. Sir

Politic is magnetized by Scoto's show. "Note, / Mark but his gesture," "Note but his bearing and contempt of these" (the turdy-facy,
etc. rogues), "Excellent! ha' you heard better language, sir?" "Is not
his language rare?" (30–31, 58, 68, 116).

The language is exquisitely pitched to the victims, each of whom
thinks he is the only true deceiver. Voltore is a most impressive ad-
vocate, with an effective "mercenary tongue" (IV, v, 95), which we
see in action in court, absolutely inverting the truth with professional inventiveness, thoroughly gulling the court and winning his
case. "I'd ha' your tongue, sir, tipped with gold for this," Mosca congratulates him (IV, vi, 64). The lawyer has himself a Puck-like professional mastery of word and action and law, so flattered by
Mosca—

> Men of your large profession, that could speak
> To every cause, and things mere contraries,
> Till they were hoarse again, yet all be law;
> That, with most quick agility, could turn,
> And re-turn; make knots, and undo them (I, iii, 53–57)

—even as Voltore is himself being gulled and in his grand success is
merely Mosca's tool. The violent Corvino, threatening his poor
wife, who has looked out the window, with having the bawdy light
dammed up, to lock in that whore he will otherwise dissect, is a few
moments later talked by Mosca into volunteering her for Volpone's
use; but, more impressively, so well does Mosca read the mind, so
cleverly does he speak, that he makes the suggestion come from
Corvino himself and marks the progress ("I hear him coming") to the
moment of confirmation of the ironic truth:

> Sir, the thing
> But that I would not seem to counsel you,
> I should have motioned to you at the first. (II, vi, 74, 81–83)

Corvino is so responsive (as the irony turns on the successful Mosca)
that he arrives at the house with his wife too soon, while Bonario is
there. "Did e'er man haste so for his horns?" Mosca wonders in exasperation. But all is yet well and Mosca has the exact word to bring
forth from the grateful Corvino's own mouth exactly what he is do-

ing. Signior Corvino is here to see you, Mosca announces to the expiring Volpone, and

> for your health, is come to offer,
> Or rather, sir, to prostitute—
> CORVINO: Thanks, sweet Mosca.
>   (III, vii, 4, 74–75)

With Corbaccio, another admirer of Mosca the mind-reader ("See,
how he should be / The very organ to express my thoughts!" I,
iv, 115–16), still other truth-telling games are possible, because
Corbaccio is deaf. That mockery has brought some complaints
against Jonson. John Dennis, who thought Jonson was the best English comic dramatist, censured him, in a letter to Congreve (1695),
and Congreve and others agreed with him, for ridiculing a personal
defect which cannot be amended; exposing it can never divert any
but half-witted men; a thinking man is brought to reflect upon the
misery of human nature. But of course Corbaccio is deaf, and blind,
and so are the others. Corbaccio is deaf as Bottom has ass's ears,
to signify the inner space of the head. Corbaccio is an old man
more impotent than Volpone can feign to be, yet hopes to hop over
Volpone's grave. Mosca replies to his opening question:

> CORBACCIO: How does your patron?
> MOSCA: Troth, as he did, sir; no amends.
> CORBACCIO: *[cupping his ear.]* What? mends he?
> MOSCA: *[shouting.]*   No, sir. He is rather worse.
> CORBACCIO: That's well.

From there Mosca works him to the concluding point where he can
insult the wretched man with truth in direct address.

> MOSCA: Rook go with you, raven!
> CORBACCIO: I know thee honest.
> MOSCA: You do lie, sir.
> CORBACCIO: And–
> MOSCA: Your knowledge is no better than your ears, sir.
> CORBACCIO: I do not doubt to be a father to thee.
> MOSCA: Nor I to gull my brother of his blessing.
> CORBACCIO: I may ha' my youth restored to me, why not?
> MOSCA: Your worship is a precious ass—
> CORBACCIO: What sayst thou?

> MOSCA: I do desire your worship to make haste, sir.
> CORBACCIO: 'Tis done, 'tis done, I go.   *[Exit.]*
>   (I, iv, 3–8, 124–32)

No, Corbaccio's knowledge is no better than his ears and interior
and exterior are so fully identified in these creatures that their animal names are both descriptive and normative, fixed and unchangeable fools as they are. In this company poor Celia cannot establish an
identity, can only hope for inexistence: "I would I could forget I
were a creature!" (IV, v, 102). We need feel no compunction for the
gulling of the rapacious fools, for in a hellish punishment they are
being given exactly what they want and deserve, what fulfills their
natures. We are happily satisfied to see Volpone and Mosca dish it
out, because in their superior knowledge and power they are revealing truths to us and because, interested as their own motives may
be, they are agents of justice. We keep watching them, waiting for
them, to see them display their wares and top themselves. It is only
at the point where they begin to operate on Celia that our sympa-
thies shift a bit. Even if we can't cheer for helpless Celia—even at
those several worst moments of her life what catches our interest is
what the rascals will do and say next—she isn't the cooperant clown
who deserves the treatment administered. Excepting her case, we
would like to be on *their* side, because otherwise we would be their
stupid victims. Part of the uneasiness we may feel in the midst of this
marvellous display of power is that we are implicated by our partici-
pation in the pleasure of it.

All this power, in the hands of such overwhelmingly superior,
dominant, spirits, is dedicated to a false love. The only love that is
deeply felt, the only kiss that is sincere, is of course in the love for
gold. We begin the play with

> Good morning to the day; and next, my gold!
> Open the shrine that I may see my saint.

The desired beloved often makes her appearance as the commonplace of the figured deity, for what higher expressive object is there?
It is what we expect when Demetrius awakes and springs from the
ground, under the spell of the fairy charm, to see the girl he has
spurned and who is now "O Helen, goddess, nymph, perfect divine"
(*Midsummer Night's Dream*, III, ii, 137). Absurd and wonderful, it

is young love. But here, with Volpone, more is being claimed, an absurd and, even in his deliberately mocking and exhilarating play-fulness, a stunning devil-worship—"Hail the world's soul, and mine!"—displacing the life-giving sun, "thy splendor darkening his." Celia's desperate prayer for survival, when her husband intro-duces her into Volpone's house, must be "Make me the heir of dark-ness" (III, vii, 26). Volpone's prayer to his god is

> O thou son of Sol,
> But brighter than thy father, let me kiss,
> With adoration, thee, and every relic
> Of sacred treasure in this blessed room.

This is a god who is not only far transcending human life but annihi-lating children, parents, friends, "Or any other waking dream on earth." It empties the world to fill it with itself. It is "the dumb god that giv'st all men tongues," can do nought yet makes men do all things. It is the "price of souls; even hell with thee to boot, / Is made worth heaven!" (I, i, 1–27). The inversion is complete, hell for heaven, dark for light, out of nothing comes everything, both creat-ing word and act, in the false dream for which there is no dawn. Gold is the remedial charm that brings new health and rebirth, trans-forms. "This is true physic, this your sacred medicine" (I, iv, 71). "Why, your gold / Is such another med'cine . . . / It transforms the most deformèd, and restores 'em lovely / As 'twere the strange po-etical girdle," the girdle of Venus; "It is the thing / Makes all the world her grace, her youth, her beauty" (V, ii, 98–105). But the med-icine is false, as Scoto's, as Lady Wouldbe's variants, and those other nostrums offered by the fools of Volpone and Mosca. The fools of Volpone and Mosca—and how many are not that?—cannot be healed because, as Volpone says, "to be a fool born is a disease incur-able" (II, ii, 157–58).

There is no journey, no movement possible for them in a world so physically thick, having no element but the one in which they want to submerge wholly. The desired sensual feeling Mosca holds out to Voltore's imagination is that he will come

> to swim in golden lard,
> Up to the arms in honey, that your chin
> Is borne up stiff with fatness of the flood . . . (I, iii, 70–72)

There is a stiff sensuality that in its diabolical passion stops the other senses, smell, touch, vision. The "strangest" thing to Volpone is how Mosca has managed the perverted trial scene that the gulls, so divided among themselves, "Should not scent somewhat . . . " Mosca understands that strange truth:

> True, they will not see't.
> Too much light blinds 'em, I think. Each of 'em
> Is so possessed and stuffed with his own hopes
> That anything unto the contrary,
> Never so true, or never so apparent,
> Never so palpable, they will resist it—
> VOLPONE: Like a temptation of the devil. (V, ii, 19–28)

It is an ironically sick possession as the 1st Avocatore finally realizes (though not seeing well how he has been blind himself).

> These possess wealth as sick men possess fevers,
> Which trulier may be said to possess them. (V, xii, 101–02)

Celia has wondered at the sudden transformation of her Corvino: "Lord, what spirit / Is this has entered him?" (III, vii, 46–47). Voltore, when he sees he has been gulled and makes a turn to vengeful recantation, to destroy himself and all, is declared by the other fools to be "possessed"—"The devil has entered him! . . . Nay, if there be possession / And obsession, he has both"; then he is gulled yet again by Volpone and under that instruction he feigns possession and recovery. "You are dispossessed," Volpone tells him so well (V, x, 10, 35, xii, 8–35). There is no way out from this unpurgeable stuffed possession, but

> Mischiefs feed
> Like beasts, till they be fat, and then they bleed. *[Exeunt.]*
> (V, xii, 150–51)

That ending in which Volpone and Mosca are gathered up with their victims into a universal shambles, which Jonson defended, insisted on, in anticipation of those who would think he had returned upon his promise of a comedy, is something of a shocker and is intended to be. Dramatically it is a question. Why hasn't the play ended at the end of Act IV? With all Venice divided into the all-powerful deceivers and the incurable fools, who can reverse that tri-

umph of Volpone and Mosca? The case has been taken to the highest
court in the land and they have won. Their fools, each of whom has a
different notion of the truth of the matter, so that it is "the strangest"
that they never suspect, are all marshalled, unknowingly, to the one
point which serves to protect their deceivers. The deceived have
forsworn themselves with passion to destroy a good wife, a good son.
Those innocents are worse than ineffective, having offended the
court, making their righteousness absurd. The lawyer, himself a
dupe, has been a glorious perverter of his professional and legal reason and responsibility, a reliable narrator of a lying and vicious fiction. It all works. Volpone and Mosca are set free again, with honor,
as themselves being vindicated victims, and the innocent are
condemned: the law is with the criminals. The Scrutineo, the last
hope of a counterforce, the only neutral authority, is hopelessly
blinded, for the Avocatori are such fools (and the second time around
one of them is ready to see Mosca as a fit match for his daughter).

It has been the greatest triumph. Volpone and Mosca, like all
great artists, have got themselves in trouble by doing much, and we
have seen earlier their skill in minor extrication, but this is a master-
piece. It is better than sex, the usual happy end. "The pleasure of all
womankind's not like it," Volpone says (V, ii, 11), to gull the court
and quite divert the torrent upon the innocent.

> MOSCA: Yes, and to make
> So rare a music out of discords— (15–18)

"How comes this gentle concord in the world," Theseus asked when
he found rival enemies lying down together in the sleep of the rec-
onciling dream (IV, i, 140); it was the magical harmony of the end of
all difficulties, which is the end of Act IV, and it is, wonderfully,
more than cool reason ever comprehends and yet more witnesseth
than fancy's images. And, again, when he was offered for his entertainment the tragical mirth of young Pyramus and his Thisbe, it was
"How shall we find the concord of this discord?" (V, i, 60), the
equally strange harmony of the human play of Act V and its concluding dance. For Volpone the resolving concord is the rare music of
the devil's dance. There can be no better chord, higher note, to be
struck, no worlds left to conquer. What else is there to do? If we
have surpassed the pleasures of sex, says Mosca,

> We must here be fixed;
> Here we must rest. This is our masterpiece;
> We cannot think to go beyond this. (12–14)

If he says it four times, in four independent clauses, in four ways, that ought to be more than enough to wind up the charm. But Volpone won't stop. "Shall we have a jig now?" he cries, but it will not be the concluding dance, it will be "jig" as one more trick. "What you please, sir," Mosca replies, and then neither will Mosca stop (59). No one is capable of defeating them, but they are, and they must be, self-defeating.

It is impossible that such perversion, such worship of a false god, such disease, can maintain itself. As with other figures who are so successful and so daring in their command of others—Dorimant would be an example of this—there has got to come a point of lost control, of moving so many creatures and strands of action, of such proud confidence in the ability to control, that the lines will cross. That happens when Volpone is drawn to Celia, the innocent who does not merit his plotting, and he leaves his house, makes his first little journey of desire and finds himself in trouble, subject to another law, and gets beaten off. He recovers and tries again, is defeated this time by Corvino's hasting to his horns and is beaten again, now by Bonario. Once again he recovers. Again he goes on, to a greater success, in the staging of the court scene. His troubles have been increasing, his successful escapes growing in brilliance, the margin narrowing. When he ventures from his house for the third time in his last act, to fulfill another desire, he is caught and can never return. "I'll go and see," he says and he exits. Mosca now makes his move.

> MOSCA: Do so. My fox
> Is out on his hole, and ere he shall re-enter,
> I'll make him languish in his borrowed case,
> Except he come to composition with me. (V, v, 5–9)

For all his forays, Volpone can survive securely only in his hole; for all his extensive imaginations, only in that narrowed space and scope of law.

He goes abroad in the last act to torment his victims. To this point he has read their minds so well that he could blind and lead them, by their own eager willingness, as he chose, and could so take his joy and their wealth *ad lib*. Now when that sport has been played out to its end he will pretend to be dead, to hang the false reward before them and then crush them: Mosca will be the counterfeit heir. For the first time he plays a profitless trick, meaningless, wanton sport; and with an ingenuous trust he makes himself vulnerable by assuming a full faith in another human being. Mosca has the game in hand: "So, now I have the keys and am possessed."

> To cozen him of all were but a cheat
> Well placed; no man would construe it a sin.
> Let his sport pay for 't. This is called the fox-trap.
>
> (V, v, 12, 16–18)

We may note that Mosca will have to learn more of what it means to be possessed. But as for Volpone, he has never understood Mosca. Now he does not understand his victims, who no longer have any false hopes, any reason to embrace deception and who round on him and one another in their ignorant desperation. Volpone is being foolish and, worse yet, he is being trivial in a not very interesting trick, requiring little skill, certainly less than the high standard he has held to in his previously illustrious career, less revealing of those he gulls, for at this point what is there that remains to be revealed? Why one more disguise and act? Old trouper that he is he never knows when to retire, but there is more in it than that.

Volpone's gold, as Mosca had told him, is the transformer, the strange poetical girdle, and strange transformations have been the amazing effective force in his career. The Avocatori have been the least comprehending, overwhelmed by the strangeness of what they have heard (Voltore has worked the word in their "strangely abused ears"): "These be strange turns!" they say, "This is strange" (IV, v, 90, 59, 115); and later it is "Still stranger! More intricate!" and when all is finally revealed, by no understanding of their own, "The knot is now undone by miracle!" (V, xii, 60–61, 95). There has been no miracle of course, and the strangeness in this play has been a series of impostures ("strange impostures," as Bonario has said, IV, v, 18), not wonderfully more than natural but perversely less than human, monstrous, unnatural. Corbaccio disavows his son as "an utter stranger to my loins" (109); Mosca wonders of that wretched old man, "What horrid, strange offense / Did he commit 'gainst nature in his youth, / Worthy this age?" (IV, vi, 89–91). Strange transformations seem so pervasive, not limited to this extraordinary place of Venice, as we are shown in the feeble imitations of the English Wouldbes; not limited to this time, as we are shown in the dramatized history of the "transmigration" and "translation" of foolishness played by Volpone's deformed family in Mosca's pretty invention (I, ii), and shown in the annals of vanity retailed by Scoto (II, ii, 232–45); not limited to our own bodies in time and space, as we are shown in the "changèd shapes" and "many shapes" of the metamorphoses of lust which Volpone offers Celia (III, vii, 220–45). But as Volpone and Mosca see, the "strangest" (V, ii, 19) is the changeless shape that seizes upon those possessed and stuffed with their own hopes, utterly blinded. And what is stranger still is that in his own endless transformations Volpone cannot see it in himself. Too much light blinds him, that worshipper of the god brighter than the sun.

The laughter he has created and enjoyed has always been aggressive, an infliction, but in the last trick it becomes gratuitously violent (V, i, 15), a rare meal (V, ii, 87), a torture, "torture 'em rarely" (111). "O, I will be a sharp disease unto 'em." He must look for curses, Mosca warns—"Till they burst," he interrupts; "The fox fares ever best when he is cursed" (V, iii, 117–19). But that voracious laughter has always been its own curse, brings on its own diseased discharge that cannot be staunched. "O, I shall burst! / Let out my sides, let out my sides." "Contain / Your flux of laughter, sir" (I, iv, 132–34). An appetite that can never be satisfied must be fed until, like beasts that fat, it must bleed. There is no point for Volpone to rest, to reach his time of fulfillment, because there is no shape in which he will realize himself. "I must / Maintain mine own shape still the same," he had said carefully at the end of Act I: "we'll think" (I, v, 128–29). But, strange transforming devil, he cannot think well enough and it is not possible that he should be ever the same. "Never but still myself," he says in Act V, but it is false self-comfort now, for it is a self that has no center of its own, and he is near his self-destruction even as he says it (V, ii, 41). There is no problem for which there is a solution to meet his desire, no desire that leads to a

happy place, no journey, no awakening from his dream, no cure for
his illness, no ordering. In the worship of the false god he deceives
perpetually and is deceived, disguise and change without end. As
he grows in gold and cunning purchase he contracts in life, cannot
be reached by any human sense:

> If you have ears that will be pierced, or eyes
> That can be opened, a heart may be touched,
> Or any part that yet sounds man about you . . .
>
> (III, vii, 240–42)

In endless transformation there is an enclosed fixity, no accession of
life, no freedom but the same repetitive and immobile thickness of
the world of his victims. He has been forced by his own devices to
submit himself to the punishing visitation of the most trivial of his
victims, the "torment on me" of Lady Wouldbe. "I fear / A second
hell too," that his loathing for her will expel his appetite for Celia.
"Lord how it threats me, what I am to suffer!" (III, iii, 25–31) Lady
Wouldbe enters and fills his house with her voice and chokes it with
herself.

> VOLPONE: [*Aside.*]   —I do feel the fever
> Ent'ring in at mine ears. O for a charm
> To fright it hence— (III, iv, 7–9)

But there is no charm for this disease; no awakening from this dream
("I dreamt / That a strange fury entered, now, my house"); no love
("Oh, if you do love me, / No more; I sweat and suffer"); no relief
from her offers of mad medicine ("Before I feigned diseases, now I
have one"); no escape ("Is everything a cause to my destruction?").
"O'y me!" is his cry. "Laugh and be lusty," she prescribes in such
precise irony. "My good angel save me!" is his prayer which none
will answer; "Some power, some fate, some fortune rescue me!"
(40–126). Mosca is his only savior: "Mosca, welcome! / Welcome to
my redemption." He must rid himself of this torture, that "everlasting voice" of hers, more noise than bells in time of pestilence, "perpetual motion."

> All my house,
> But now, steamed like a bath with her thick breath.
>
> (III, v, 1–8)

He creates his own choking world and he creates his own punishment, and he is, in his final act, caught in his own noose (V, x. 13–14).

> To make a snare for mine own neck! And run
> My head into it wilfully, with laughter!

So he has turned the violent laughter on himself, after escaping "free and clear," and has done it "Out of mere wantonness!" He's been a clever devil but

> O, the dull devil
> Was in this brain of mine when I devised it,
> And Mosca gave it second . . .

But Mosca gave it second not in support but in his own plot. The desperate (and foolish) hope that Mosca "must now / Help to sear up this vein, or we bleed dead" is the fate of his victims now come upon him (V, xi, 1–7). With him, as with all the possessed, there is no fairy in this world but the devil within.

Each victim, each plotter, has his appropriate end, and a series of reversals of the usual conclusions. No rewards here but punishments. No freedom but, with Mosca, life as perpetual prisoner. No wedding but a divorce, not a liberating event for the husband, though he has done all he can to un-husband himself and will wear a cap with fair long ass's ears instead of horns; we cannot even hope that Celia regards it as desirable: poor thing, she is still pleading "And mercy" for Corvino, as though this were *Measure for Measure*, but the judge here dismisses that. No eye-opening, except as Corvino's eyes may be opened now at the point where they will be beat out with stinking fish: " 'Tis well, I'm glad / I shall not see my shame yet" (V, xii, 105, 141–42). No journey to a better condition but expulsion, as Voltore, officer of the state is driven from the state. No young lover beginning a new life but old Corbaccio, who knew not how to live well here and tried to reverse the course of life, is confined in the monastery to learn to die well for another world, where it is unlikely he will be received with honor. We are left with a cleansed but rather depopulated Venice.

Volpone of course loses all, his substance confiscate "To the hospital of the *Incurabili*"—this is his journey, for as he had said in his own contempt of fools, to be a fool born is a disease incurable. Having got his substance by feigning diseases he will lie "cramped with irons" till he be sick and lame indeed. "Remove him." There is no countercharm, nothing to free him from his prison, present or past— he has never been able to "live free." There is no mortification in a middle passage that ends an old life and begins a new. Here the mortification comes at the last and the devourer is now dead meat. "This is called the mortifying of a fox," he tells us (V, xii, 120–25).

Mosca had always been the more clever devil, "O my fine devil!" (V, iii, 46), the better inventor of devices, the more resourceful one in crisis when Volpone panics; from the opening scene he understands Volpone and profits from him as the self-conscious, self-loving parasite, that most precious thing dropped from above, the fine elegant rascal.

> This is the creature had the art born with him;
> Toils not to learn it, but doth practice it
> Out of most excellent nature; and such sparks
> Are the true parasites, others but their zanies. (III, i, 30–33)

When the parasite thinks he is above his natural condition, and is ready to destroy his host, comes to the fatal point of foolish pride, and when he will not accept half ("I cannot now / Afford it you so cheap," V, xii, 69–70), he becomes the zany. The devil is an ass, Jonson knew.

Health is refreshened, as the Prologue had said it would be, with what we may feel has been a somewhat vigorous rubbing of salt in our cheeks. We know—how could we have doubted?—that such disease incurable cannot, by nature, thrive. Volpone's saint and dumb god of false light cannot close the eye of heaven. "Are heaven and saints then nothing?" Celia had asked, "Will they be blind, or stupid?" (III, vii, 53–54). "Heaven could not long let such gross crimes be hid," Bonario concludes, with more truth than he has earned, as they two have been pronounced innocent and curtly dismissed: "Give 'em their liberty" (V, xii, 97–98). But it is not clear that they will know what to do with it.

The text is Ben Jonson, *Volpone,* ed. Alvin B. Kernan (New Haven, 1962). References are to act, scene and line numbers; where successive quotations in the same paragraph are from the same scene the act and scene numbers are not repeated.

Coleridge on Bonario and Celia is in one of his lectures of 1818, *Coleridge's Miscellaneous Criticism*, ed. T. M. Raysor (London, 1936), p. 55; also in one of his marginalia, *Coleridge on the Seventeenth Century*, ed. Roberta Brinkley (Duke University, 1955), p. 644.

Dennis on Corbaccio is in his *Critical Works*, ed. E. N. Hooker (Baltimore, 1939–43), II, 384. Congreve's agreement is in "Concerning Humour in Comedy," also 1695, *Works*, ed. Montague Summers (London, 1923), III, 163.

Barish, Jonas, "The Double Plot in *Volpone*," *Modern Philology*, LI (1953), 83–92

Barton, Anne, *Ben Jonson, Dramatist* (Cambridge, 1984)

Beaurline, L. A., *Jonson and Elizabethan Comedy* (San Marino, 1978)

Creaser, John, "*Volpone:* The Mortifying of the Fox," *Essays in Criticism*, XXV (1975), 329–56

Dolan, Frances, "'We Must Here Be Fixed': Discovering a Self behind the Mask in *Volpone*," *Iowa State Journal of Research*, LX (1986), 355–67

Donaldson, Ian, "*Volpone:* Quick and Dead," *Essays in Criticism*, XXI (1971), 121–34

Empson, William, "*Volpone*," *Hudson Review*, XXI (1968), 651–66

Enck, John J., *Jonson and the Comic Truth* (Madison, 1957)

Garner, Jr., Stanton B., *The Absent Voice: Narrative Comprehension in the Theater* (Urbana, 1989)

Greenblatt, Stephen J., "The False Ending in *Volpone*," *Journal of English and Germanic Philology*, LXXV (1976), 90–104

Greene, Thomas M., "Ben Jonson and the Centered Self," *Studies in English Literature*, X (1970), 325–48

Hawkins, Hariett, "Folly, Incurable Disease, and *Volpone*," *Studies in English Literature*, VIII (1968), 335–48

Kernan, Alvin, "Introduction" to his edition (New Haven, 1962)

Leggatt, Alexander, "The Suicide of Volpone," *University of Toronto Quarterly*, XXXIX (1969), 19–32

———, *Ben Jonson: His Vision and His Art* (London, 1981)

Leonard, Nancy S., "Shakespeare and Jonson Again: The Comic Forms," *Renaissance Drama*, N.S. X (1979), 45–69

Levin, Harry, "Jonson's Metempsychosis," *Philological Quarterly*, XXII (1943), 231–39

Parker, R. B., Introduction to *Volpone*, "Revels Plays" (Manchester, 1983)

Partridge, Edward B., *The Broken Compass: A Study of the Major Comedies of Ben Jonson* (New York, 1958)

Schell, Edgar, *Strangers and Pilgrims: From* The Castle of Perseverance *to* King Lear (Chicago, 1983)

Skulsky, Harold, "Cannibals vs. Demons in *Volpone*," *Studies in English Literature*, XXIX (1989), 291–308

Sweeney, John, "*Volpone* and the Theater of Self-Interest," *English Literary Renaissance*, XII (1982), 220–41

Watson, Robert N., *Ben Jonson's Parodic Strategy* (Cambridge, Mass., 1987)

Chapter Eight

The wrong time to give a dance

The Cherry Orchard

The Cherry Orchard must be a most difficult play to produce. It had problems in the first effort, with Stanislavsky, who wept when he read it, insisting to Chekhov that it was a "tragedy," Nemirovich-Danchenko complaining to him that whatever it was it had too many weeping characters, Chekhov upset that it was being advertised as a "drama" and not the "comedy" he said he had written. But at every level of production, right to the prop-man, it must be a difficult act to get together (or maybe prop-men delight in these things, I don't know). The amount of dropping and breaking that goes on is astonishing. A character like Epihodov, who is called "two and twenty misfortunes," on his first entrance drops a nosegay, then stumbles against a chair and knocks it over, in a later act evidently invites himself to play billiards and breaks a cue stick (offstage, fortunately) and in the last act, to help the family in its departure, puts a trunk down on a cardboard hat box and crushes it. "There, now, of course—I knew it would be so." A bit after that he rather charmingly even loses his voice with suppressed emotion. "I've just had a drink of water, and I choked over something," but that's the actor's problem and the character certainly gets no sympathy from anyone else (IV, 69, 76). He does have difficulties with small objects, external and internal, but these are part of a large drama in which he plays his role heroically. "There! *(as though triumphant)*," as he hits the chair, "There you see now, excuse the expression, an accident like that among others. . . . It's positively remarkable *(goes out)*" (I, 5). Destiny behaves mercilessly to him but he accepts. "Every day some misfortune befalls me and I have long ago grown accustomed to it, so that I look upon my fate with a smile," "if I may venture to express myself, I merely smile at it, I even laugh" (III, 58). There is a com-

forting tragedy in this endless confrontation at the highest level, but
it does require the proper equipment:

> I'm a cultivated man, I read remarkable books of all sorts, but I
> can never make out the tendency I am myself precisely in-
> clined for, whether to live or to shoot myself, speaking pre-
> cisely, but nevertheless, I always carry a revolver. Here it
> is . . . (*shows revolver*). (II, 29)

If this were Ibsen (or another Chekhov play) we and the prop-man
might be certain that the gun would go off in the last act, but we can
feel easy with Epihodov, because the gun probably doesn't work, or
he doesn't know how it works, and if he did try to shoot himself he'd
surely miss; and that's well, because otherwise he might hurt himself and we wouldn't want that.

The prop-man has to keep track only of the objects he himself actually needs, but for us the distinctions among onstage and offstage
things, and breakings which are not, or not fully, physical, and
losses which are not reported or felt or perceived by characters, are
less easy to separate. In the first act Anya does lose her hairpins as
she stands there and Dunyasha breaks a saucer, and in the next act
Madame Ranevsky (Lyubov Andreyevna) drops and scatters her
money. But then in the act following Pishtchik loses his money, falls
into a fright and tears and sweat, and then gleefully finds it himself,
behind the lining of his coat, so we don't need to see that scattering,
except in his wits. We do need a little table for Lopahin to tip over
accidentally, and the candelabra which he almost upsets, when he
has bought the cherry orchard and can pay for everything; but then
to start the play he has missed a (naturally) unseen train. Well, we do
need Firs's stick with which Varya tries to hit Epihodov, but misses,
at the very moment triumphant Lopahin is entering to announce his
purchase and take the blow. "Very much obliged to you!" "I haven't
hurt you?" "Oh, no! Not at all! There's an immense bump coming
up, though!" (III, 59–60). And though it is an offstage event we do
need sound effects for Trofimov falling down the stairs. But the thermometer which in the last act is said to be broken doesn't have to be
repaired for each performance. We can't expect to be shown the rec-
ipe for the preserved cherries which they used to send to Moscow
and Harkov by the wagon-load—"That brought the money in!"—

soft and juicy, sweet and fragrant—". . . They knew the way to do them then . . . " It's forgotten. Nobody remembers it (I, 16). The villa at Mentone which Madame Ranevsky lost to debt, in preparation for her present difficulties in hanging on to real estate, is in another country. And then there are some *people* who get lost, notably aged and faithful Firs; with all the careful inquiries which the characters make about him, each assured that someone else has taken care or will take care of him, he does get forgotten and left alone, in a locked room, to conclude all. At the other end of life, there was once a little boy, Madame Ranevsky's son Grisha, who drowned in the river, "such a pretty boy he was, only seven" (I, 11), for whom she still weeps when she is reminded of that. We can all agree that the accidental death of a child is a sad event, must be wept for, but of course this happened a while ago and we have never known him, and, in this family, he does seem to have been one more object that slipped through their fingers somehow. That wayfarer who wanders in and out, a self-proclaimed Russian brother, not quite knowing if he's on the road to the station, or so he says, has come to the right place, for his brief moment. The harp-string that snaps, half way through the play and again at the very end—what is it? in the sky? in the pits? somewhere far away—in another play might be a kind of easy and obvious reaching for an effect, but here it seems just right, at home. The prop-man better get that distant, mournful, dying sound right (Chekhov was insistent). And among other cosmic effects he will need two pair of old goloshes, one a wrong pair, not Trofimov's, to be thrown in from the wings by Varya, then the right pair for her to find after that, so he can march off into the future. Trofimov had lost them and they'd been worrying us. In this play that delayed finding and recovery is almost a note of hope.

It must be a difficult play for the actors. There must be twenty-five or thirty moments for tears, varied occasions and kinds of tears, some happy, some bitter, most just tears—in tears, through his/her tears—and only a few of the family or servants or friends are exempted from them (Chekhov was angry at Stanislavsky for taking all these stage directions too literally). Then too there is great deal of laughter, if not quite as much as the tears yet very close to that (not counting the joyfullys, gleefullys and gailys), sometimes in the same speeches as the tears, to be produced both individually and, several

times, in a chorus of "(*All laugh*)." There are specifically noted directions for excitement, wonder, triumph, despair, ecstasy, anxiety, anger, horror, and calls to sigh, scream, shake the fist, clutch the head,
kiss, embrace, dance, shout dance-calls, hum, sing, play a guitar
(and call it a mandolin), play imaginary billiard games, start reciting
a poem about a sinful woman, listen to a little Jewish "orchestra," do
parlor tricks, smoke a cigar, eat, drink, fling things, swing things.
The contrast between the little that happens and the large emotional activity and the stage-busyness is wonderful. Maybe actors
delight in these things (again I don't know), but then in that broken
dialogue, the odd sequence of speeches, remembering one's cues
cannot be easy; and the cues must be fed just right because if they
are not, then, in a special and peculiar way, one will be throwing off
the other actors, who in turn have to keep the thing moving in the
right way or there will be a complete breakdown. It seems that this
might be an easy play in which to ad-lib if there were a hitch, but I
should think that this is not so at all. The words have got to be right.
The rhythm has got to be right: time is so important in this play. The
most common stage direction, and it is certainly common, has to do
with rhythm: "(*a pause*)." Maybe it's a little less common than one or
another variation of tears, but then they too have to do with the syncopated rhythms. The ritardando of the three dots, three dots, that
pace the dialogue is a continual notation. (In this chapter, contrary
to normal practice and necessarily so, three dots are part of the
quoted text unless otherwise indicated.)

There must be a certain problem in keeping things moving on the
stage. Sleeping is an important activity. We begin with Lopahin
yawning and stretching, having fallen asleep over his book, and so
missing the train he was supposed to meet at the station. Anya arrives, without his help, staggers in exhaustion, later ends the act falling asleep as she sits down, returns to a half-sleep to say a few words.
Pishtchik is the best performer in this mode, on two occasions actually falling asleep while he is talking (I, 19; III, 47). Yasha is a great
yawner, five, six times. It is one of the few reassuring comforts at the
end of the last act, as Gaev leaves his lost home, that he sleeps better
now, though one would think he'd already been doing well at that,
or at least yawning well. But there is a limit to what can be done on
the stage with sleeping so there is rather more of dreaming. When

Lopahin, who knows he has some difficulties with language, peeps
in at the door at Varya and Anya and moos like a cow and disappears,
Anya is reminded by his expressiveness that he loves Varya; she
wonders what they two are waiting for, and everyone is congratulat-
ing Varya, but Varya knows there is really nothing to it: "It's all like a
dream." She has another dream, "I keep dreaming all the time," of
marrying Anya to a rich man and then going off by herself on a pil-
grimage (I, 10). Anya has her own way, speaking in Act I, *"dreamily"*
of the past, in the last act *"dreamily"* of the future (11, 71). And between she echoes Madame Ranevsky.

> LYUBOV: (*dreamily*). There goes Epihodov.
> ANYA: (*dreamily*). There goes Epihodov. (II, 40)

Lyubov tells Lopahin he is well aware of her hopes for him and
Varya, "I dreamed of marrying her to you" (IV, 73). He doesn't understand it himself, he confesses, and he's ready, but his dreams
have run in other directions. "My God, the cherry orchard's mine!
Tell me that I'm drunk, that I'm out of my mind, that it's all a dream
(*stamps with his feet*)," "I am asleep, I am dreaming!" though one
mustn't have the impression that he is happy, or not that only, because he ends with tears for his own miserable disjointed life (III,
61–62). But the money keeps coming to the last, even Pishtchik re-
paying him 400 roubles, almost a third of the debt he owes. Lopahin
is amazed. "It's like a dream" (IV, 72).

It is a puzzling matter for these characters to locate themselves
and they can't work it out. If in *A Midsummer Night's Dream* every
character is a member of a class, a definitive classification, with political, social, economic, cultural, linguistic coordinates, and no possibility, or desire, of moving from that order; and if in that play any
confusions of class are delightful because they are seen to be minor
and temporary aberrations which will be set straight, in this play
there is hardly anyone who has not been declassed and, far from lib-
erated, has not been permanently confused by that loss. Old Firs is,
naturally enough, the most lost. He remembers how things were
before the calamity.

> GAEV: Before what calamity?
> FIRS: Before the emancipation (*a pause*).

He was the head footman before the emancipation came: "I wouldn't consent to be set free then; I stayed on with the old master . . . " Poor fellow, his new master doesn't know much of mastering either. "The peasants knew their place," Firs says, "and the masters knew theirs; but now they're all at sixes and sevens, there's no making it out" (II, 41, 37). He has an impossible job now trying to get the servants to do their work, feckless and uncaring as they are. Dunyasha drops things, forgets things, no longer a peasant, not a lady, a useless combination of both:

> I am so nervous, I'm always in a flutter. I was a little girl when I was taken into our lady's house, and now I have quite grown out of peasant ways, and my hands are white, as white as a lady's. I'm such a delicate, sensitive creature, I'm afraid of everything. I'm so frightened. (31)

One can hardly blame her—in a house where she is impressed into dancing with the guests, to fill out the party.

> My young lady tells me to dance. There are plenty of gentlemen, and too few ladies, but dancing makes me giddy and makes my heart beat.

Like her dreaming betters, and going them one better, she can say "I am lost in reverie (*plays with her fan*)" (III, 57–58). Yasha, Madame Ranevsky's valet, has been entirely spoiled by the mistress, in Paris, is mad to return there from the uncultured Russia he now cannot bear (he no longer wants to see even his old mother—he's the one genuinely contemptible character in the play), trifles in his stupid and callous way with Dunyasha, is insubordinate with Gaev.

Lopahin is the one former peasant who has made a significant move, is a rich man; in his white waistcoat and brown shoes he feels like a pig in a bun-shop and, for all his money, "come to think, a peasant I was, and a peasant I am." In reality, he says, hard in his self-judgment, he's just another blockhead, like his father. "I've learned nothing properly. I write a wretched hand. I write so that I feel ashamed before folks, like a pig" (I, 4; II, 36). There is, offstage, an indeterminately large number of people who in their way are moving up too. They are the customers Lopahin has in mind when he plans the redevelopment of the cherry orchard, clearing out the old buildings, this house too, which is really good for nothing, and cutting down the orchard. Now that the railway runs close by, if the cherry orchard and the land along the river were cut up into plots and leased for summer villas the family could make 25,000 roubles a year out of it. (That must mean a thousand renters because it would be 25 roubles for a three-acre plot from summer visitors; it must also be then 3,000 acres, so it's not a little estate we're talking about here). It's a perfect situation with that deep river (yes, *that* deep river). There used to be only the gentlefolks and the peasants in the country, he says, but now there are these summer people; all the towns are surrounded now by these summer villas. And in another twenty years there'll be more people and they'll be everywhere. At present the summer visitor only drinks tea in his verandah, but maybe he'll take to working his bit of land too, this new member of the landed class, and that Lopahin thinks will make Lyubov's orchard a success (I, 15–17). Lopahin himself, it turns out, is the one who will make a lot of money from this subdivision (and no doubt it will be called Cherry Orchard Estates, after the fashion of developers, who christen their creations for the beauty they have destroyed). He is a good fellow, Lopahin, and he would help Lyubov and Gaev, he even begs them, would do that job not for his but their benefit. They can't understand what he means.

> LYUBOV: Cut down? My dear fellow, forgive me, but you don't know what you are talking about. If there is one thing interesting—remarkable indeed—in the whole province, it's just our cherry orchard. (15)

That's not just a silly response (Matthew Arnold tested an age by asking how interesting it was). But here it's a hopeless case. Lyubov married out of her class, below it, and has now descended into worse. Gaev, still being taken care of, like a boy, by Firs, is going to become a bank clerk, but that won't last.

There is a flotsam, drifting, quality to these people who cannot locate themselves. That wayfarer who wanders from nowhere to nowhere and frightens them is their brother. Varya wants to spend her life going from one holy place to another; "I would go on and on . . . What bliss!" (I, 10). Domestically the wandering is done by Charlotta Ivanovna, the ungoverning governess, who begins the second act, when plans to save the estate are to be formulated, with her own musing, with no identity card.

> I haven't a real passport of my own, and I don't know how old I am, and I always feel that I'm a young thing.

Of course she is not a young thing, young things have a future, with love, marriage. But not she:

> where I came from, and who I am, I don't know . . . Who my parents were, very likely they weren't married . . . I don't know (*takes a cucumber out of her pocket and eats*). I know nothing at all (*a pause*). One wants to talk and has no one to talk to . . . I have nobody.

She does have the cucumber so we needn't worry about her survival.

Also, Charlotta Ivanovna does have one admirer of her talents, the magic charm upon him:

> PISHTCHIK: (*wonderingly*). Fancy that now! Most enchanting Charlotta Ivanovna. I'm simply in love with you.
> CHARLOTTA: In love? (*shrugging her shoulders*). What do you know of love, guter Mensch, aber schlechter Musikant.
>
> (III, 49)

That's true enough and it is a fair account of most, all, of the men— good men, but love is not the kind of music they can make. There is a remarkable number of such affairs going, one cannot say in progress. Epihodov is ineffectively in love with Dunyasha ("He does love me, he does love me so!"), but she is ineffectively in love with Yasha ("I'm passionately in love with you, Yasha; you are a man of culture—you can give your opinion about anything (*a pause*)"; and Yasha agrees, "(*yawns*). Yes, that's so. My opinion is this: if a girl loves anyone, that means she has no principles (*a pause*)" (I, 8; II, 31). Yasha will steal a kiss, but he is in love with no one but himself and is happy to get away at the end. Not much hope in the cast of that incomplete *ronde*. Madame Ranevsky does not have a history which indicates past or future success, or sets much of an example for her children. Her marriage was a disaster, to a man who drank himself dead, made nothing but debts. Then to her misery she loved another man (and little Grisha had to die to punish her for that sin). That pitiless, brutal lover wore her out with his illness, dried her soul, in Paris robbed and abandoned her, brought her to a try at poison and suicide (II, 34–35). And now that he is sick and poor and begging for her again she will be going back to him, which does seem like a generous act—and she is a generous woman, in the sense of one who throws away money, throws away herself—but it also seems like a seeking which can never be happily satisfied. "I love him, that's clear. I love him! I love him!" is neither a clear nor a convincing cry, not even to herself. He is, as she says, a millstone about the neck and she is going to the bottom with him, "but I love that stone" (III, 53–54). Anya and Trofimov appear to be the one traditional young pair who offer a hopeful possibility, both eager, looking to the future; but, as with the others, it is an appearance only, all the more frustrating because of its conventional signs of an expected reality. Madame Ranevsky would gladly let Trofimov marry Anya, "I swear I would," but "you must do something with your beard to make it grow somehow (*laughs*). You look so funny!" (53). He has no wish to be a beauty, he says, and his sort of beardless immaturity isn't a sign of youth. When she sees him in the first act, and he had been the tutor of her Grisha, she looks at him in perplexity until he has to introduce himself. "Can I have changed so much?"

> LYUBOV: . . . But, Petya? Why have you grown so ugly? Why
>   do you look so old? [my dots]
> TROFIMOV: A peasant-woman in the train called me a mangy-
>   looking gentleman.
> LYUBOV: You were quite a boy then, a pretty little student, and
>   now your hair's thin—and spectacles. Are you really a stu-
>   dent still? (*goes towards the door*).
> TROFIMOV: I seem likely to be a perpetual student. (I, 21–22)

(I have a special fondness for Trofimov, I must admit. The professor has always been a comic figure, at least since Aristophanes hung up Socrates in a basket, but Trofimov must be one of the first examples of the graduate student as comic character.) Not a promising candidate for young love, and, still worse, he is above love. He preaches that to Anya, contemptuous of how Varya is afraid he and Anya will fall in love: "With her narrow brain she can't grasp that we are above love" (II, 43), and he repeats his line to Lyubov: "Such triviality is not in my line. We are above love!" "And I suppose," she says, "I am beneath love," a fine, pointed, deserved retort, with a bit of truth in it for herself too (III, 52). We expect the man who declares himself to be above love, above the trivial human mode, to fall at last, having grown to the point of self-knowledge and so fulfilling his humanity—but not here, because Trofimov will never grow up, will fall only downstairs.

The pervasive uncompleted love affair is of course between Varya and Lopahin, introduced as a hope in the early part of the first act, and a hope near the very end of the last act, but more in the minds of others and not much of a hope for the participants. Both express willingness, no one else raises any objections or sees the match as anything other than appropriate, neither he nor she understands why it doesn't come to a marriage. They are caring, hard-working people, which makes them quite different from the others around them and gives them something in common, but if they are both the same type in that regard it is a type that works because it doesn't know what else to do, can't do anything to a satisfying end. "But I can't do without work, mamma," she says, "I must have something to do every minute" (III, 51). "I can't get on without work," he says, "I don't know what to do with my hands, they flap about so queerly, as if they didn't belong to me" (IV, 66). That's something less than a human being who is able to love and to find another touch for his hands. Varya offers an explanation, that he's absorbed in business, and what she says is plausible, but there is no question of definite reason. The thing just doesn't happen. She is not the marrying kind, looks like a nun, wants to go to a nunnery, she says, but she won't do that either, hasn't any vocation. He is very good with money, and he is a good man, as she says, but he is not very good with people, freely offers money to Lyubov, without understanding her enough to see why she won't take it, freely offers money to Trofimov and can't see why he won't take it, usually says the wrong thing. He says Moo. It just can't happen. At the final moment when it seems it may finally happen, with the traditional family arrangement to leave two lovers alone for the understood specific purpose of the proposal, there is not much warmth to work with; the thermometer is broken, and anyhow there is three degrees of frost; and though there is champagne on hand it isn't very good champagne and it too is the wrong temperature, and besides Yasha has drunk it all up. And besides, Madame Ranevsky has never been a successful matchmaker, not for anyone. Lopahin had remembered, as the play began and he waited for her to return, what a splendid woman she is, a good-natured, kind-hearted woman, and how she comforted him when he was fifteen and his father punched him in the face and made his nose bleed. He can see her now—she was a slim young girl then—as she took him to wash his face and brought him to the nursery: "'Don't cry, little peasant,' says she, 'it will be well in time for your wedding day' . . . (a pause)" (I, 4). When will his wedding day be? He'll have a bloody nose all his life. If he was ever in love it may have been then, with her, maybe still now.

There is a remarkable amount of kissing that goes on in this play, and of course one must understand that the conventions of the society call for that, but none is a lover's kiss. There are no lovers, no lovers who can ever come together, no marriages, no real possibility of a marriage. Like the other things which are disappearing, forgotten, lost, dropped, broken, the family has fallen and will fall further as this old, interesting, beautiful home is going. They are losing the garden; one can get up in the morning and run into the garden; "The birds are singing in the garden." And "What a ravishing orchard! White masses of blossom, blue sky . . . " (I, 8, 10, 21). It is a thing worth weeping for, worth saving. What we need is a character of some competence, of some power and ability to understand and control, take charge, establish a way to the future. There are no bad people around, no devil or anything like that—an identifiable unfriendly force would be something of a relief, someone to overcome—only nice people, so if there were one good fairy this problem could be solved. Partly solved? a little solved? There are candidates for the position too.

Lopahin is certainly one—he is the central character, Chekhov said—because he is the one character who has an ability to be successful, and has been successful in a remarkable way as the peasant boy, son of a serf, who is now rich and growing continually richer. Everything he touches turns to money, which is both rewarding and unfortunate. He sowed three thousand acres with poppies in the spring and in the last act, the first time we hear of it, casually, he has cleared 40,000 roubles in profit. "And when my poppies were in flower, wasn't it a picture!" That's pleasant to hear, that enjoyment, picture of profit, picture of beauty. "After all, I am fond of you," Trofimov says, "you have fine delicate fingers like an artist, you've a fine delicate soul." That's more difficult to believe, but still pleasant to hear, does credit to them both (IV, 67, 66). Lopahin is the only character who has a specific and practical device to save Madame Ranevsky and the family property, not only save it but convert it into a source of income and put an end to their continually deteriorating fortune which is about to become the final disaster of dispossession. He sees the cherry orchard becoming the good place, "happy, rich and prosperous . . . " (I, 17). The major difficulty is his utter inability to convince those he would help, because, apart from their inability to accept him as their saver, his solution requires the end of what it is that they desire to save. They cannot understand him, he cannot understand them. It is an insoluble problem. He is incapable as a lover and incapable as a man of any power to direct the lives of others, not the man above but, in his own unhappy characterization, a pig.

Trofimov is more than ready to volunteer as the director of the lives of others. One of his deficiencies in that role, in common with Lopahin, is that his solution leads to the loss of what is to be saved, and with him it is a superior approval and pleasure that the cherry orchard will go.

> What does it matter whether the estate is sold to-day or not?
> That's all done with long ago. There's no turning back, the path
> is overgrown. Don't worry yourself, dear Lyubov Andreyevna.
> (III, 52)

For him the cherry orchard was never a good worth saving, has always been an instrument of oppression. That, like Lopahin's project, is a potentially hopeful sign, a replacement of an old and dying order by the coming of the new. Trofimov has the message. "One must give up glorification of self. One should work, and nothing else." Self-knowledge and effective power, that's how the bright comic heroes hope to achieve their desire. "One must die in any case," says Gaev, but not Trofimov, the hero who is not defeated by death but is reborn to a fuller life in a better world.

> Who knows? And what does it mean—dying? Perhaps man has
> a hundred senses, and only the five we know are lost at death,
> while the other ninety-five remain alive.

He has the vision of the mythic comic hero, rather like his contemporary Don Juan of *Man and Superman,* the development to the truth, to a mythic perfection.

> Humanity progresses, perfecting its powers. Everything that
> is beyond its ken now will one day become familiar and com-
> prehensible; only we must work, we must with all our powers
> aid the seeker after truth.

He detects, in the vast majority, the difference between the high pretense and illusion of their fine talk and the reality of their lives. So much talk of grand things that only exist in novels: in real life there are none of them. "I am afraid of serious conversations. We should do better to be silent." All this in a very long speech (II, 38–39).

And from a man who does nothing. Himself above the triviality of love, he can, from his superior vision, undeceived, tell Lyubov, "You mustn't deceive yourself; for once in your life you must face the truth!" True enough—these people say so many true things—but with little meaning as coming from him. He thinks he sees what is wrong with her, but he is blind to her feelings and to himself. "What truth?" she asks:

> You see where the truth lies, but I seem to have lost my sight, I
> see nothing. You settle every great problem so boldly, but tell
> me, my dear boy, isn't it because you're young—because you
> haven't yet understood one of your problems through suffer-
> ing? You look forward boldly, and isn't it that you don't see and
> don't expect anything dreadful because life is still hidden from
> your young eyes?

Her appeal for understanding is touching, sentimental and self-deceiving, too, but touching.

> You're bolder, more honest, deeper than we are, but think, be
> just a little magnanimous, have pity on me. I was born here,
> you know, my father and mother lived here, my grandfather

lived here, I love this house. I can't conceive of life without the
cherry orchard, and if it really must be sold, then sell me with
the orchard (*embraces* TROFIMOV, *kisses him on the forehead*).
My boy was drowned here (*weeps*). Pity me, my dear kind fellow. (III, 52–53)

He's a decent fellow and he says, sincerely, "You know I feel for you
with all my heart." But it's poor language, words, not music, because he doesn't see her, and she hears his shallowness. "But that
should have been said differently, so differently." She wants to make
it up to him, "Don't be hard on me, Petya . . . I love you as though
you were one of ourselves," because it will be too painful if they go
on telling truths to one another. She would gladly let him marry
Anya, but he, for all his talk does nothing, as lover or man: "only my
dear boy, you must take your degree, you do nothing—you're simply tossed by fate from place to place. That's so strange. It is, isn't
it?" And then there is that infertile beard, so funny. Her own immediate anxiety is the sale of the cherry orchard, going on at the moment, and her decision to go back to Paris and her faithless lover, so
that she is deficient in credentials for what she is telling him, doesn't
want to hear his truth about her love and must tell him truths about
himself. "You're twenty-six or twenty-seven years old, but you're
still a schoolboy." "Possibly," he says, with the neutral equanimity of
an intellectual. That's a bit much for her restrained anger:

> You should be a man at your age! You should understand what
> love means! And you ought to be in love yourself. You ought to
> fall in love! (*angrily*). Yes, yes, and it's not purity in you, you're
> simply a prude, a comic fool, a freak.

Now that truth, the accurate classification of comic fool, does upset
him, quite upsets him:

> (*in horror*). This is awful! The things she is saying! (*goes rapidly
> into the larger drawing-room clutching his head*). This is awful!
> I can't stand it! I'm going. (*goes off, but at once returns.*) All is
> over between us! (*goes off into the ante-room*).

She shouts after him, trying to call him back. "Petya! Wait a minute!
You funny creature! I was joking! Petya!" And the next we hear is the

sound of "*somebody running quickly downstairs and suddenly fall-ing with a crash.*" Anya and Varya scream but there is a sound of laughter at once. What has happened?

> ANYA: (*laughing*). Petya's fallen downstairs! (*runs out.*)
> LYUBOV: What a queer fellow that Petya is!

He comes back and Lyubov invites him, "Come, Petya—come, pure heart! I beg your pardon. Let's have a dance! (*dances with* PETYA)" (II, 53–55). Nobody will be following this talker as he runs off into the future, downstairs, falling with a crash. He has equal dif-ficulty at the end as his departure for the future is delayed. "The devil only knows what's become of my goloshes; they're lost . . . I can't find them" (my dots). Lopahin wants to give him money for his journey and he is too proudly self-sufficient for that, but "(*anxiously*) but where can my goloshes be!" Varya flings in goloshes from the next room. "Take the nasty things!" "Why are you so cross, Varya? h'm! . . . but these aren't my goloshes." He still won't take the money for the journey. "I am an independent man" (IV, 65–67). It is Varya who does at last manage to see his goloshes, with tears, "And what dirty old things they are!" He puts them on: "Let us go, friends!" (77).

The value and effectiveness of Trofimov's words are defined for us by Anya's admiration. We are above love, as he tells her, and

> To eliminate the petty and transitory which hinders us from being free and happy—that is the aim and meaning of our life. Forward! We go forward irresistibly towards the bright star that shines yonder in the distance. Forward! Do not lag behind, friends.
> ANYA (*claps her hands*). How well you speak! (*a pause*).

And he goes on and on, to his own rather oversized new garden. "All Russia is our garden."

> If you have the house keys, fling them into the well and go away. Be free as the wind.
> ANYA (*in ecstasy*). How beautifully you said that! (II, 43–44)

Lyubov too has complimented him on his exposition of the ninety-five senses that remain after death. "How clever you are, Petya" (39).

We know, we have seen it in Jack Tanner, for example, what it means when someone is admired for speaking so well (a Great Communicator, as we now say). It can only mean that no one there is hearing what is being said, because there is no substance to distract the mind. The scene in which Trofimov has his longest, grandest speeches, about life after death and humanity progressing and perfecting its powers, is in Act II, where the decision is to be made on how to solve the problem of the cherry orchard. Trofimov finishes his irrelevant apocalypse, and then Lopahin makes his, happily shorter, grand-vision speech, on how he works from morning to night, money passing through his hands, and "I see what people are made of all round me." And

> Sometimes when I lie awake at night, I think: "Oh! Lord, thou hast given us immense forests, boundless plains, the widest horizons, and living here we ourselves ought really to be giants."

He too, this hard-working man, has his romance or myth of more than mortal power. "You ask for giants!" Lyubov says; "They are no good except in story-books; in real life they frighten us," which, for the moment, takes her closer to the truth, away from an illusion. No giants. Who advances, who goes there?

> (EPIHODOV *advances in the background, playing on the guitar.*)
> LYUBOV: (*dreamily*). There goes Epihodov.
> ANYA: (*dreamily*). There goes Epihodov.
> GAEV: The sun has set, my friends.
> TROFIMOV. Yes. (40)

That sets off another speech-maker.

> GAEV: (*not loudly, but, as it were, declaiming*). O nature, divine nature, thou art bright with eternal lustre beautiful and indifferent! Thou, whom we call mother, thou dost unite within thee life and death! Thou dost give life and doth destroy!

"Uncle!" "Uncle, you are at it again." Yes, he knows. "I'll hold my tongue, I will." Poor Gaev, hasn't he as much right as the others to talk great nonsense? In the perfect stillness that follows him the

string snaps. What more is there to be said? There's more, there's
always more to be said. Along comes the wayfarer, slightly drunk,
and he "(*Declaims*) My brother, my suffering brother! . . . Come
out to the Volga! Whose groan do you hear? . . . " (40–41). Another
speech-maker in the grand manner, declaimer, making his comment on the significance of the others. He is rather more effective
because he at least gets from his talk something he wants, taking
money from his audience.

Gaev gets sat on almost every time he opens his mouth, which is
not infrequently, and really he does deserve better treatment because he is the one character who is aware, when he is reminded,
though he can't control it, that he talks too much and to little purpose. If an effective command of language is a mark of the effective
figure there is none here, but then language here is hardly a means
of communication. Each character seems to be living along a line of
his own and not often getting through to anyone else, sometimes not
really interested in getting through, rarely understanding anyone
else. "What do you say?" We begin with Lopahin reading, not reading, a book, not making head or tail of it, falling asleep over it; with
Dunyasha reporting a proposal from Epihodov, "He's a harmless fellow, but sometimes when he begins talking, there's no making anything of it. It's all very fine and expressive, only there's no
understanding it" (and as Anya says, "It's always the same thing with
you"); with Firs crossing the stage and, we are told, as he goes "*He
says something to himself, but not a word can be distinguished*" (I,
5–7). Firs is deaf, doesn't hear, mishears, and he can't be understood. "What is he saying?" Lyubov asks (I, 18). But then she doesn't
hear or understand very well either. "I don't quite understand you,"
she says to Lopahin (15). He tells her in plain Russian, he says, "and
you seem not to understand it" (II, 33). She covers her ears not to
listen to what Trofimov says (III, 54). Fine speakers may get compliments but they do not get hearers, and some are just not properly
appreciated. Epihodov, that cultivated man, reads remarkable
books of all sorts and has a sense of the delicacies of language, "excuse the expression" and "speaking precisely," but never quite a
sense of meanings. "But of course, if one looks at it from that point of
view, if I may so express myself, you have, excuse my plain speaking, reduced me to a complete state of mind" (58).

Lopahin has his device to overcome the present difficulty and reach to the future, Trofimov has his, even Gaev has his and a multiple move it is that Gaev has. He has been in the District Court and, in talking to people he met, of one thing and another (of course), he believes it will be possible to raise a loan on an I.O.U. to pay the arrears on the mortgage; Lyubov will talk to Lopahin and he will help; and Anya will go to Yaroslavl to the Countess, her very, very rich old great aunt.

> So we shall all set to work in three directions at once, and the business is done. We shall pay off arrears, I'm convinced of it (*puts a caramel in his mouth*). I swear on my honour, I swear by anything you like, the estate shan't be sold (*excitedly*). By my own happiness, I swear it! Here's my hand on it, call me the basest, vilest of men, if I let it come to an auction! Upon my soul I swear it!

Anya is restored to happiness. "How good you are, uncle, and how clever! (*embraces her uncle*). I'm at peace now! Quite at peace! I'm happy!!" (I, 25). But three directions at once are not the most promising path to a goal and, except for this one evanescent moment with Anya, no one, including Anya, even thinks Gaev is capable of anything useful. Gaev himself is speaking only to be speaking, and to say something comforting to Anya, a caramel for her mouth, because he's a nice man, but he doesn't expect anything to happen. He has just before offered his best diagnosis and prognosis:

> Yes (*a pause*). If a great many remedies are suggested for some disease, it means that the disease is incurable. I keep thinking and racking my brains; I have many schemes, a great many, and that really means none. (23)

There are no remedies for this expiring family and its house and orchard. Pishtchik, in his good old horsey way, knows all about medicines. He takes away Madame Ranevsky's pills.

> You shouldn't take medicines, my dear madam . . . they do no harm and no good. Give them here . . . honoured lady (*takes the pill-box, pours the pills into the hollow of his hand, blows on them, puts them in his mouth and drinks off some kvass*). There!

Lyubov is alarmed, he must be out of his mind. Doesn't bother him: "I have taken all the pills." "What a glutton!" Lopahin says, and "*(All laugh)*". Like the other devices they do no harm and they do no good. Firs remembers how "His honour," whoever he was, stayed with them in Easter week, ate a gallon and a half of cucumbers. He mutters. "What is he saying?" (18). Makes no difference. But then perhaps they should listen to Firs, because he has had a proven nostrum. "The old master, the grandfather," he says, "used to give sealing-wax for all complaints. I have been taking sealing-wax for twenty years or more. Perhaps that's what's kept me alive" (III, 55–66). Pishtchik has no faith in medicines, but he does have several large philosophical ideas of his own about how to overcome all difficulties, miscellaneous ideas, sort of, he's picked up, vaguely, in the main it would seem from his daughter Dashenka, a clever offstage thinker (" . . . she says . . . various things"), or from anonymous people he has met briefly, out there. "Nietzsche, the philosopher, a very great and celebrated man . . . of enormous intellect . . . says in his works, that one can make forged bank-notes" (I, 19; III, 47). "A young man in the train was telling me just now that a great philosopher advises jumping off a house-top. 'Jump!' says he; 'the whole gist of the problem lies in that.' *(Wonderingly)* Fancy that, now! Water, please!" (IV, 72). Actually Pishtchik ends up better than the others, not by any of his deep thoughts or plans, which may be his best trick.

Among all these advocates and heralds of a new life there is, it happens, one character who is capable of producing that trick. "These clever fellows are all so stupid," Charlotta Ivanovna says at the beginning of Act II (30), the act in which they will present their big speeches. Charlotta, who doesn't know who she is, is the best performer, does card tricks, ventriloquism, impersonations, appearances, disappearances. Pishtchik is her best audience, spellbound in the wonder and fancy of it; he sees the real Puck: "Mischievous creature! Fancy!" (III, 48–50). Unhappily, all this magic is inconsequential, domestic vaudeville, while the cherry orchard is at that moment being auctioned away offstage. In the next and last act she produces a miracle. While Anya is talking to her mother, dreamily, of the wonderful new worlds which will open out before them, Charlotta enters softly humming a song. "Charlotta's happy; she's singing!"

> CHARLOTTA: (*picks up a bundle like a swaddled baby*). Bye, bye, my baby. (*A baby is heard crying: "Ooah! ooah!"*) Hush, hush, my pretty boy! (*Ooah! ooah!*) Poor little thing!

A happy mother, a pretty new baby boy, a new life, the future—it is startling, where can it have come from? Clever Charlotta throws the bundle back. Just a throwaway trick, another illusion. The reality is that Charlotta, who doesn't know who she is, has no place to go. "You must please find me a situation. I can't go on like this." "We'll find you one, Charlotta Ivanovna," Lopahin says. "Don't you worry yourself" (IV, 71).

We meet here no lovers but the incomplete, no fairies but the ineffective. What remains is a cast of all clowns, each a "good-for-nothing," in Firs's refrain (and he doesn't except himself). Nice people all of them, but they don't see and they can't do. All blind and deaf, and there is no countercharm that can get through, open the eyes, no language they can hear. Gaev, talking inappropriately as usual, this time about his sister (who is good and kind and nice, he says, and he loves her, but there is no denying she is an immoral woman), doesn't see Anya until Varya whispers to him. "What do you say? (*a pause*). It's queer, there seems to be something wrong with my right eye. I don't see as well as I did. And on Thursday when I was in the district Court . . . " (I, 24). And of course as Lyubov says to Trofimov, "I seem to have lost my sight, I see nothing," and she knows that Trofimov the bold seer doesn't have better eyes but only more ignorance: " . . . you don't see and don't expect anything dreadful because life is still hidden from your young eyes." Firs has lost his hearing to old age, but she stops her own and when Trofimov tells her truths about herself, it is "No! No! No! You mustn't speak like that (*covers her ears*)" (III, 52, 54).

Without eyes or ears that can open, without anyone who has the power to do something for them, with no medicine for the incurable, in a dream, in a sleep from which they cannot wake, there is no way to change. They are continually telling one another that they haven't changed. "Varya's just the same as ever, like a nun,"

Madame Ranevsky says on her return. "You're just the same as ever, Varya." To Gaev, "You are just the same as ever, Leonid"; and the grinning Yasha agrees, "just the same as ever" (I, 7, 13, 17, 23). Varya says the same of Lyubov: "Mamma's just the same as ever, she hasn't changed a bit" (23). Lyubov finds comfort in that as she looks out of the window into the garden and sees her childhood, her innocence; in this nursery where she used to sleep, from here looked out into the orchard, happiness waking with her every morning, "and in those days the orchard was just the same, nothing has changed (*laughs with delight*)." (20). A great deal has changed, even if the cherry orchard still looks the same and she still throws away her money and Varya still has the habit of a nun. Time doesn't move for them, except as they are its victims, as the world around them changes, as they grow older without much other change. The one character Lyubov doesn't recognize when she returns is Trofimov, because he was young enough when she left to have become old in his twenties. "Can I have changed so much? . . . " Why does he look so old, that mangy-looking gentleman, likely to be a perpetual student?—and in essentials the same as ever and will be the same forever (21–22).

Time is presented dramatically in this play as though we were engaged in a critical action with a limited period in which a decision must be made, a deed done. There are four days, Theseus declares, between now and his wedding, when Hermia must move to find her fate, and indeed it is accomplished magically faster than that. Elizabeth Bennet, Dorimant, the Duke Vincentio, must use their time, in an hour, a day, or perhaps some months by a series of stages, but always by the clock or the calendar, to gain their desire or lose it for all time. And so it seems here, because if nothing is done to save the cherry orchard it will be sold on August 22, as Lopahin announces in Act I, and repeats in Act II, and then August 22 is the day of Act III. But in the rhythms and its pauses of this play time slips by in a leisurely way: from Act I in May, with the cherry trees in flower; to Act II, about three weeks later, a summery scene, everyone out of doors in glorious weather; to Act III, the aforesaid August 22, when they dance; to the concluding Act IV, October but still good weather for his building business, Lopahin says happily. The pressure of time as a continuum in which critical decisions and actions must be taken is there to be felt only as an absence. There is no movement to that pressing end. Trofimov concludes Act I with a tender word to the half asleep Anya, "My sunshine! My spring," but we go in a dying fall, not to a new spring but from spring to fall. The sun rises in Act I, goes down in Act II and it is the night of August 22 in Act III. Act II—following the first act when the problem is presented and the action would seem to begin, and preceding the third act when the cherry orchard is to be sold and the action would seem to end— would seem to be the moment when the turning move, the right word, ought to come.

In Act II all the characters have gone out to what would seem to be the right sort of place to seek a solution not to be found at home, to the open country, and quite beautiful, perhaps with hope from another realm. But it is at *"An old shrine, long abandoned and fallen out of the perpendicular."* Sweeter than Volpone's shrine certainly, but if his was a false god they have long abandoned theirs (though they still do appeal occasionally, with little faith, for magic or divine help to come from wherever that may be). Near the shrine is a well, a source, perhaps, except that in this setting it doesn't seem to be used; among large stones *"that have apparently once been tombstones"* (now that *is* gone); and an old garden seat (of course). They even have what seems to be a suggestive (and, as always, indecisive) map for the journey. The road to the house is seen, and on one side the beginning of the cherry orchard, and far, far away on the horizon, faintly outlined, a great town, visible only in fine weather. But it is near sunset. No one moves. *"All sit plunged in thought."* (II, 28). Thinking about what? Lots of things. Lopahin enters with Lyubov and Gaev and he tries to concentrate their minds.

> You must make up your mind once for all—there's no time to lose. It's quite a simple question, you know. Will you consent to letting the land for building or not? One word in answer: Yes or No? Only one word!

Lyubov wonders who has been smoking such horrible cigars here; it's been Yasha, her useless valet, but she never knows. Gaev says that now the railway line has been brought near it has made things

very convenient. They've been over and lunched in town.
(Lopahin's point about the railway, but not quite what he intended.)
Gaev would like to go home now and have a game of billiards.

> LYUBOV: You have plenty of time.
> LOPAHIN: Only one word! (*Beseechingly*) Give me an answer!
> GAEV: (*yawning*). What do you say? (31–32)

Lyubov drops her purse, scattering gold pieces. Lopahin finally gets
back their attention for a moment. Maybe the aunt in Yaroslavl will
send help, Gaev volunteers, but when and how much we don't
know. How much? a hundred thousand, two hundred? Oh well, ten
or fifteen, and we must be thankful to get that.

> LOPAHIN: Forgive me, but such reckless people as you are—
> such queer, unbusiness-like people—I never met in my
> life. One tells you in plain Russian your estate is going to be
> sold, and you seem not to understand it.

He's right about that. "What are we to do?" Lyubov asks. "Tell us
what to do."

> I do tell you every day. Every day I say the same thing. You
> absolutely must let the cherry orchard and the land on building
> leases; and do it at once, as quick as may be—the auction's
> close upon us! Do understand! Once make up your mind to
> build villas, and you can raise as much money as you like, and
> then you are saved.

These absolutes, only one word, and do it at once, and quick as may
be, make up your mind, be saved, are simply incomprehensible,
not their language. It's so vulgar, she says, and Gaev perfectly
agrees. "I shall sob," Lopahin sobs, "or scream, or fall into a fit. I
can't stand it! You drive me mad!" He calls Gaev an old woman,
which is sort of precise, and sort of heard ("What do you say?"), and
gets up to go. Lyubov is in dismay. "No, don't go! Do stay, my dear
friend! Perhaps we shall think of something." What is there to think
of? Well, with him there "it's more cheerful, anyway (*a pause*)"
(33–34).

Lopahin, the one businessman in the place, is subject to time,
very busy with time, and not only of calendar but of clock. In Act I
he is "(*glancing at his watch*)," saying "there's no time to say

much . . . well, I can say it in a couple of words," and he tells them of the coming date of the sale; "(*glancing at his watch*)" once again, decide, he says, to take some steps, August 22 is coming; and "(*looking at his watch*)" once again, "Well, it's time I was off" (I, 14, 16, 17). In the last act he is looking at his watch again, now warning everyone that the train goes in forty-seven minutes, so they ought to start for the station in twenty minutes, "You must hurry up!" (IV, 65). The play began with him asking what time it is and complaining that the train is late, but then, yawning and stretching, he missed the train. " . . . what a fool I've been. Came here on purpose to meet them at the station and dropped asleep . . . " (I, 3). He missed his train again in the third act, after buying the cherry orchard. With himself, and with other people, his clock doesn't work too well. He won't be well in time for his wedding day. If there's still time at the end he's ready to propose, "now at once," "(*looking at his watch*). Yes" (IV, 73–74). He has interesting things to say about time. "Yes, time flies," he says. "What do you say?" Gaev asks. "Time, I say, flies." "What a smell of patchouli" (I, 12).

The scent of this self-made rich man offends Gaev, who has his own sense of time, of time past and time to come and of their relations. That old bookcase, for example. Last week he pulled out the bottom drawer and found the date branded on it, made "just a hundred years ago. What do you say to that? We might have celebrated its jubilee. Though it's an inanimate object, still it is a *book* case." Pishtchik is amazed. "A hundred years! Fancy that now."

> GAEV: Yes . . . It is a thing . . . (*feeling the bookcase*). Dear, honoured bookcase! Hail to thee who for more than a hundred years hast served the pure ideals of good and justice; thy silent call to fruitful labour has never flagged in those hundred years, maintaining (*in tears*) in the generations of man, courage and faith in a brighter future and fostering in us ideals of good and social consciousness (*a pause*). (I, 17)

If he has not much of that silent call and fruitful labor and if a brighter future will not be his, still it is a thing, and it brings tears. He, like the others, is a man of a period, in his case of an outdated liberalism (a Russian Roebuck Ramsden). "I'm a man of the eighties. They run down that period, but still I can say I have had to suffer not a little for my convictions in my life. It's not for nothing that the peasant loves me. One must know the peasant! One must know how . . . " "At it again, uncle!" (25–26). Firs's life came to an end in the sixties, in "the catastrophe." Epihodov is a man of the future; he may make his entrance in new boots that creak so that there is no tolerating them, and he may be a man who is the brave present sport of less than heroic misfortunes, but after all he is a reader of the much translated Englishman's rational, progressive history of civilization: when he takes up a jug of kvass, "to quench my thirst," in it "there is something in the highest degree unseemly of the nature of a cockroach (*a pause*). Have you read Buckle? (*a pause*)" (II, 30). But past, present or future nothing in these people changes. It was three degrees of frost in the first act and it is three degrees of frost in the last act. If how to marry Varya and Lopahin and how to provide for Firs were problems in the first act they are still there in the last and they will never be solved. We begin in the comforting nursery and we end in the empty nursery.

There is no turning back, Lopahin says to Lyubov, with tears, and "oh, if our miserable disjointed life could somehow be changed!" He has just bought the estate, the end of Act III (62). In a disjointed life the time is out of joint. Act III began with a dance and a dance is what one may well expect in a comedy. But not now, at the wrong time, but later, later, when all has been worked out harmoniously and everyone celebrates a new order. While this dance is in progress the cherry orchard is being sold offstage. "It's the wrong time to have the orchestra," Lyubov says, "and the wrong time to give a dance. Well, never mind (*sits down and hums softly*)" (48).

When Chekhov calls this a comedy he knows very well what he is doing, and that should hardly surprise us. He is writing a play for an audience which knows what is expected in comedies—lovers and marriages, and incompetent clowns, and effective fairies with power to create and to resolve problems, a dream, a journey, a sickness to be lived through to a new life in good time, a dance to conclude, and the language of nonsense and the higher language of wit and poetry: and Chekhov holds out all these expectations and then deliberately leaves them incomplete, rearranged, without their expected effects. And he does it so beautifully. The characters themselves really wish they were in another kind of comedy, and, here as one might expect from them, it would be a sentimental comedy. All their difficulties would end without the need to do anything. If only somebody would leave us a legacy. Maybe Anya could marry a rich man. Maybe our aunt, that good fairy in Yaroslavl, will give us the money. Maybe a lottery ticket will win. If God would help us. Gaev has his own happy place, that game he plays in his mind, in which he is almost always a successful shot-maker. And caramels are always sweet in the mouth. Pishtchik, in fact the most bumbling character, gentle sponger, but always wondering, never losing faith that something will happen, does get the money he needs by a stroke of fortune, " . . . a most extraordinary occurrence." Some Englishmen came along and found in his land some sort of white clay, " . . . most lovely . . . wonderful (*gives money*)" (IV, 72). That sort of thing had happened to him once before; he thought everything was over, he was a ruined man, "and lo and behold—the railway passed through my land and . . . they paid me for it"; and as he said then, "something else will turn up again, if not to-day, then to-morrow . . . " (I, 19). So evidently such things do happen to some people and there is this happy stroke at the end: but he's the wrong man, not that we have anything against him, good old horse (and a horse is a fine beast, it can always be sold), but his fortunes are not what had held our attention. Besides, he has solved his problems by selling off, first, part of his land, and now his rights (and this time for twenty-four years, ominous figure!). Then he discovers that everyone else is leaving and it agitates him, but

> No matter . . . (*through his tears*) . . . no matter . . . men of enormous intellect . . . these Englishmen . . . Never mind . . . be happy. God will succour you . . . no matter . . . everything in this world must have an end. (IV, 73)

"Heyday!" says Congreve's Witwoud at the end of the last act, "what, are you all got together, like players at the end of the last act?" (*The Way of the World*, V, iii). A good question for anyone, wit or fool, who knows what happens at the end of comedies. But here all disperse: Varya to Yashnovo, seventy miles away, and as Lopahin notes, "(*a pause*). So this is the end of life in this house!" (74);

Lopahin to Harkov for now; Trofimov back to Moscow to his university; Gaev to a job at the bank, where he won't last; Anya to school;
Lyubov back to Paris.

> LYUBOV: Now we can start on our travels.
> ANYA: (*joyfully*). On our travels!

Anya and Trofimov are excited: "Good-bye, home! Good-bye to the
old life!" and Trofimov, in his old refrain, cheers her on with "Welcome to the new life!" (75, 77); but this is not a journey to a new life
but a round-trip on the railway. Lyubov is completing her circle,
back to what she had just left last May, that faithless lover, that place
on the fifth floor, smelling of tobacco and so comfortless (I, 9), just
the same as ever. We have followed the telegrams from that begging
lover, the only messages she responds to, as they called her back,
from Act I (17), when she tore them without reading, to Act II (35),
when she carried them in her pocket and read them before tearing,
to Act III (53), when they fell from her pocket, as she was getting one
every day, and she knew she really ought to go. The modern tele-
graph is the one form of communication that seems to work effectively, as the railroad is the one form of movement, and both take
her around to where she was. She can live there on the money their
Yaroslavl auntie sent the family to buy the estate with, "—hurrah for
auntie!—but that money won't last long" (IV, 71). One last moment
for "Oh, my orchard!—my sweet, beautiful orchard!" and it *was*
that, "My life, my youth, my happiness, good-bye! good-bye!" (77),
and it *is* that.

The stage is empty, silent, and in the stillness the dull stroke of an
axe in a tree. The footsteps of an old man, locked in. "They have
forgotten me . . . Never mind," and "There's no strength in you,
nothing left you—all gone! Ech! I'm good for nothing (*lies motionless*)." And now the concluding music. We've had a succession of increasing discords from act to act: the shepherd's pipe far away
beyond the orchard, beautiful in itself, melancholy in implication,
to end the first act; Epihodov's mournful guitar to begin and then,
following the mournful breaking harp-string, end the second act;
the Jewish orchestra, hired by the family with nothing to pay
them, playing its wrong-time dance music to begin the third act,
and then again, but this time at the ironic order of the new master, to

end it; in finale, to punctuate the strokes of the axe far away in the orchard, again the sound from the sky like a breaking harp-string dying away mournfully (IV, 78), the concluding refrain. Never mind, as motionless Firs says, and, as Pishtchik said, no matter.

The translation is by Constance Garnett (sorry, but I still like it), *The Cherry Orchard and Other Plays* (London, 1928). References are to act and page number; where successive quotations in the same paragraph are from the same act the act number is not repeated.

Barricelli, Jean-Pierre, "Counterpoint of the Snapping String: Chekhov's *The Cherry Orchard*," *California Slavic Studies*, X (1977), 121–36

Brustein, Robert, *The Theatre of Revolt: An Approach to Modern Drama* (Boston, 1964)

Fergusson, Francis, *The Idea of a Theater* (Princeton, 1949)

Gerould, Daniel Charles, "*The Cherry Orchard* as a Comedy," *Journal of General Education*, XI (1958), 109–22

Goldberg, Lea, "Chekhov's Comedy *The Cherry Orchard*," *Scripta Hierosolymitana*, XIX (1967), 100–25

Hahn, Beverly, *Chekhov: A Study of the Major Plays and Stories* (Cambridge, 1977)

Kramer, Karl D., "Love and Comic Instability in *The Cherry Orchard*," in *Russian Literature and American Critics*, ed. Kenneth N. Brostrom (Ann Arbor, 1984)

Latham, Jacqueline E. M., "*The Cherry Orchard* as Comedy," *Educational Theatre Journal*, X (1958), 21–29

Magarschack, David, *Chekhov the Dramatist* (New York, 1960 ed.)

Peace, Richard, *Chekhov: A Study of the Four Major Plays* (New Haven, 1983)

Pitcher, Harvey, *The Chekhov Play: A New Interpretation* (London, 1973)

Rayfield, Donald, *Chekhov: The Evolution of His Art* (London, 1975)

Styan, J. L., *Chekhov in Performance: A Commentary on the Major Plays* (Cambridge, 1971)

A pause

Having got to a stasis, motionless, we may be at a good place to look back to where we have been and how we have come here. We have been following the fortunes of characters of certain sorts as they go through actions of a certain sort. One sort of characters are those we have been calling lovers because in the form in which we have seen them, and this is after all very common in art and life, their desire is for union with another human being. They often find that to achieve their desire in coming together they have a problem or more to solve along their way, people or circumstances that stand in their course, and therefore, they, or someone or something, must bring about a change to a state in which they can be satisfied. Sometimes the obstructions are within themselves and they must be capable of changing to solve their problem. In any case they need to attain a freedom from the forces which frustrate them and to start a happier life. These are usually characters of an upper class, in that sense the center of the society, perhaps socially upper class, or if not that then higher class in the scale of values by which we judge the characters among whom we find them: perhaps more intelligent, perhaps more moral, but in any case usually those with whom we sympathize because we would like to see them arrive at what they desire, even if they themselves don't always understand that very well.

Another sort of characters are those we have been calling clowns, or fools, or if we wanted to adopt Theseus's terminology we might say lunatics. These are lower class characters, and again they may be of the lower social class of their society, or if not that, because some of them may in fact have honorific titles, then lower class in the scale of values by which we judge. They have inferior minds and frequently are not merely unconscious of this but think of themselves as members of the better class, imitating that class to improve their state but incapable of the reality. Even if their fortunes improve it is usually not by their own abilities, though they may think so, and more probably it is in spite of themselves. They cannot change themselves. We may be contemptuous of them, as they are mean and offensive, or we may like them, as they are innocuous, or pleasantly helpful to others, and even wonderfully instructive in the ways they are revealing of others (and of us).

A third sort we have been calling fairies, or, if we were to continue with Theseus's categories, we might say poets because they have abilities to shape things. They can hinder or promote change in the action, prevent or invent movement. They have superior power to direct the actions of others, have a life above what they see as the limiting human condition from which they are exempt: sometimes because they really are more than human; sometimes because they have a superior social status or force; but most notably because they have superior minds, able to see into and read the minds of others and thereby to predict or shape other characters' thoughts and actions. They can be clever, witty, inventive. They are capable of trickery. With the higher liveliness, which they usually have, they exercise powers, which we have been designating as charms or countercharms, with which they can change the visions of lovers or clowns, blind them or open their eyes to the truth: sometimes acting to deceive their victims, complicate the problems, for pleasure or profit, sometimes acting to provide a beneficent solution for otherwise insoluble problems. They delight in match-making, or breaking. They are dramatic artists. Sometimes they discover that they are not so much more than mortal as they have thought themselves to be and are brought back to earth. For on earth characters of these sorts we have been distinguishing as lovers, clowns and fairies may change roles, playing in different capacities as they stand in different relations to different people, or to themselves at different times, finding that they have miscast themselves. Only the author can be the true Puck and sometimes he too mistakes his trade, in incapacity or bad faith.

These characters are usually distinguishable from one another by their language. As they are superior or inferior they are heard to speak accordingly. Their language is a sign of, expression of, their knowledge and intelligence, and offers them and us the pleasures of an art in action, as it proceeds, skillful or clumsy. In its most effective practice language is significant power of mind, the readiest form of mastery even for those who are otherwise marginal in the society, as it is able to control ideas, feelings, lives; it can discern and manipulate levels of reality, and thereby dominate and move the action, bring the changes.

The changes in fortune that we see can appear in varied expressive shapes. Time is the most obvious measure of change, of growth. Actions and characters of different kinds proceed at different paces, in the differing conditions of their time and such pressures as their time puts upon them, by using or failing to use time well for their ends. Some characters develop, naturally or artfully, to their fulfilling maturity. Time is human, and the story gives it that human form, in the fullness of time on this earth. The movement can be measured and displayed also in the coordinate terms of space, by the common figure of a journey. Characters can go from place to place as they and their fortunes change, sometimes to heaven, like Don Juan, to be the master of reality, sometimes more modestly, like Elizabeth Bennet, to be the mistress of Pemberley (which, after all, *is* something). Lovers try to travel the course of true love, always so difficult to negotiate; if happiness cannot be found here at home, and it never can be, then there is a desired place to which they can depart. But there are surprises along the way as they try to find that other realm, stranger than they have ever imagined, and they are lost in knots or mazes until in their denouement they can emerge in a new amazement. Sometimes they return, home again, but now they are changed in a changed home. Another figure of governing movement is the law, the laws of the state, or of social authorities, more generally the laws by which human life seems to be governed, sometimes an edict in destiny, which restrain, hold lovers from their desire. Those laws must be escaped, altered, transcended, in movement to a higher law which demands freedom for love and life. Once again the attempted solution is not so easy as it promises, often develops unforeseen complications as it brings its own law. Or, in the figure of another liberal art which attempts to manage the human in its passage through the difficulties of fulfilling its nature, the changes can be seen in medical terms; there are unnatural diseases to be cured, remedies to be found, in characters, in societies, in the world they inhabit, sometimes to remove the noxious elements, and usually to restore a proper healthy condition. Medicine is another art that at times seems to cross its normal limits, works to save in mysterious ways. In these several human ventures there is likely to be an unexpected encounter at the border with what is not fully understandable, with something more than what is assumed to be natural, with the strange, the bewitching, indeed magical. The apprehension of the more than comprehensible, what cannot be explained by reason and cannot be dismissed, enters the scene in varied forms, sometimes as luck or chance, sometimes as dream or shadow, as transfiguring imagination. Its strangeness may be deeply disconcerting, frustrating, or may be joyfully received, fulfilling, or may be both at different stages. It is an unknown force, beyond ready control, threatening or rewarding uncertainly except as the art of the storyteller gives it a shape that scrambles the pieces and then puts them together anew. That art is the power bringing a larger shape, a form that gives freedom and love. At its best the magic is absorbed as an access of experience, an increase that lifts the spirit with a new delight, or a sobering realization, in the marvelous unrealized potencies of human life.

In quite general terms the changes can be seen as a movement from a disordered to an ordered life. The order is likely to be a very active order, a more lively life, often with the promise of producing new life, but one that moves within its desired pattern, as when discords play into concord, or as in the mazes of a dance which sets free its participants in communal celebration. For the character who must change in order to join in this order the movement is figured in one or more of several ways. It manifests itself in a moment, which may be long in preparation, when a blindness ends and the eyes are opened to their vision. It can be the end of a dream and the time of awakening, from the night to the dawn, to the realization of a dream. Who seemed gone is come again, re-born. The experience of the eye-opening, awakening, rebirth, may be chastening, humiliating, said to be mortifying as the old character goes and the new comes. In those terms it is the classic movement from ignorance to knowledge, most importantly from self-ignorance to self-knowledge. The journeying characters arrive at themselves, as far as they are able. Some are never able, some ask amazed questions of themselves, some discover themselves. "Am I not Hermia?" asks the bewildered girl. "What art thou, Angelo?" asks the disgusted deputy. "I! I!! I!!!" cries Jack Tanner, beginning to realize his ignorance, in character- istic crescendo. "Till this moment I never knew myself," says Elizabeth Bennet in mortification. "I fear I shall begin to grow in love with myself," says Mosca with delight, fatally losing his way. "Who are you?" Tristram Shandy is interrogated; "Don't puzzle me," says he, wise enough to be puzzled, as we shall see. They must, in that puzzling way, lose themselves to find themselves. In the most general terms, our characters go from unreality to reality, illusion to truth, but these terms become less useful as they become more general, because in their particular manifestations they are so often strange mixtures.

The outcome may be the laughter that rejoices in the achieved conclusion, the "universal laughter" which greets the hero of one of our plays at its end, though of course it does not wait for that period and appears along the way in several forms and moments. It has value as it has meaning when it appears, because often the move- ments of the characters and their actions have taken them through passages of pain and a pain that we have felt with sympathy. It has value along the way as it expresses our joy, in seeing the exercise of skilled powers of life as they succeed, or in appreciating just how they fall short with practitioners who only think they have power. In the kinds of terms we have been using, the most interesting laugh- ter arises in the perception of the difference between the blindness and the vision and those other similar pairs: in that revelation where laughter is the moment of truth. To laugh is to be the Puck, in pos- session of the insight. And, in the way laughter turns and circles, laughers are often mistaken in their perceptions.

The categories we have been using are subdivisible into many fur- ther and finer distinctions, all kinds of clowns or fools, for example, and these more precise analyses must be made in each instance to arrive at the level of this unique particular within this unique work. What one emphasizes or neglects, and the consequent shape that emerges, depends on one's interest and that will always mean that the result will be unsatisfactory to others who have different con-

cerns and ways of beginning and proceeding. The ways we have
gone here allow for some considerations of a succession of works,
some means of seeing them as a group and of distinguishing them
from one another, and of noting the response of our feelings to
them. We have looked at characters with desires of certain sorts
which require actions of certain sorts to meet the problems presented by their desires and by those forces which stand in their way.
So the works can be characterized by the kinds of desire and
whether, as they are presented to us, we think they can or ought to
be fulfilled. They are further distinguished by the kinds of problems
to be solved. There are different degrees of solubility: characters
have capabilities of different sorts and effectiveness; the balance of
forces between opposing elements can vary; the means by which the
solution is obtained, so far as it is obtained, can differ; the ease or
difficulty by which the end is attained, the completeness of the solution and the satisfactions it offers can have many degrees. In general
terms these are questions of the possibilities of change, of movement to an end. In the succession of works we have followed it is
apparent that the ways in which movement can be effected become
more and more difficult and the full achievement of a shape that fulfills desire becomes less possible: the desires tend to become less
attractive of sympathy; or they are such that it seems less possible
they will be reached; the problems become more intractable, the
characters less competent, their means less effective; the possibility
of movement is reduced, or more violence is needed to produce a
change. The elements we have come to expect from having seen
them in one or more works are shifted in another, are rearranged,
have variant qualities, are changed in emphasis in their relations
with one another, are surprisingly absent, though they continually
recall the features of a family resemblance by insistent or nagging
resemblances or by what is obviously missing. These elements are
certainly not all coordinate with one another as one goes from work
to work, for there are an indeterminate number of combinations of
elements which are themselves variant, so what we are pointing at
can be only tendencies.

In the examples chosen here *A Midsummer Night's Dream* is a
beginning point for this way of looking at things because it has a clarity, a symmetry, of elements, in the way the three kinds of charac-

ters, distinguished in status and language, are set before us and carry out their action. The lovers play out their course of true love, winning through the problems presented both by the restraint upon their desire and by their own blindness. The clowns, eager to play another role, speak a finer word, may be translated for us but are essentially incapable of change. Both groups set forth to find a better place to attain their ends and there they meet the fairies, beings from a more than mortal realm with a magical power over the mortals and their limits of time and space: the fairies are able to see into them, alter their vision, and thus direct their movements, with a distorting charm; but they have the coordinate power of a counter-charm to open the eye, and all is finally resolved, all disorders remedied, in a complete harmony. It is all done by a power beyond human comprehension, in the strangeness of a dream and the return. *Man and Superman* too takes the action to a dream, to another realm where problems can be worked out, by the central character, free of human limitations. But here the attainment of that perfection is not available in life on earth, that level of reality bound by the conditions of a body in space and time. The young lover who thinks he is the spirit above that condition must learn that he can't expect perfection, least of all in himself. It requires a process of time to the moment when the eye-opening force changes that vision. In *Pride and Prejudice* that journey to another place, where the limits of human deficiencies and their frustrations can be escaped, is appealing but not possible. It is a more testing, slower, course now, harder to find one's happy end. Here essential changes must occur within, a more surprising journey, in a work of controlled time, in a mortifying process of learning to see others precisely, to distinguish the proper objects of laughter, and above all to see oneself. With *The Man of Mode* the possibilities of movement are further enclosed in a tight space and time, where there is no quarter for clowns who do not understand these conditions; the power here is exercised by a dominant figure, seen by others as a charming devil, for his own ends of dominance in love, matched only by a young woman who can understand and laugh at him.

There follow several works which are more problematic, in the sense that the problems faced and the ways in which these are solved, or not solved, can leave not satisfied desires but dissatisfac-

tions for the characters and the audience. Traditionally there has
been often a reluctance or unwillingness in calling them comedies.
The special difficulty with *The Conscious Lovers* is not that the end
is short of completing the desires of the characters but rather that it
comes too easily. The levels of reality are shifted on us as the young
lover is also the superior spirit, at once completely at home in town
and above the mortal foolishness; for this virtue the solution to his
problem is provided by a kind of Providential violence. In *Measure
for Measure* the problems run so deep and are so extensive, in the
very polity, a corrupt and sick society, flouting the law in a false freedom, that they can hardly be brought to a pleasantly desirable end.
Only the most extraordinary measures can save. The counterforce to
open the eyes of subjects must be an extraordinary force, and the
emphasis is on this figure, wielding both secular and sacred power,
working from below. His remedy is to move them, these lovers and
clowns of Vienna, to the face and the acceptance of death, that mortification, before they can be new made. In the Venice of *Volpone*
the sickness is so pervasive and dominant that the cast of characters
is reduced, with no lovers except the perverse, only fools and victims subject to the powerful and vicious, remarkable, deceivers.
The only remedy is the severest punishment, divorce, expulsion,
prospective death for the blind deceived, and for the deceivers who
are themselves necessarily their own greatest fools, incurable. The
characters of *The Cherry Orchard,* so much more likeable than anyone in Venice, are even more limited and incapable in meeting their
difficulties. We find no lovers able to move and no superior power,
no sight of how to solve the problem that dissolves the home estate.
All things break for them, time slips away, all are fools, and, with no
better place to go, all depart in separate directions. With *The
Cherry Orchard* we seem to have come to a stop, but it is only, in the
characteristic term of that play, a pause.

   We are familiar today with works which, unlike *The Cherry Orchard*, do not want to be called comedies, where we meet rather
more than a pause, where problems with clocks seem to be permanent. We are in a "play" where "I need a clock to tell the time! How
can I tell the time without a clock? I can't do it! . . . I mean, if you
can't tell what time you're at you don't know where you are, you understand my meaning?" (Pinter, *The Caretaker*, III). No, we don't

understand his meaning. What difference would it make to that shambling old man anyway? He's not going to Sidcup, or anywhere, to get his references; he'll never have the right pair of shoes. Or we are in an "Anti-play" where the clock strikes 17 or 29 or "The clock strikes seven times. Silence. The clock strikes three times. Silence. The clock doesn't strike" (Ionesco, *The Bald Soprano*). Or we are in "a tragicomedy" where there are problems with the calendar, and no one can tell what season it is; and, unlike *A Midsummer Night's Dream,* this is not a temporary aberration which we know will be corrected.

Waiting for Godot is a tragicomedy, but not in the sense of a work which begins as though it might end tragically for the characters and then pulls out the solution for them. It is, rather, a work that gives us things that look as though they ought to be comic, is deliberately, mockingly, very traditional in its references, and we know quickly that these parts are not going to work: they don't come together, they don't come in the right order, they're not going to fulfill the conventional expectations; the play depends on our recognizing these echoes and the fascination is in watching how cleverly it will defeat their false promises. And it is always dangerous to quote Beckett; every time you stop you've stopped too soon; what follows qualifies, contradicts, the point you think you're making. Here are clowns, these specimens more immediately and obviously identifiable than most we have seen, but seeming to be more from the circus or the music-hall than the drama, doing their short turns, not playing out an action. They fall down, lose their pants, exchange their hats, wear the wrong boots; as ever, the state of shoes, boots, goloshes, not the right color or squeaky or ill-fitting or lost, is important for characters who can't move well (at a later point in Beckett they don't have legs). When they go beyond that, in attempts to put on little play routines, it is not to give an effective shape to life but to give themselves, briefly, the impression that they exist. Not much of a cast: one clown, then another clown, and that, it seems, pretty well exhausts it. The first one is himself already exhausted, can't get the boot off, giving up, says the first words: "Nothing to be done." The second advances with an advanced prostate, in short, stiff strides, legs wide apart. They seem to be on a journey but we can't have much hope of successful movement. They are meeting—"Together again at last!"—so perhaps we have, if not lovers certainly, at least a pair who can embrace and resume the struggle. "We'll have to celebrate this." A little early for a celebration, we may think, since we are more accustomed to enjoying that sort of delight at a final moment when difficulties have been happily overcome, or at least in that anticipation. "But how? (*He reflects*). Get up till I embrace you." And the other replies "(*irritably*). Not now, not now" (I, 9). He's right. It's not the right time and this effort isn't going to succeed. The union they form, as we follow it through the play, comes and goes, with moments that seem almost touching but which touch and go with disconcerting lack of any developing pattern, and with moments of hostility which might frighten except that they don't have any issue either; and all seems to repeat endlessly, so there's no point in continuing for long. A "tragicomedy in two acts" will be enough to work out all the possibilities and bring us back. What's their problem? The first clown, *"with a supreme effort succeeds in pulling off his boot,"* which is perhaps a first good move, but he can't find anything in the boot. "There's a man all over for you," says the other, "blaming on his boots the faults of his feet": he takes off his own hat and can't find anything in it. We might expect a clown to be able to laugh—many do, even if the joke is, unknowingly, on them, because a laugh is an assumption of understanding—and one now *"breaks into a hearty laugh which he immediately suppresses, his hand pressed to his stomach, his face contorted."* He realizes "One daren't even laugh any more." "Dreadful privation," says the other. "Merely smile," is the second attempt. That doesn't work either. "It's not the same thing. Nothing to be done. (*Pause*)" (11). He tries the laugh again a bit later with the same repression, less the smile. "You'd make me laugh, if it wasn't prohibited . . . *Silence*" (19).

They are essential clowns, incapable of change of any sort, incapable of moving anywhere, of finding a place, of existing in a time with any meaning. They wait. "Let's go." "We can't." "Why not?" "We're waiting for Godot" (I, 13), an exchange that returns a number of times. But it's not clear that they are waiting in the right place, by the leafless tree. "What are you insinuating? That we've come to the wrong place?" Nor that it's the right time. "You're sure it was this evening? . . . He said Saturday. (*Pause*.) I think. . . . But what Saturday? And is it Saturday? Is it not Sunday? (*Pause*.) Or Monday?

(*Pause.*) Or Friday?" (14–15). Time, a concern of Beckett's from his start, is always flowing or always stopped, never controllable, never to be shaped to a satisfactory end. Identities, names of course, are difficult or impossible to establish. Everything changes, so nothing changes, in a zero-sum game. "The tears of the world are a constant quantity. For each one who begins to weep, somewhere else another stops. The same is true of the laugh. (*He laughs.*)" (32). The traditional comforts of time are contradicted as they are uttered: "One can bide one's time," knowing what to expect, no need to worry, simply wait (37), because nothing will come; "Well, I suppose in the end I'll get up under my own steam. (*He tries, fails.*) In the fullness of time" (II, 82). If one has been accustomed to the gently syncopated "a pause" of the dialogue of *The Cherry Orchard*, "Pause" here jerks time to a stop, it seems, any time a word or two attempts to go. If *The Cherry Orchard*, at a couple of key points, before the harp-string breaks, comes to a silence, language here resolves itself into ever-returning "Silence." Like everything else it is endlessly repetitive. The dialogue has a characteristically circular pattern that cuts off any brief hint of a development. "It's worse than being at the theatre." "The circus." "The music-hall." "The circus" (I, 34; or II, 62–63, quite beautifully, or 69). Perhaps there will be a dream, one of those shared dreams we have seen, which may offer a way out, to another world where things are done differently; dreams are surprising to dreamers and in their differences bring even more confusion, but when they are told out they may outgo expectations in bringing a better order.

> "I had a dream."
> "Don't tell me!"
> "I dreamt that—"
> "DON'T TELL ME!"
> "(*gesture towards universe*). This one is enough for you? (*Silence.*) . . . Who am I to tell my private nightmares to if I can't tell them to you."
> "Let them remain private" (I, 15–16)

From whom, from where, then, will help come? "Well? What do we do?" "Don't let's do anything. It's safer." "Let's wait and see what he says." "Who?" "Godot." "Good idea." A very good idea, but what

DeWitt Wallace Library
Macalester College
1600 Grand Avenue
St. Paul, Minnesota

DUE DATE:

good is it they seek in this non-journey? "What exactly did we ask
him to do for us?" (18). In *The Cherry Orchard* there seems to be a
more or less determinate desire, at least to save the orchard, even if
that hardly promises much in the way of continuing stability, if the
incapable characters would only do something, and a particular
something; here that sort of option doesn't even get to the point of
being formulable.

The one hope that appears at all possible is that some figure of
power will appear, someone who understands the clowns and their
problem better then they, knows how to speak and act effectively,
who perhaps has been fooling them until now, but who has the will
and ability to save. Godot, with his initially impressive but then di-
minished name (if it is English), may be that fairy power. But what
we've heard of previous communication—their sending "A kind of
prayer." "Precisely." "A vague supplication." "Exactly."—and his
response—"That he'd see." "That he couldn't promise anything" (I,
18)—isn't the best language. It does not seem at all promising that
he will ever arrive; what one might expect to be the major controlling
character is now the resident absentee. He does not come. Pozzo
comes. A great figure of power, with all sorts of paraphernalia, including a whip, a long rope around the neck of an abject slave, violent in act, terrifying in voice, a being of a higher order, dangerous
in his graciousness. "You are human beings none the less. (*He puts
on his spectacles.*) As far as one can see. (*He takes off his spectacles.*)
Of the same species as myself. (*He bursts into an enormous laugh.*)"
Obviously a superior being, of deeper vision, able to dominate and
to laugh at what fools all these mortals are (21–22). They took him for
Godot, this unmeaning, brutal creature. "I am perhaps not particularly human, but who cares?" (28). Whatever he is, unlike them he
is in control. He is aware of time, understands the importance of
time on the grand scale, has a watch, remarkable watch—"That was
nearly sixty years ago . . . (*he consults his watch*) . . . yes, nearly
sixty" [his dots] (33). He consults his watch again, because he really
must be getting along if he is to observe his schedule. "Time has
stopped," a clown tells him out of his inferior experience. But not for
Pozzo, "(*cuddling his watch to his ear*). Don't you believe it, sir,
don't you believe it. (*He puts his watch back in his pocket.*) Whatever you like, but not that" (36). He laughs, pleased with his own

wit. As other powerful wits may, he has his servant and agent, this one with the felicitous tag-name Lucky, from whom he can command dance or thought. Perhaps he could dance first and think afterwards, one of the clowns requests, if it's not too much for him. "By all means, nothing simpler," Pozzo agrees, "It's the natural order. *Brief laugh.*" No, we know that is not the natural order; first some superior power figures out how to move things into the right place, then one celebrates the free order. It's the wrong time to give a dance. "Dance, misery!" Lucky presents his very brief and poor dance. He used to dance the farandole, Pozzo says, the fling, brawl, jig, fandango, even the hornpipe. "He capered. For joy." Do you know what he calls this? Pozzo asks. The clowns can name it well, in their own terms. "The Scapegoat's Agony." "The Hard Stool." No freedom and order in this dance, no movement. "The Net," Pozzo explains; "He thinks he's entangled in a net." The dance is over, but we're not even out of Act I. Silence. "Nothing happens, nobody comes, nobody goes, it's awful!" (39–41).

Now Lucky, according to the promised amusement, must think. "Think, pig!" And then, astonishingly, this hitherto wordless, less than human, creature speaks. Pozzo had said that it was his Lucky who had taught him all the beautiful things. "But for him all my thoughts, all my feelings, would have been of common things" (I, 32–33). Not much of an endorsement, coming from that source, but will we hear now, strangely, the words of the servant with his mind wiser than the master's? And Lucky launches into the most learned monologue, all the hard words and authorities which ought to be able to solve the great problems of this world; and indeed he brings news from the world beyond the human condition—"of a personal God quaquaquaqua with white beard quaquaquaqua outside time without extension Who from the heights of divine apathia divine athambia divine aphasia loves us dearly with some exceptions for reasons unknown but time will tell," and so on, running downhill with a divinity who seems quite without power or even interest to do much at all, in an absolute whirl of the more and more meaningless, louder and louder, unpunctuated until the speaker is forcibly stopped (42–44). Before we have done with this traveling pair Pozzo is fumbling about, sobbing, having lost his genuine watch, given him by his granpa (45–46). (Perhaps Pozzo, who seemed to enter as

the knowing power—a deep well?—is pazzo, a patched fool?) Even
the appearance of power—he was certainly never in control of
himself—doesn't seem very impressive by now, as they depart.
"How they've changed!" says one clown. "Who? . . . What?"
"Changed." "Very likely. They all change. Only we can't" (48). And
so to the messenger from Mr. Godot, with the word that he won't
come this evening but surely tomorrow.

> "Well, shall we go?"
> "Yes, let's go."
> *They do not move.*

End of first act. Perhaps the next and last act will get them moving.

Act II. Next day. Same time. Same place. "What am I to say?"
"Say, I am happy." "I am happy." "So am I." "So am I." "We are
happy." "We are happy. (*Silence.*) What do we do now, now that
we're happy?" "Wait for Godot" (II, 60). Things have changed since
yesterday, is the next assertion, which does seem to have some
promising evidence because the tree has four or five leaves, but that
dissipates because without a corroborating memory there's no way
of measuring time or verifying change. Any possibility that the
second time around will be a change has been a brief and feeble
joke—disconcerting but never taking us in—because obviously all
that can happen is that we are going to ring the changes. There will
be no magic, dismissed before it comes into existence. "We always
find something, eh, Didi, to give us the impression that we exist?"
"(*impatiently*). Yes yes, we're magicians. But let us persevere in
what we have resolved, before we forget" (69). Dreams are still
frightening, "Don't tell me!" dance is still a writhing, "I can't!" (70,
73). The coming of Godot, "We're saved!" (73), is still an illusion.
"You must have had a vision" is an irony that hardly needs emphasis
but will have it: "What?" "(*louder*). You must have had a vision!" "No
need to shout . . . *Long silence*" (75). Is there anyone with vision?
"Do you think God sees me?" "You must close your eyes." Here
comes Pozzo again, and he doesn't see. "Is it Godot?" " . . . Now it's
over. It's already tomorrow . . . Time flows already." No, it's Pozzo,
crying "Help!" (76–77). He's blind, in a reverse eye-opening. The
possibility of their being able to see or do anything to help another,
even for gain, is quickly lost; and so too the wonderful possibility of

his having any power to help them. If he is blind "Perhaps he can see
into the future." He used to have wonderful sight. They laugh
noisily at him. "What time is it?" Pozzo wants to know, his watch
long gone. They don't know what season it is. "The blind have no
notion of time," he says, "The things of time are hidden from them
too" (85–86). Their continual questions about what has happened
make him furious. "Have you not done tormenting me with your ac-
cursed time?" There is no time: one day is like any other, we are
born, we die, the same day, the same second, "the light gleams an
instant, then it's night once more," and he exits (89). Like the lightning in the collied sky of *A Midsummer Night's Dream* the jaws of
darkness do devour it up, there as an obstacle to run in the course
of the time of true love, here as a repetition in an unending circle of
unchanging time. One of the clowns has fallen asleep, is shaken
awake. "I was dreaming. I was happy." The other doesn't want to
hear, has his own wonder of whether Pozzo saw them, is in turn re-
jected. "You dreamt it." "Was I sleeping? . . . Am I sleeping now?"
(90). As with other dreamers we have met it seems they were both
dreaming, but here it was not the shared dream; as with other
dreamers they are now uncertain of the bounds of sleeping and waking, but here it is not the magic of the transformed reality but an
unending confusion. Here they will never come out of dream, but
then it is not clear that they have ever entered it. Here for the
second time is Godot's messenger. "Off we go again. (*Pause.*) Do you
not recognize me?" Will we now have the surprising anagnorisis?
"No, sir." Same message as yesterday. "What does he do, Mr. Godot?
(*Silence.*) Do you hear me? . . . Well?" "He does nothing, sir." "*Silence.*" That we might have guessed from his performance. But now
a new question, "(*softly.*) Has he a beard, Mr. Godot?" "Yes, sir."
"Fair or . . . (*he hesitates*) . . . or black?" "I think it's white, sir"
"*Silence.*" "Christ have mercy on us!" "*Silence.*" (91–92). What else
can be said, unless quaquaquaqua? What else can be done, except
hang ourselves tomorrow? "(*Pause.*) Unless Godot comes." "And if
he comes?" "We'll be saved." So that's hopeful and we can start moving again.

> "Well? Shall we go?"
> "Yes, let's go."
> *They do not move.* (94)

Actually it's not as hopeless as it may seem. As we were told early, "One of the thieves was saved. (*Pause.*) It's a reasonable percentage" (I, 11). The source for that is in what Beckett said was a wonderful sentence in Augustine: "Do not despair; one of the thieves was saved. Do not presume; one of the thieves was damned." Augustine, like other great men, has always been loaded with a lot of things he never said, and if he did say this his sentence carried a difference, not a question of reasonable percentage, but a matter of significant human or divine action. In the play it's a matter not of effort or plan, or reward, or an act of any sentient being, but of random statistics; it is hardly even what could be called happy chance. (In fact it may not be that good a bet because only one of the four gospels is willing to offer those odds.) "Let us not waste our time in idle discourse! (*Pause. Vehemently.*) Let us do something, while we have the chance!" (II, 79). These are clowns who are capable only of idle discourse, who cannot act, cannot take the offering of chance. But then the author has his power, the marvellous effectiveness of art; he has wit, point, remarkable control of language. The very repetitions of his very repetitious play have a rhythm, symmetries, a varied, moving and satisfying balance; the play has its closures of form. The art itself is not chance. The ineffectual clumsiness of the clowns, as in the skillful presentation of all trained clowns, is a practiced, time-honored, performance of those who play (try, if you like, that intricate exchanging of hats and see if you and your company can get the sequence and the timing just right). Chance here, as in all well-shaped works, whatever it may be for the characters, is subsumed in the shape of the art, in which we have confidence and find pleasure. "I am interested in the shape of ideas even if I do not believe them," Beckett said of Augustine's idea: "That sentence has a wonderful shape. It is the shape that matters" (*International Theatre Annual*, I [1956], 153).

There is a limit, though, to the development of a shape when there is nothing to be done, two acts as we have seen it here, or a play in one act, or one character talking to himself and listening to himself replayed, or one character in an act without words, stopped in every direction, reduced to paying no attention. For a more capacious form a larger acceptance is needed and the confidence that if problems are endless and we do not seem to be going anywhere, such clowns as we are here on earth, there is such variety of complication that chance is as likely to help as to hinder, and there is such a mixture of pains and pleasures in the process, that it all resolves strangely to a wonderful shape. We circle to perfection again and the story can go on forever. Losing and finding our way we get on in two journeys together. We end with an author whose name pops up in the literature about Beckett, and, characteristically of both authors, the other way around too.

The text is Samuel Beckett, *Waiting for Godot* (London, 1959). References are to act and page number; where successive quotations in the same paragraph are from the same act the act number is not repeated.

Cohn, Ruby, *Samuel Beckett: The Comic Gamut* (New Brunswick, 1962)

Cousineau, Thomas, *Waiting for Godot: Form in Movement* (Boston, 1990)

Esslin, Martin, *The Theater of the Absurd* (New York, 1961)

Fletcher, John, and John Spurling, *Beckett: A Study of His Plays* (London, 1972)

Gilman, Richard, *The Making of Modern Drama* (New York, 1974)

Graver, Lawrence, *Samuel Beckett: Waiting for Godot* (Cambridge, 1989)

Guicharnaud, Jacques, with June Guicharnaud, *Modern French Theatre from Giraudoux to Genet*, rev. ed., (New Haven, 1969)

Iser, Wolfgang, "The Art of Failure: The Stifled Laugh in Beckett's Theater," in Harry R. Garvin, ed., *Theories of Reading, Looking, and Listening, Bucknell Review*, XXVI, No. 1 (1981), 139–89

Kenner, Hugh, *Samuel Beckett: A Critical Study*, new ed. (Berkeley, 1973)

———, *A Reader's Guide to Samuel Beckett* (New York, 1973)

Nealon, Jeffrey, "Samuel Beckett and the Postmodern: Language Games, Play and *Waiting for Godot*," *Modern Drama*, XXXI (1988), 520–28

Peter, John, *Vladimir's Carrot* (Chicago, 1987)

Robinson, Michael, *The Long Sonata of the Dead: A Study of Samuel Beckett* (New York, 1969)

Schricker, Gale, "The Antinomic Quest of *Waiting for Godot*," *CEA Critic*, XLIX, Nos. 2–4 (1986–87), 124–33

States, Bert O., *The Shape of Paradox: An Essay on* Waiting for Godot (Berkeley, 1978)

Chapter Nine

Getting forwards in two different
journies together

Tristram Shandy

If one is looking for a world where there is no successful movement towards an end *Tristram Shandy* is rather more spectacular than anything we've seen. Characters in *The Cherry Orchard* have difficulty handling objects or ideas, and in *Waiting for Godot* they are feebly incompetent, but in *Tristram Shandy* things material and mental not only seem to be defeating the characters at every turn but sometimes attacking them with startling and even violent result. Knots which cast obstructions in our way in getting through life, indeed into life, cannot be untied and any attempt at a heroic solution can lead only to cutting one's thumb ("quite across to the very bone," III, x, 168); noses are broken down ("crush'd . . . as flat as a pancake"), before they can even emerge into this world, and thus break down the fortunes of a house (III, xxvii; IV, ix, 280); names leak out of heads, forever depressing the character and conduct of a life ("'tis not my fault . . . I told him it was *Tristram-gistus*," IV, xvi,); hot chestnuts take on a rotundity and life of their own and fall perpendicularly into apertures, to raise a terrifying disorder of passion ("a warning to all mankind," IV, xxvii); slap comes the sash-window down like lightning upon us ("Nothing is left . . . nothing is left," V, xvii). This sort of active business reduces the likelihood of our young hero's ever becoming a successful lover and it is notorious that impotence is a shadow over Tristram, his father, his uncle and the bull, deservedly or not. Tristram certainly has a fiasco (VII, xxix). Even the expectations for the favorite little mare, a most beautiful Arabian, by some neglect or other in Obadiah is answered with nothing better than a mule ("and as ugly a beast of the kind as ever was produced," V, iii, 352). Obadiah, falsely accused with the mare, has a better result in his own marriage; though even then, when his wife is brought to bed, he runs into some confusion with the bull ("Now, said *Obadiah*, I shall have a calf")—and there is a premature accusation of the bull's lack of performance (IX, xxxiii, 646). Attempts at remedies are not always successful and wounds are long in recovery ("But what do you mean by a recovery?" she would say, IX, xxvi); illnesses pervade (one can get an asthma skating against the wind in Flanders, a vile cough that torments to this hour, I, v, 10; VIII, vi, 545). And death pursues, trying to catch up on the journey.

It is a journey that gets off, setting the pace, to an unfortunate start. We begin, unusually, after the curtain of the happy end of most comedies, after the moment of "Lovers, to bed," as Theseus had enjoined, and whence, as Oberon and the fairies had promised, "the blots of Nature's hand / Shall not in their issue stand"; here it is something late in the married life and not the life of a young lover but of a less than eager progenitor and his less than fully responsive spouse. This is not a concluding moment when her answer is yes and not a joyous gathering or a move to a happy place, but a beginning when a very unseasonable question has "scattered and dispersed" the animal spirits, whose business it was to have escorted the *HO-MUNCULUS* and conducted him safe "to the place destined for his reception." In his way alone, through accident and terror "natural to so young a traveller," the little gentleman "got to his journey's end miserably spent," not at the end of a dream but, in his sad disordered state of nerves, subject to "a series of melancholy dreams" for nine long months together; a foundation has been laid for a thousand weaknesses both of body and mind which "no skill of the physician" or the philosopher, can ever set thoroughly to rights (I, ii). As we would expect, those who have no mastery over movement in space have none in time, so that the initiating difficulty here has an immediate cause in a clock-related confusion of ideas. (And actually the effect is not a term of nine months, which raises other questions, but we must not digress.)

Journeys in this story do tend to be without successful issue, or with none at all, as in that journey of Tristram's mother which preceded his begetting and which may have been a cause of one of the disasters which accompanied his arrival. By her marriage articles Mrs. Shandy was granted the option of having her lying-in in London, but she exercised that right to go up when, it turned out, there

was no valid call—to my father's disappointment and expense, a vile
trick and imposition he fancied it, weakness, as he kept telling her
on the way back, so "that my mother, whatever was her journey up,
had but an uneasy journey of it down" (I, xvi). That kind of return-
trip or up-and-down motion, circling around in one place, is the
characteristic progress. It is, in its most common version here, the
journey of the hobby-horse. The wisest men in all ages, not excepting Solomon himself, have had their hobby-horses, riding them
along the King's highway, and Tristram keeps a couple of pads himself, though sometimes, to his shame be it spoken, he takes "somewhat longer journies" than what a wise man would think altogether
right (I, vii–viii, 13–14). When the hobby-horse grows head-strong
then farewell cool reason and fair discretion. When it fires my uncle
Toby's imagination he cannot shut his eyes, and it becomes "bewitching," he posts to it with the heat and expectation of a lover to a
"belov'd mistress" (II, v, 93, 98). It takes the lover-like quality of the
"magic" in the mind, the "dream," and it is only the superior love
effect of widow Wadman which can for a time weaken it (VI, xxxv,
465–66). My father rides his hobby-horse of names (and several
other things) and for him too it has this fatal attraction. He is of the
opinion that there is "a strange kind of magick bias" in names which
irresistibly imposes upon our characters and conduct—argues the
point as seriously as Don Quixote and his faith in the powers of nec-
romancy or of Dulcinea's name; Christian names have that "magic
bias" (I, xix, 50; IV, viii, 279).

The hobby-horse with its magic power, the love and the dream,
that leads one on strange journeys, is the charm that controls the
vision, blinds the eye in that manner which makes its victim think
he is being most rational, most powerfully understanding. My father would see nothing in the light in which others placed it: "—he
placed things in his own light" (II, xix, 145). It gave him of course, in
his own eye, the insight to truth possessed by the superior spirit, the
one who can read minds. If we had the fixture of Momus's glass we
would have a window through which we could take a man's character, as with a dioptrical beehive look in and view the soul stark naked. But this is not an advantage to be had in this planet—in
Mercury the intense heat of the country may have vitrified the
bodies of the inhabitants, but here minds do not shine through the

body but are wrapped up in the dark covering of uncrystallized flesh and blood. Here we must go some other way to work and draw the character from the hobby-horse (I, xxiii). To my father's vision my uncle Toby, by his own hobby-horse, makes himself the readiest subject of reading. "Had my *Uncle Toby*'s head been a *Savoyard*'s box [peep-show], and my father peeping in all the time at one end of it,—it could not have given him a more distinct conception of the operations in my uncle *Toby*'s imagination, than what he had" (III, xxvi). My father was a great motive-monger and consequently a very dangerous person for a man to sit by, laughing or crying, "—for he generally knew your motive for doing both, much better than you knew it yourself" (VI, xxxi, 458). But then, seeing from his own hobby-horse, my father is in these insights consistently mistaken. And with my mother he is married to such a head-piece that he cannot hang up a single inference "within side of it" to save his soul from destruction (II, xix, 147).

Now the larger problem my father has which brings him to this failure of vision is (in this story which is nothing if not serious) epistemological—is a large question of knowledge, of locating Truth. The form it takes in my father is peculiar to him, but that is a general quality in the mind of all men in this world. "Endless is the Search of Truth!" as my uncle Toby found as he was drawn into his study of ballistics, of which road the cannonball did not go, which road it did go, that precise truth, and further into that thorny and bewildered track. " . . . intricate are the mases of this labyrinth! intricate are the troubles which the pursuit of this bewitching phantom, KNOWLEDGE," brings upon him (II, iii, 90) as he begins to mount his hobby-horse. As he tries to arrange his necessary equipment on the table—the maps, the compasses, the case of instruments, the books and odds and ends—in the customary series of accident they get thrown down or fall and in his endeavoring to catch them he makes things worse ("see what confusion"); the immediate problem is that the table is small "for that infinity of great and small instruments of knowledge which usually lay crouded upon it" (II, v, 93–94). "'Tis a pity," as my father cries, after a three-hours painful translation of Slawkenbergius, 'tis a pity "that truth, brother *Toby*, should shut herself up in such impregnable fastnesses, and be so obstinate as not to surrender herself sometimes up upon the closest

siege—" (which word in turn "like a talismanic power, in my father's
metaphor" crosses the divergent path of Toby's mind, III, xli, 238–
39). But my father always had some favorite notion to himself "out of
the high-way of thinking," and, taking a road of his own, entered
into the minutiae of philosophy. Knowledge, like matter, he would
affirm, was divisible *in infinitum,* to the grains and scruples; error
was error and "'twas alike fatal to truth, and she was kept down at the
bottom of her well," as inevitably by a mistake in the dust of a but-
terfly's wing as in the sun, moon and all the stars of heaven together
(II, xix, 145, 149). Once infinite possibilities are opened in this
search for truth—the bewildered track, the mazes of labyrinth, the
impregnable, the inaccessible bottom or height—we are in for an
endless journey.

If, as the story bears out my father's understanding of the matter,
truth is infinitely divisible, then the number of divergent roads to be
followed is rather large, and the chances of error on the way are
quite high or, as my father's career suggests, inevitable. And again
this is not something limited to my father. If the objects of knowledge are infinite, hitting the right point in any one act or word will
certainly be a rare event. "Ten thousand, and ten thousand times
ten thousand (for matter and motion are infinite) are the ways by
which a hat may be dropped upon the ground, without any effect"
(V, vii, 362). " . . . there are such an infinitude of notes, tunes,
cants, chants, airs, looks, and accents with which the word *fid-
dlestick* may be pronounced . . . every one of 'em impressing a
sense and meaning as different from the other, as *dirt* from
cleanliness—That Casuists (for it is an affair of conscience on that
score) reckon up no less than fourteen thousand in which you may
do either right or wrong" (IX, Chapter the Nineteenth, which, as
things can go in this story, is between xxv and xxvi, 635). My father
himself, as an object of knowledge, will of course present the same
problem. As many pictures as have been given of him, however like
him in different airs and attitudes, not one of them, or all, can ever
help the reader to any kind of preconception of how he would think
or speak or act on any untried occasion. "There was that infinitude of
oddities in him, and of chances along with it, by which handle he
would take a thing,—it baffled, Sir, all calculations.—The truth
was, his road lay so very far on one side, from that wherein most men

travelled,—that every object before him presented a face and sec-
tion of itself to his eye, altogether different from the plan and eleva-
tion of it seen by the rest of mankind.—In other words, 'twas a
different object,—and in course was differently considered." But
this is also the true reason Jenny and I, as well as all the world besides us, have such eternal squabbles about nothing (V, xxiv).

So this infinite world opens all sorts of possibilities of misconcep-
tion and misfortune, is certainly beyond the power of man to grasp
and control. It is not only that almost anything might and probably
will go wrong, but it is as though some mischievous power is at play,
usually with the cooperation of the victim, like "the father of mischief" who hammers at my father (III, ii, 159). It is certainly part of
Tristram's life, from the moment of his conception, that he has been
and will be "the continual sport of what the world calls fortune,"
pelting him with a set of as pitiful "misadventures and cross accidents" as ever small hero sustained (I, v, 10). From the moment before and during his delivery, "Sport of small accidents, *Tristram
Shandy!* that thou art, and ever will be!" (III, viii, 166), to the last
volume, "all the powers of time and chance, which severally check
us in our careers in this world" are at work on him (IX, i, 599). But
then in an infinite world where sport and the powers of time and
chance work there do seem to be, and it makes sense, possibilities
other than disaster. There are built-in limits. Diego, with his monstrous or glorious or true or false nose, did not want to be the sport of
fortune (IV, "Slawkenbergius's Tale," 253); and in the learned disputation on the reality of his nose there were those who amicably
laid it down that the just and geometrical arrangement and proportions of the human frame could not be transgressed "but within certain limits—that nature, though she sported—she sported within a
certain circle;—and they could not agree about the diameter of it"
(259). But "God's power is infinite, cried the Nosarians, he can do
any thing." "He can do nothing, replied the Antinosarians, which
implies contradictions." It was not a matter that could be decided
and it had religious significance. "Infinite power is infinite power,
said the [*Popish*] doctors who maintained the *reality* of the nose.—
It extends only to all possible things, replied the *Lutherans*" (263–
64). Catholics are absolutists (and therefore terrible cursers) so we
can't take their word; and if there will not be a precise description of

the certain circle or of the limits of the sport which we can all agree on, it does not seem that this resolution is essential. Indeed, while the Strasburgers were preoccupied and their men, women and children marched out to follow the stranger's nose, the French followed their own and marched in to take the city: in tracing the true springs of this and such like revolutions, as Slawkenbergius says, the vulgar look too high for them and statesmen look too low, but on this occasion "Truth (for once) lies in the middle" (271). The one thing that seems evident is that we don't really understand how it all works.

But it does work. Misfortunes fall heavily upon our heads and noses and whatever, for Nature sports with us, but she, dear Goddess, on large occasions and small, also gives us ease:

> But mark, madam, we live amongst riddles and mysteries—
> the most obvious things, which come in our way, have dark
> sides, which the quickest sight cannot penetrate into; and even
> the clearest and most exalted understandings amongst us find
> ourselves puzzled and at a loss in almost every cranny of na-
> ture's works; so that this, like a thousand other things, falls out
> for us in a way, which tho' we cannot reason upon it,—yet we
> find the good of it, may it please your reverences and your
> worships—and that's enough for us (IV, xvii, 293).

If my father is stopped by a finite sum—he can either enclose the Ox-moor or educate my brother Bobby—and in a world of infinite possibilities a finite sum is a stopper, he is rescued by a fresh misfortune: the death of Bobby. If Tristram on his journey through France enters Lyons with his chaise all broke to pieces he finds the misfortune will save him money, for indeed he gains a mine of wealth by selling the thing to the chaise-undertaker. It is his usual method of bookkeeping with disasters: "—Do, my dear *Jenny,* tell the world for me," knowing how he behaved under one of the most oppressive of its kind which could befall a man proud of his manhood. Coming close up to him as he stood there with his garters in his hand, reflecting on what had *not* passed, she said, "'Tis enough, *Tristram,* and I am satisfied," whispering these words in his ear: "**** ** **** *** ******;—**** ** ****—" Any other man would have sunk down to the center, but not Tristram. "Every thing is good for something, quoth I." He would go to Wales for six weeks to drink goat's whey and gain seven years longer life for the accident. For which reason he thinks himself inexcusable for blaming Fortune so often for pelting him all his life long with so many small evils: surely if he has any cause to be angry with her it is that she has not sent him great ones—a score of that kind would have been as good as a pension to him (VII, xxix, 517–18). Pensions may be given for service, as to Toby, or evidently for non-service, as here, though we cannot reason upon it.

Jenny can tell the world. We might like her to tell us who she is and just what is her relation to Tristram (and how I wish a Dutch commentator would tell me what her stars are whispering), but as with so much else we cannot know. What we do learn is both that he and she may squabble eternally about nothing and that, in the most disastrous moments that seem to keep them from joining, she is most kind and loving. In this world of mysteries the infinite possibilities work in both directions, in misfortunes and in comings together, alternating and, still better, interacting. Jenny can tell the world how her human response remedies the broken moment which did not happen, gives a natural ease. And she is not the only one. In the pain of my uncle Toby's wound, the infliction of the blow of the broken stone, my father's care and sincere affection brought visitors to discourse with my uncle: "These conversations were infinitely kind." Toby received great relief from them; of course they brought him into some unforeseen perplexities (which are not yet told to us, who are left guessing); but he hit upon an expedient to extricate himself (I, xxv, 79); that leads him to further difficulties, as we find, and then to comforts, and to succeeding problems, in those endless alternations. If, in later days, my father ridicules his brother's hobby-horse Toby never attempts any defense but that of redoubling the vehemence of smoking his pipe; and if that produces in my somewhat phthisical father a violent fit of coughing, Toby leaps up, without feeling the pain upon his groin and, "with infinite pity," stands beside his brother and cares for him in that affectionate and endearing manner that rebukes my father for the pain he has given. May my brains be knocked out, quoth my father to himself, if ever I insult this worthy soul more (III, xxiv, 211–12), though of course he will. The people, the events, the sequences are a strangely rich mixture.

In Toby the mixture is such that it can absorb almost anything, a harmony that will make concord out of any discord, a depth of goodness that appears to be infinite. He has an "infinite patience" with my father (III, xxxix, 236), "infinite was his pity" (IX, iii), "infinite benevolence" (IX, xxxii, 644). It does indeed seem that in comparison with anyone else's tender parts his wounded groin is "infinitely more sensible," there being so "many tendons and what-d'ye-call-'ems . . . about it—but moreover * * *—" (VIII, xix, 569). He feels an insult as feelingly as any man could feel but his nature is such that there is "no jarring element in it,—all was mix'd up so kindly within him." He had scarce heart to retaliate upon a fly, and in this peaceful, placid man the metaphor comes to life. "—Go— says he, one day at dinner," to an overgrown fly which has been buzzing about his nose and tormenting him cruelly; he does not retaliate but "after infinite attempts" he catches it at last. "Go, says he, lifting up the sash, and opening his hand as he spoke, to let it escape;—go poor devil, get thee gone, why should I hurt thee?— This world surely is wide enough to hold both thee and me." Tristram was but a boy when this happened but his whole frame was instantly set into one vibration by the action—or the manner and expression might go towards the effect—"or in what degree, or by what secret magic,—a tone of voice and harmony of movement, attuned by mercy, might find a passage to my heart, I know not"; but he knows that the lesson of "universal good-will" then taught and imprinted has never since been worn out of his mind, by "that one accidental impression" (II, xii, 113–14). This touching human inclusiveness has been stretched as far as it will go and a bit more, past reason, infinitely absurd, in the vibration that harmonizes even the dissonance that other experiences seem to obtrude forcibly. This universal good will, in a world wide enough to hold everything, not hurting a fly, pitying the devil himself—"he is cursed, and damn'd already, to all eternity," says Dr. Slop; "I am sorry for it, quoth my uncle *Toby*" (III, xi, 179)—does seem to be infinitely inclusive. Infinity in *Tristram Shandy*, its Shandean sense, is a world of endlessness in which objects, ideas, events, accidents are always multiplying—in short, there is no end of it (I, xiv, 37)—crossing one another to make incalculable confusions or unpredictably happy combinations. In this world things are so disconnected because they are so connected that the multiple meanings of any word, thought, happening, can take us into another digressive round. Things go too far and begin to return upon themselves, circle back, so that misfortune turns into good, or the reverse, pathos passes over into humor, or the reverse, or they join. My uncle Toby is certainly not always successful and could not possibly be; there are things he cannot hold onto, or does not see, and, in one instance, when the blister breaks it leads him to an unanticipated painful moment: with his innocence of the full meaning of that infinitely sensible groin, he will be shocked. But he does have a way of creating one accidental impression when all things come together, when, this time, the sash stays open, when an escape is made, when there is a tone and harmony, attuned. There is communication.

If my father and my uncle Toby are so often missing one another's track that does help them get on together. Childbirth is a heavy tax upon half our fellow-creatures, my uncle Toby says, shaking his head; yes, yes, a painful thing, my father agrees, shaking his head too. But each is thinking of a different sex:

> certainly since shaking of heads came into fashion, never did
> two heads shake together, in concert, from two such different
> springs.
>   God bless ⎫ 'em all—said my uncle Toby, and my
>   Duce take ⎭ father, each to himself. (IV, xii)

When they seem farthest from each other, each to himself, and because they are so far, there is no problem of miscommunication. They are in concert, two voices in a musical brace. It is not a unique occasion. The illustrative lesson of the buzzing fly, in which the characters of the two brothers reflect light on each, is set in a passage which arose about Stevinus, the inventor of the wonderfully fast sailing chariot. The "irreconcileable pulsations" of the ringing of the bell and the rap on the door—like my author I can't go into that now, reader; you will have to look it up yourself—instantly brought that man into my uncle Toby's mind. What business Stevinus had in this affair, Tristram says, is the greatest problem of all; "—it shall be solved,—but not in the next chapter" (II, x, 108). It doesn't have to be solved with any speed. We run into Stevinus again some volumes later, when my father refers to the great Piereskius—the very man,

Toby says, I once told you of, who walked so far to see Stevinus's chariot. "He was a very great man! added my uncle *Toby;* (meaning *Stevinus*)—He was so; brother *Toby,* said my father, (meaning *Piereskius*)" (VI, ii, 410). Irreconcilable pulsations are resolved in remarkable harmonies.

Or again, time and space are great problems, but they can be dissolved too. My father consoled himself for the death of Bobby by recalling how many great cities of the ancient past are now no more, how the world itself must come to an end. "'Returning out of *Asia,* when I sailed from *Ægina* towards *Megara,*' (*when can this have been? thought my uncle Toby*) 'I began to view the country round about. *Ægina* was behind me, *Megara* was before, *Pyræus* on the right hand, *Corinth* on the left,'" and so on for a paragraph. This last is an extract from Servius Sulpicius's consolatory letter to Cicero upon the loss of a daughter, but Toby had no skill in such fragments of antiquity. And as my father had once been a merchant in that part of the world Toby naturally concluded that this was nothing more than the true course of my father's voyage and reflections. And pray, brother, he asks, laying the end of his pipe upon my father's hand in his friendly way, "what year of our Lord was this?—'Twas no year of our Lord, replied my father.—That's impossible, cried my uncle *Toby.*—Simpleton! said my father,—'twas forty years before Christ was born." Toby has a dilemma. Either his brother is the wandering Jew or his misfortunes have disordered his brain. "'May the Lord God of heaven and earth protect him and restore him,' said my uncle *Toby,* praying silently for my father, and with tears in his eyes." But "My father placed the tears to a proper account, and went on with his harangue with great spirit" (V, iii, 354–55). Impossibilities are no obstacle in the relations of these brothers. There is no wandering, no fatal disorder of the brain. The Lord God of heaven and earth protects and restores and the world does not come to an end. We may wonder how someone so gentle as my uncle Toby can follow a profession and hobby of war—but he can tell us. Toby is not eloquent, as his nephew has said but with the usual contradiction: there are occasions when his uncle can be at least equal to Tertullus (or perhaps it is Tertullian—whatever) and in others "infinitely above him." We cannot write off my uncle Toby's apologetical oration on war, which, like the rest of the book, does see the contradictions and accepts them as parts of the unending whole. His thoughts and feelings are derived both from his own life and from a larger story, from epic and romance and history past and present, and like them he knows the glory and the desolation, the laurels and the cypress. He knows further that all are part of a greater story.

> And heaven is my witness, brother *Shandy*, that the pleasure I have taken in these things,—and that infinite delight, in particular, which has attended my sieges in my bowling green, has arose within me, and I hope in the corporal too, from the consciousness we both had, that in carrying them on, we were answering the great ends of our creation. (VI, xxxi–ii, 458–62)

There is then a secret cause that makes and holds together this strange world and Toby understands what that is well enough to smoke his pipe with unvarying composure. For him there is no cause but one why one man's nose is longer than another's, "but because that God pleases to have it so." For him it is God "who makes us all, and frames and puts us together in such forms and proportions, and for such ends, as is agreeable to his infinite wisdom." My father thinks he knows more. "'Tis a pious account, cried my father, but not philosophical,—there is more religion in it than sound science." My uncle Toby feared God and reverenced religion, so the moment my father finished my uncle "fell a whistling *Lillabulero,* with more zeal (though more out of tune) than usual.—" (III, xli, 240–41). Toby has his own music, which is his own kind of argument, the *Argumentum Fistulatorium,* whistling half a dozen bars of Lillabulero (which in its historical origin had been a very mocking song). "You must know it was the usual channel thro' which his passions got vent, when any thing shocked or surprised him;—but especially when any thing, which he deem'd very absurd, was offered" (I, xxi, 69, 71). Out of tune as it must be in a more than unusually shocking or absurd moment, with it he brings his moment back to concord.

In this book in which human cause is continually frustrated and at best impenetrably remote from effect, in this infinitude of oddities and chances, in all the powers of time and chance, there is a superior power that both complicates and resolves all things. "Time and Chance" is the title of one of the *Sermons of Mr. Yorick.* " . . . there are some secret and unseen workings in human affairs, which baffle all our endeavours," the most likely causes disappoint and fail to produce the effect we wish and naturally expect (128–29). Some men, the sermon goes on, from a superficial view atheistically infer from this lottery in life that the providence of God is unconcerned in the workings of our affairs, leaving them to the mercy of time and chance, such blind agents. But in truth the very opposite conclusion follows, for "if a superior intelligent Power did not sometimes cross and overrule events in this world" then human designs would always answer to our wisdom and causes would produce their natural effects; but since this is not so it follows that "there is some other cause which mingles itself in human affairs," governing and turning them as it pleases: "which cause can be no other than the First Cause of all things, and the secret and overruling Providence of that Almighty God" who raises the lowest of men and overthrows the projects of the wisest. Time and chance happeneth to all; "—you must call on the Deity to untie this knot . . . " The events the profane call Chance are designed, what the Almighty Being's "infinite wisdom" sees necessary for the world over which Providence perpetually presides (131–33). When we see whose goodness it is that is invisibly conducting us to the best and greatest ends of the happiness of his creatures, then we understand that, as a great reasoner [Samuel Clarke] has justly distinguished on this point, "It is not only religiously speaking, but with the strictest and most philosophical truth of expression," that God commands the ravens, the winds and the seas (136–37). This secret, invisible, power at work in human affairs to baffle our endeavors is, as we have seen it in the other works we have looked at, a superior mischief-maker; and here again, as with Puck, in his other and Goodfellow quality, and here as a far higher and greater being, this power can not only untie the knot of seeming chance and lead to happiness but do it all with infinite wisdom.

The distinction of religion and philosophy made in the sermon, and the subsumption of the lower in the higher, is an important truth. When the evil of the world falls upon Tristram, crushing his nose at the start of his second disastrous attempt to get on with his journey, my father the philosopher finds his own great and secret power. When "I reflect," he says, "upon MAN; and take a view of that dark side of him which represents his life as open to so many causes of trouble—when I consider, brother *Toby*, how oft we eat the bread of affliction, and that we are born to it," to that catalogue of all the cross-reckonings and sorrowful items by which the heart of man is overcharged, "'tis wonderful by what hidden resources the mind is enabled to stand it out, and bear itself up, as it does against the impositions laid upon our nature." This human and natural account is not Toby's. "'Tis by the assistance of Almighty God, cried my uncle *Toby*, looking up, and pressing the palms of his hands close together—'tis not from our own strength, brother *Shandy* . . . " "— That is cutting the knot, said my father, instead of untying it." We do recall that the nose went down because the incompetent scientific Dr. Slop began with the self-wound of a clumsy attempt at cutting the knot. Toby does seem to know more of its untying. My father relies on his own magic. "Though man is of all others the most curious vehicle, said my father, yet at the same time 'tis of so slight a frame and so totteringly put together, that the sudden jerks and hard jostlings it unavoidably meets with in this rugged journey, would overset and tear it to pieces a dozen times a day—was it not, brother *Toby*, that there is a secret spring within us—Which spring, said my uncle *Toby*, I take to be Religion.—Will that set my child's nose on? cried my father . . .—It makes every thing straight for us, answered my uncle *Toby* . . . " "Figuratively speaking," it may, my father replies, rejecting that unphilosophical mode of speech before completing his own figure: "the spring I am speaking of, is that great and elastic power within us of counterbalancing evil, which like a secret spring in a well-ordered machine, though it can't prevent the shock—at least it imposes upon our sense of it" (IV, vii–viii).

This dialogue between philosophy and religion on the journey through life appears in one of Mr. Yorick's sermons too, "Trust in God," which begins, with verbal identities, as my father begins to my uncle Toby: "Whoever seriously reflects upon the state and condition of man, and looks upon the dark side of it, which represents his life as open to so many causes of trouble;—when he sees how often he eats the bread of affliction, and that he is born to it, . . . would not one wonder,—how the spirit of man could bear the infirmities of his nature, and what it is that supports him" under the accidents he meets in his passage. Without some certain aid to bear us up, this sermon continues, "so tender a frame as ours would be but ill fitted to encounter what generally befalls it in this rugged journey." Accordingly we find that we are so curiously wrought by an all-wise hand that in the very composition and texture of our nature there is a remedy against most of the evils we suffer (211–12). The introduction of the all-wise hand indicates that we have here taken a turn from my father's to my uncle Toby's line, but the sermon, without the abrupt interruption of the dialogue, develops my father's case more fully and draws out the source of his remedy. We are so "ordered," it says, in its explanation of my father's well-ordered machine, that the principle of self-love, given us for preservation comes to our aid, by opening the door of hope, and in the worst emergencies flattering us with a belief we shall extricate ourselves. This expectation in no way alters the nature of the cross accidents, "yet imposes upon the sense of them, and like a secret spring in a well-contrived machine, though it cannot prevent, at least it counterbalances the pressure,—and so bears up this tottering, tender frame under many a violent shock and hard jostling, which otherwise would unavoidably overwhelm it" (212). This flattering propensity in us is built upon one of the most deceitful of human passions—self-love, which inclines us to think better of ourselves and our conditions than there is ground for. And since it often disappoints, finally, in our severer trials we find a necessity of calling in something to aid and direct it, so that it will fix itself upon a proper object of trust, able to fulfill our desires. Reason and religion are called in at length and join with Nature in exhorting us to hope—but to hope in God, who has power to help and the goodness always to incline him to do so, this infinite Being, this "infinitely kind and powerful Being" (214–17).

My father, in his moments of shock, has the remedy of human hope, the self-love that is deceitful, and for him it seems to work, the secret spring that imposes on the sense. If evil has fallen on his son's nose, for my father a great evil, he can turn to the "the magic bias" of names. " . . . as the greatest evil has befallen him—I must counteract and undo it with the greatest good." He shall be christened *Trismegistus.* "I wish it may answer—replied my uncle *Toby*, rising up" (IV, viii). But then it doesn't, when accident intervenes again as Susannah, that leaky vessel, scatters the name. And in this affliction my father might have fallen ill, had not his thoughts been critically drawn off "and his health rescued by a fresh train of disquietudes left him, with a legacy of a thousand pounds by my aunt *Dinah*" (IV, xxxi, 332)—in the usual unexpected alternations of misfortune and fortune where it is not always evident which is which (and this series which begins with the legacy still has several turns to run). But then if the great good name doesn't counteract the undoing of the nose, the ill luck of the breaking down of that part was not the greatest evil; chance could have done worse. "What a chapter of chances, said my father, turning himself about upon the first landing, as he and my uncle *Toby* were going down stairs—what a long chapter of chances do the events of this world lay open to us! Take pen and ink in hand, brother *Toby*, and calculate it fairly—," the philosopher's limited notion that this is a matter within human determination. "I know no more of calculations than this balluster, said my uncle *Toby*, (striking short of it with his crutch, and hitting my father a desperate blow souse upon his shin-bone)— 'Twas a hundred to one—cried my uncle *Toby*." It is another unfortunate blow and Toby's comment doesn't seem to be helpful—but he has said the right thing. "I thought, quoth my father, (rubbing his shin) you had known nothing of calculations, brother *Toby*. — 'Twas a meer chance, said my uncle *Toby*—Then it adds one to the chapter—replied my father." And that solves the immediate problem. "The double success of my father's repartees tickled off the pain of his shin at once—it was well it so fell out—(chance! again)—or the world to this day had never known the subject of my father's calculation—to guess it—there was no chance—What a lucky chapter of chances has this turned out! for it has saved me the trouble of writing one express . . . "

> Take pen and ink in hand, and calculate it fairly, brother *Toby*, said my father, and it will turn out a million to one, that of all the parts of the body, the edge of the forceps should have the ill luck just to fall upon and break down that one part, which should break down the fortunes of our house with it.
>
> It might have been worse, replied my uncle *Toby*—I don't comprehend, said my father—Suppose the hip had presented, replied my uncle *Toby*, as Dr. *Slop* foreboded.
>
> My father reflected half a minute—looked down—touched the middle of his forehead slightly with his finger—
>
> –True, said he. (IV, ix)

And again it's not quite true, because on another occasion another chance, with a closer implication of Toby, will present that other part of young Tristram to its misfortune too. But for the time being—and what else is there?—the philosophical and the religious man have agreed, in their way of harmony, that it was well it so fell out.

And even more happily for the present moment of writing, it has been, as Tristram sees, a lucky chapter of chances for him as author. It has saved him the writing of a chapter when he has enough already on his hands—the promise to the world of a chapter of knots, two chapters on the right and wrong end of a woman, a chapter on whiskers, a chapter on wishes, a chapter on noses (no, he's done that), a chapter on my uncle Toby's modesty, to say nothing of a chapter on chapters (IV, ix). He needs all the lucky chance he can get in writing, and he gets it. We must follow this writer in his own curious vehicle on his rugged journey.

The originating journey of Tristram's life has a deep effect upon his opinions and, since he is the author, the problem becomes a problem in the telling of the tale. He is not alone as imperfect narrator, in oral or written attempts. For my uncle Toby, in explaining what happened to him at Namur, there are "almost insurmountable difficulties he found in telling his story intelligibly" (II, i, 82). The day before yesterday Trim was telling the story of the King of Bohemia: "What became of that story, *Trim?*—We lost it, an' please your honour, somehow betwixt us." (VII, xxviii, 581). My father as author of the *Tristra-paedia* found that, "Like all other writers, he met with disappointments"; he imagined that he could bring it into a small compass, but "Matter grows under our hands.—Let no man say,—'Come—I'll write a *duodecimo*,'" for the boy grew faster than the book and every day a page or two became of no consequence (V, xvi). Like his father Tristram can't get on with it. In "a strange state of affairs" between the reader and himself he loses time at an even more spectacular rate, living 364 times faster than he can write, in an endlessly self-defeating regression where the more he writes the more he will have to write (IV, xiii). As it turns out, the pace is not quite that frantic but it does happen that when he has come to the end of his ninth and last volume, seven years after writing the first, he has circled back behind his start. He makes no doubt, having got to his sixth volume, that he will be able to get on with his uncle Toby's story, and his own, in a tolerable straight line. But the indeterminate diagrams of the otherwise indescribable lines he has followed in the first four volumes—and his confidence of how much he has improved in the fifth, when the precise line he has described there does not really appear to be greatly more regular—and his insistence that in the sixth he has scarce stepped a yard out of his way and that if he mends at this rate it is not impossible he may arrive hereafter at a line straight as he could draw it with a ruler—all these are not very convincing. We are more ready to accept his exclamation of "—What a journey!" (VI, xl).

The lines of his story, like the lines of thought of the characters, are forever crossing. A passage on a bridge must be, one realizes, an impasse. If my uncle Toby assumes from Trim's report of Dr. Slop's making a bridge that it must be a military miniature, when actually it is a bridge for Tristram's nose (my father is already confused and does not yet know the worst), then to understand how such a mistake occurs "I fear I must give you an exact account of the road which led to it." Or to drop the metaphor, as he adds (empirical philosopher that he is, scrupulously honest in his use of language), to establish the probability of the error he must give some account of an adventure of Trim's. But that story is in one sense certainly out of its place here, because it should come in either amongst the anecdotes of my uncle Toby's amours with Mrs. Wadman, or else in the middle of the campaign on the bowling green—it will do very well either place—but if he reserves it for either of those parts of his story he ruins the story he is now upon, and if he tells it here by anticipation he ruins it there. What would we have him do? "—Tell it, Mr. *Shandy*, by all means.—You are a fool, *Tristram*, if you do." The Powers (for powers there are and great ones too) who enable mortal man to tell a story worth the hearing, who kindly show him what to put in, leave out, how much to cast in the shade, whereabouts to throw the light, and who see how many scrapes and plunges their subjects fall into, could do at least one thing for him, he begs—that whenever in their dominions of story-telling three several roads meet in one point, at least set up a guide-post in mere charity to direct an uncertain devil which of the three he is to take (III, xxiii).

But these Puckish powers of story-telling are not going to help an author find a road who has a problem beyond their help. He cannot get a fix in language at any prior level. Words may give his characters difficulties, but the deeper problem is that the teller of the tale is himself a clown, and the harder he tries, the more precision and control he insists on, the deeper he sinks. Let him define the word *nose* with all possible exactness and precision, to leave nothing equivocal, and see where it gets him (III, xxxi). Anything he begins to talk about sprouts new possibilities of its own, new paths to be followed, so that it becomes syntactically impossible to come to the end of a sentence. Volume VI—that volume he will conclude shortly by declaring he has scarce stepped a yard out of his way—Chapter xxxiii, starts:

> I told the Christian reader—[and now "Christian" beckons with a needed qualification] I say *Christian*—hoping he is one—and if he is not, I am sorry for it—and only beg he will consider the matter with himself, and not lay the blame entirely upon this book,—

Start again, new paragraph:

> I told him, Sir [and now "told" calls]—for in good truth, when a man is telling a story in the strange way I do mine, he is obliged continually to be going backwards and forwards to keep all tight together in the reader's fancy—which [off now to a relative clause, sort of], for my own part, if I did not take heed to do more than at first, there is so much unfixed and equivocal matter starting up, with so many breaks and gaps in it,—and [parenthetical qualification] so little service do the stars afford [to qualify the unfixed and equivocal], which [a relative branch within the parenthetical qualification] nevertheless [futile as the effort is, we already know], I hang up in some of the darkest passages, knowing [in participial explanation] that the world is apt to lose its way, with all the lights the sun itself at noon day can give it—and now [and now perhaps we will have an object for the main verb with which we began? but no, because he has forgotten the start], you see, I am lost myself!—

All this—the present confusion, not the still unknown object of the sentence he had started—requires some explanation. So we get a new paragraph: "—But 'tis my father's fault," because of the distant original begetting, and so forth until, "All which being considered, and that you see 'tis morally impracticable for me to wind this round to where I set out—" So we get a new paragraph: "I begin the chapter over again." And so to Chapter xxxiv:

> I told the Christian reader . . .

He is, he's quite right, telling a story in a strange way. We are familiar with characters who cannot handle language well, the clowns who are incompetent in communication, and with those among them who have a mistakenly high opinion of their ability to speak the best language, but here we have an author of his own book who is an incompetent fool. It is not only his characters whose lives are put in danger by words. He is absolutely reduced to non-verbal means. He keeps changing roles on us. What is more disconcerting is that as we read, superior as we are to this fool, we are tricked into becoming this fool's fool. We wander and stumble on our own way. We have to keep changing *our* roles. With him, he tells us, we "shall lead a couple of fine lives together" (IV, xiii, 286). We are reduced to becoming that inattentive Madam, punished for our ignorance by being forced to turn back and read the whole chapter over again, and we are still incapable of observing what, we are told, we have been told already (I, xx, 56–57). We are never able to guess at anything, and if we were able to form the least judgment or probable conjecture of what was to come in the next page he would tear it out of his book (I, xxv, 80). If there are more than fifty points left yet unraveled we may endeavor to solve them if we have time, but he tells us beforehand that it will be in vain; not the sage Alquife, the magician Don Belianis of Greece, nor Urganda, the sorceress his wife, could pretend to come within a league of the truth (II, xix, 154), so what hope have we who must wait until next year for the next volume (but what help will *any* time be?). It is in vain to leave the comprehension of difficult propositions to our imagination: to form any kind of hypothesis that would render these propositions feasible we must cudgel our brains sore, and to do it without we must have such brains as no reader ever had before (V, xviii). We must count the stars he hangs up to light us in our darkest passages, some counts so obvious and so mildly naughty that we feel silly to have played the game, some of them so tantalizing in their call for ingenuity (especially if they offer four-star words), some of them impossible (probably the juiciest too). In these knots we are implicated.

Getting through his book is, for him and for us, a difficult and dangerous journey. Stop two moments, my dear Sir, at the beginning of Volume VI and "let us just look back upon the country we have pass'd through—What a wilderness has it been! and what a mercy that we have not both of us been lost, or devoured by wild beasts in it." But then the wild beasts have been those Jack Asses (such a number of them in the world), the critics of his volumes, so the problem of escaping them has had its pleasures too. Telling a story in his strange way he is continually obliged to be going backwards and forwards to keep all tight together in the reader's fancy but he can do it, even as he is tripping over his syntax, and do it well. The machinery of his work is of a species by itself: "two contrary motions are . . . reconciled, which were thought to be at variance with each other. In a word, my work is digressive, and it is progressive too,—and at the same time" (I, xxii, 73). Provided he keeps along the line of *his* story, "he may go backwards and forwards as he will,—'tis still held to be no digression" (V, xxv). If he is at a loss to make ends meet and to torture a chapter presently writing to the service of the chapter following, "one would think I took a pleasure in running into difficulties of this kind, merely to make fresh experiments of getting out of 'em" (VIII, vi, 545). This is a wandering fool who seems to be very much in control of his way. If he travels through Auxerre he writes himself in the most puzzled skein of all—"getting forwards in two different journies together, and with the same dash of the pen," he is in fact, remarkably, moving two ways at once. "There is but a certain degree of perfection in every thing" and he has pushed it something beyond that, has brought himself into a situation where no traveller ever stood before him: for at this moment he is in Auxerre with my father and my uncle Toby, entering Lyons with his post-chaise broke into a thousand pieces, and upon the banks of the Garonne where he now sits rhapsodizing all these affairs, three places at once. "—Let me collect myself, and pursue my journey" (VII, xxviii).

He is his own Power in the dominion of story-telling and he has no need to beg a guide-post. He is at once the lost mortal clown and the spirit with the Puck-like ability to be in three places at once. He can mislead the reader, and no magician can come within a league of the truth, but he is the good fellow too, and if he blinds us he will bring us to a better vision. If he implicates us, to laugh at us, he also takes us into his confidence, raises us to that level where we can make league with him in a superior understanding of the scene, to enjoy with him, laughing at the Jack Asses, the art behind the scene. We, like him, are both fools and higher spirits. The author pays the truest respect to the reader's understanding, "to halve this matter amicably, and leave him something to imagine, in his turn, as well as yourself" (II, xi, 109): on the journey with him we do lead a couple of fine lives together. He fulfills the promise given early that as we proceed with him the slight acquaintance will grow into familiarity and terminate in friendship; let him go on and tell his story in his own way and if upon the road he sometimes puts on a fool's cap courteously give him credit for a little more wisdom than appears, "and as we jogg on, either laugh with me, or at me, or in short, do any thing,—only keep your temper" (I, vi, 11). We need not be upset, nor congratulate ourselves, at the invitation to join knowingly in the sexual play for that is a matter—my father does happen on truths— "which couples and equals wise men with fools" (IX, xxxiii, 645). If we find confusion in words, like my father and my uncle Toby, for there is an infinity of meanings, like them we find harmony. Double-entendres work both ways, catch us out and unite meanings. Yorick rides a meek-spirited jade of a broken-winded horse, for a reason he will not explain, "But upon his steed—he could unite and reconcile every thing,—he could compose his sermon,—he could compose his cough,—and, in case nature gave a call that way, he could likewise compose himself to sleep" (I, x, 20). Attitudes are nothing, madam, 'tis the transition from one to another, "like the preparation and resolution of the discord into harmony, which is all in all" (IV, vi). For his own part he is just set up in the business and knows little about it "—but, in my opinion, to write a book is for all the world like humming a song—be but in tune with yourself, madam, 'tis no matter how high or how low you take it" (IV, xxv, 315). It is a book as good as the *Argumentum Fistulatorium*.

He has the perfect freedom from rules of the great artist, none but his own. He is "shandy," meaning somewhat crack-brained, but also meaning wild, that unrestrained free spirit we have met before who has the controlling power and will be held by no one's law but his

own. If he is the sport of accident, he sports well himself. If his re-
sorts to non-verbal means have been signs of his incompetence in
language, they are devices that have extended his range of expression. If time has given him trouble, as he has conquered space he
has conquered time. At the beginning when he sits down to write
his history, he finds all the confounded hindrances he meets with
in his way, can't go straight forward and can't tell when he will "get to
his journey's end," for "the thing is, morally speaking, impossible,"
no end of it (I, xiv); but he comes to see that there is great pleasure in
this, that he can write two volumes every year, that his book can be
kept going these forty years if it but pleases the fountain of life to
bless him (VII, i, 479). The careful confusions of time in his telling
are no problem, not merely because he has worked out a chronology
but because he has done it to the end of eliminating time. (As my
father has said, without understanding what time is aright we never
can comprehend infinity, III, xviii, 190). For all the revolving events
and characters nothing essential changes. All times are present, the
time of his art at the moment he writes—March 9, 1759; March 26,
1759 (and betwixt the hours of nine and ten in the morning); August
the 10th, 1761; this 12th day of August, 1766 (in a purple jerkin and
yellow pair of slippers); or "where I now sit, unskrewing my ink-
horn to write my uncle *Toby's* amours . . . " (I, xviii, 44; I, xxi, 64; V,
xvii; IX, i, 600; VIII, i).

Not Death itself can stop him on his way. When my brother
Bobby dies my father knows, having read Burton, " 'Tis an inevitable chance," it is a law, "—the first statute in *Magnâ Chartâ*—it is
an everlasting act of parliament. . . . –*All must die*" (V, iii, 353).
Death is a continual presence in this book, now or past or to come, the
one chance every mortal must meet in time. But, as Slawkenbergius
has said, "chance . . . as often directs us to remedies as to *diseases*"
(IV, 269). Misfortune which sets loose my father's tongue with a
good grace is equal to and sometimes better than a blessing that ties
it up, and he is as well off again as if misfortune had never befallen
him, soon returning out of Asia with great spirit. But Tristram does
better than that. When Death himself knocked at the door Tristram
bade him come again, in so gay a tone of careless indifference that
Death doubted his commission: there must be some mistake in the
matter, quoth he—and was himself embarrassed, so grave a per-

266

Two different journies together

sonage getting in so vile a scrape. "Thou hast had a narrow escape, *Tristram*, said Eugenius," but if the son of a whore (by Sin he entered the world) has found out Tristram's lodgings, Tristram will fly. " . . . then by heaven! I will lead him a dance he little thinks of—" (VII, i), and off he goes in this dance which is a flight and finds "I had left Death, the lord knows—and He only—how far behind me." Still Death follows and still Tristram flees, "but I fled him chearfully—still he pursued—but like one who pursued his prey without hope" (VII, xlii, 534). Tristram dances through France, to the end of the Volume. At the sound of fife and tabourin the mule is frightened to death, but Tristram sees that the nymphs and swains are running at the ring of pleasure (yes, that), and so kicking off one boot in this ditch and t'other into that, "I'll take a dance, said I." His inviting partner's hair is tied up in a knot, all but one tress which she asks him to tie: "It taught me to forget I was a stranger—the whole knot fell down—We had been seven years acquainted." The knot down, a transient spark of amity shot across the space betwixt us. 'Twas a Gascoigne roundelay. "Why could I not live and end my days thus," why could not a man "dance, and sing, and say his prayers, and go to heaven with this nut brown maid?" But no, Nanette dances up "insiduous" (lovely word), the petticoat with that cursed slit— and, as happens continually, the spark across the space is transient, he must leave the ring of pleasure, the roundelay, and "Then 'tis time to dance off, quoth I; so changing only partners and tunes, I danced it away . . . I danced it along . . . till at last I danced my-self . . . that I might go on straight forwards, without digression or parenthesis, in my uncle *Toby*'s amours—" (VII, xliii, 537–38).

With the amours of his uncle Toby running in his head as if they had been his own "I was in the most perfect state . . . felt the kind-liest harmony vibrating . . . every thing I saw, or had to do with, touch'd upon some secret spring either of sentiment or rapture." He hears the sweetest notes he ever heard. It is poor Maria, sitting upon a bank, playing her vespers upon a pipe, with her little goat beside her, as he is told by his young postilion, with an accent and look "perfectly in tune" to a feeling heart. He hears her sad story and her sweet song and sits between her and her goat. She looks wist-fully at him, then at her goat, "and so on, alternately—Well, *Maria*, said I softly—What resemblance do you find?" (IX, xxiv; 629–

31). The tune, with the note we have always heard, is composed of alternations, such a continual form of its own that it seems to sport with its objects both ways, in good or bad, making them objects of laughter or pity, or of one passing into the other, or of both at once. They all live in junctures of strangely textured fortunes and feelings. The scrapes Tristram's family is perpetually getting into in consequence of my father's systems are "of so odd, so mixed and tragicomical a contexture" (VII, xxvii, 512). For my mother the stages of the journey with my father "were so truly tragi-comical, that she did nothing but laugh and cry in a breath" (I, xvi, 42). Tristram himself is "a most tragicomical completion" of his father's prediction that he should neither think nor act like any other man's child (IX, i, 600). In Bridget's close encounter with Trim, it is a momentary contest, as in an April morning, "Whether *Bridget* should laugh or cry" (IX, xxix). One would think that Tristram the author takes a pleasure in running into difficulties, merely to make fresh experiments in getting out of them, must entangle himself still more—and this is the man tormented with the vile asthma got in skating against the wind, who but two months ago in a fit of laughter lost quarts of blood (VIII, vi, 545).

So there is that harmony, secret spring, the perfection that brings all together, but always in the mixtures, in the ups and downs and the endless turns and returns. The perfection is in the renewal and repetition of the circle. There is something of great constancy here too, but in its, as always, strange way. As some man once observed, there is "great inconstancy" in the air and climate of England; but, as another added some time later, it is this which has furnished us with such a variety of odd and whimsical characters; and again, as another discovered, this copious store-house of original materials is the true and natural cause that our English comedies are so much better than any others; but that "this strange irregularity in our climate, producing so strange an irregularity in our characters" thereby in some sort makes us amends by giving us somewhat to make us merry when the weather confines, that observation is his own, Tristram says. Thus our kinds of knowledge have been gradually "creeping upwards towards that Ακμὴ of their perfections" from which we cannot possibly be far off. When that happens it will put an end to all kind of writings, and thus to all kind of reading, and must in course put an end to all kind of knowledge, "—and then—we shall have all to begin over again; or, in other words, be exactly where we started." "Happy! thrice happy Times!" (I, xxi, 63–64). So the renewing happy circle turns, in this work (as in the heavenly spheres): digressive and progressive at the same time, contrary motions reconciled, one wheel within another (xxii, 73), the journey on a hobby-horse, enclosed by God and country. Of all ways of beginning a book now in practice throughout the world Tristram is confident his own way of doing it is the best—"I'm sure it is the most religious—for I begin with writing the first sentence—and trusting to Almighty God for the second" (VIII, ii, 540). It does seem to be a chancy way of doing things, but God is with him all the way.

Within that circle, the human story is always subject to time and inevitable chance. Toby's innocence, like his groin, is not invulnerable any more than anyone can live in a garden and a green forever uninvaded by the widow Wadman. With her a new "magic" seems to enter his life, leaves the mind weaker; "No more was he to dream" of war, but "Softer visions,—gentler vibrations stole sweetly in upon his slumbers," in this epic descent when the trumpet falls out of his hands and he takes up the lute (VI, xxxv). Tristram will not offer a definition of love, a mystic labyrinth (VI, xxxvii), and in my father's theories love is a disease for which he offers arcane scientific remedies (VI, xxxvi; VIII, xxxiv): for my uncle Toby it is no mystery and when the blister breaks he knows it is love (VIII, xxvii; VIII, xxxii). But he does not know so much as the right end of a woman from the wrong. There is a moment when the double entendres do not harmonize, when there is a miscommunication and a shock: it might be the moment of the eye-opener, that counter-charm. But not here. We see it, but he doesn't and he doesn't need to, for with him as with my father there is no need to change. "Unhappy Mrs. *Wadman!*—" (IX, xxvi, 638). At Shandy Hall some hinges will never work properly but where else would one want to go and not return? It is the place where desires are never and ever fulfilled. The hobby-horse is both the charm and the counter-charm, at once encloses the mind and sets it free, as Nature sports within a circle. In that round God makes everything straight for us and all stories, going their different ways, come together, at last as at first. What is all this story about? " . . . as chance would have it," as it always does, a cock and a bull, two different journeys together, and two of the best of its kind I ever heard.

The text is Laurence Sterne, *The Life and Opinions of Tristram Shandy, Gentleman*, ed. James Work (New York, 1940). References are to volume and chapter (*Tristram Shandy* being *Tristram Shandy* that is often all that is needed) and page number. Further extensive notes are in the "Florida Edition," Vol. III (1984), ed. Melvyn New with Richard A. Davis and W. G. Day.

The text of the *Sermons* is in the edition of Sterne's *Works* by Wilbur L. Cross (1904; New York, 1970, reprint), Vol. V. "Time and Chance" is Sermon VIII and "Trust in God" is Sermon XXXIV in the numbering of this edition; references for the first of these are to pages in Part I and for the second to pages in Part II of Vol. V.

Alter, Robert, "*Tristram Shandy* and the Game of Love," *American Scholar*, XXXVII (1968), 316–23

Anderson, Howard, "Structure, Language, Experience in the Novels of Laurence Sterne," *Tennessee Studies in Literature*, XXIX (1985), 185–223

Bloom, Edward A., and Lillian D. Bloom, "Hostage to Fortune: Time, Chance and Laurence Sterne," *Modern Philology*, LXXXV (1988), 499–513

Booth, Wayne, *The Rhetoric of Fiction*, 2nd ed. (Chicago, 1983)

Burckhardt, Sigurd, "*Tristram Shandy's* Law of Gravity," *ELH*, XXVIII (1961), 70–81

Byrd, Max, *Tristram Shandy* (London, 1985)

Fluchère, Henri, *Laurence Sterne: From Tristram to Yorick*, trans. Barbara Bray (London, 1965)

Golden, Morris, "Sterne's Journeys and Sallies," *Studies in Burke and His Time*, XVI (1974), 47–62

Hammond, Lansing, *Laurence Sterne's* Sermons of Mr. Yorick (New Haven, 1948)

Iser, Wolfgang, *Laurence Sterne: Tristram Shandy*, trans. David Henry Wilson (Cambridge, 1988)

Lamb, Jonathan, *Sterne's Fiction and the Double Principle* (Cambridge, 1989)

Lanham, Richard A., Tristram Shandy: *The Games of Pleasure* (Berkeley, 1973)

Loveridge, Mark, *Laurence Sterne and the Argument about Design* (Totowa, N. J., 1982)

McKillop, Alan Dugald, *The Early Masters of English Fiction* (Lawrence, 1956)

Mayoux, Jean-Jacques, "Variations on the Time-Sense in *Tristram Shandy*," in *The Winged Skull,* edd. Arthur H. Cash, and John M. Stedmond (London, 1971)

Mendilow, A. A., *Time and the Novel* (London, 1952)

New, Melvyn, *Laurence Sterne as Satirist: A Reading of "Tristram Shandy"* (Gainesville, 1969)

Price, Martin, *To the Palace of Wisdom* (New York, 1964)

Rothstein, Eric, *Systems of Order and Inquiry in Later Eighteenth-Century Fiction* (Berkeley, 1975)

Simpson, K. G., "At this Moment in Space: Time, Space and Values in *Tristram Shandy,*" in *Laurence Sterne: Riddles and Mysteries,* ed. Valerie Myer (London, 1984)

Stedmond, John M., *The Comic Art of Laurence Sterne* (Toronto, 1967)

Tave, Stuart M., *The Amiable Humorist: A Study in the Comic Theory and Criticism of the Eighteenth and Early Nineteenth Centuries* (Chicago, 1960)

Traugott, John, *Tristram Shandy's World: Sterne's Philosophic Rhetoric* (Berkeley, 1954)

Watt, Ian, "The Comic Syntax of *Tristram Shandy,*" in *Studies in Criticism and Aesthetics,* 1660–1800, edd. Howard Anderson, and John Shea (Minneapolis, 1967)

Index

This is not a book that needs an index, but it may be useful to have a brief and partial word-list of terms repeated in the several chapters. (Semicolons between page numbers denote chapter breaks.) The Preface and then the first part of the inter-chapter "A pause" (pp. 226–34), which are general and inclusive, are not indexed here.